WOMEN ON HUNTING

EDITED BY

Pam Houston

THE ECCO PRESS

THE ECCO PRESS
100 West Broad Street
Hopewell, New Jersey 08525
Published simultaneously in Canada by
Penguin Books Canada Ltd., Ontario
Printed in the United States of America
Designed by Richard Oriolo
FIRST EDITION

Some of the works in this volume have originally
appeared in the following publications: *Antæus;
Indiana Review; Salamander; Shenandoah; Witness*

Library of Congress Cataloging-in-Publication Data

Women on hunting / edited by Pam Houston. — 1st ed.
     p.   cm. — (Ecco companions)
     1. Hunting—Literary collections.   2. American literature—Women
authors.   3. Canadian literature—Women authors.   I. Houston, Pam.
II. Series.
PS509.H85W66   1994
810.9'355—dc20   94-35028
     ISBN 0-88001-332-X

The text of this book is set in Bodoni Book

Pages 335 and 336 constitute an extension of this page

CONTENTS

Pam Houston

INTRODUCTION

When I was twenty-six years old, and just catching on to the fact that my life wasn't going to be something that came at me like opposing traffic, but something I actually had to take control of and shape, I fell in love with a man who was a hunting guide for a living. We didn't have what you would call the healthiest of relationships. He was selfish, evasive, and unfaithful. I was demanding, manipulative, and self-pitying. He was a republican, and I was a democrat. He was a Texan and I was not. I belonged to the Sierra Club and he belonged to the

NRA. Yet somehow we managed to stay together for three years of our lives, and to spend two solid months of each of those three years hunting for Dall sheep in Alaska.

I was always quick, in those days, to make the distinction between a hunter and a hunting guide, for though I was indirectly responsible for the deaths of a total of five animals, I have never killed an animal myself, and never intend to. I had the opportunity once to shoot a Dall ram whose horns were so big it would have likely gotten my name into the record books. I had three decent men applying every kind of peer pressure they could come up with, and I even went so far as to raise the rifle to my eye, unsure in that moment what I would do next. But once I got it up there I couldn't think of one good reason to pull the trigger.

I learned about bullets and guns and calibers and spotting scopes, and I was a good hunting guide simply because I'm good at the outdoors. I can carry a heavy pack long distances. I can cook decent meals on a backpacker's stove. I keep my humor pretty well for weeks without a toilet and a shower. I can sleep, if I have to, on a forty-five-degree ledge of ice. I know how to move in the wilderness, and because of this I understand how the sheep move. I'm a decent tracker. I've got what they call animal sense.

When I was hunting Dall sheep in Alaska it was one on one on one. One hunter, one guide, one ram that we tracked, normally for ten days, before we got close enough to shoot it. My obvious responsibility was to the hunter. It was my job to keep him from falling into a crevasse or getting eaten by a grizzly bear, to carry his gun when he got too tired, to keep him fed and watered, to listen to his stories, to get him up at three in the morning and keep him on his feet till midnight, to drag him fifteen miles and sometimes as much as four thousand vertical feet a day, and if everything went well, to get him in position to shoot a sheep to take home and put on his wall. My other job, though understated, was to protect the sheep from the hunters, to guarantee that the hunter shot only the oldest ram in the herd, that he only shot at one animal, and that he only fired when he was close enough to make a killing shot. A hunter can't walk down a wounded animal across the glaciers in Alaska the way he can through the trees in the Pennsylvania woods. A bad shot in Alaska almost always means a lost ram.

I describe those months in the Alaska Range now as the most conflicted time of my life. I would spend seventy days testing myself in all the ways I love, moving through the Alaska wilderness, a place of such power and vastness it is incomprehensible even to my memory. I watched a mama grizzly bear feed wild blueberries to her cubs, I woke to the footfall of a hungry-eyed silver wolf whispering through our campsite, I watched a bull moose rub the velvet off his bloody antlers, and a bald eagle dive for a parka squirrel. I watched the happy chaos that is a herd of caribou for hours, and the contrastingly calculated movements of the sheep for days.

I learned from the animals their wilderness survival skills, learned, of course, a few of my own. I learned, in those days, my place in the universe, learned why I need the wilderness, not why "we" need it, but why I do. That I need the opportunity to give in to something bigger than myself, like falling into love, something bigger, even, than I can define. This had to do not at all with shooting an animal (though it would have, of course, in its purest form, had we not packages and packages of freeze-dried chicken stew), but with simpler skills: keeping warm in subzero temperatures the predominant one, avoiding the grizzly bears that were everywhere and unpredictable, and not panicking when the shale started sliding underneath my boot soles in a slide longer and steeper than anything I'd ever seen in the lower forty-eight, finally riding that shale slide out like a surfer on a giant gray wave.

I listened to the stories of the hunters, the precision and passion with which the best among them could bring the memories of past hunting camps to life. I understood that part of what we were about in hunting camp was making new stories, stories that were the closest these men ever got to something sacred, stories that would grace years, maybe even generations, of orange campfire light.

But underneath all that wonder and wildness and the telling of tales, the fact remains that in payment for my Alaskan experience I watched five of the most beautiful, smartest, and wildest animals I'd ever seen die, most of them slowly and in unspeakable pain. And regardless of the fact that it was the hunter who pulled the trigger, I was the party responsible for their deaths. And though I eat meat and wear leather, though I understand every ethical argument there is about hunting, including the one that says it is hunters who will ultimately save the animals because it is the NRA that has the money and the power to protect what is left of America's wilderness, it will never be okay with me that I led my hunters to those animals. There is no amount of learning that can, in my heart, justify their deaths.

So when I remember that time in my life, I try to think not only of the killing, but also of the hunting, which is a work of art, a feat of imagination, a flight of spirit, and a test of endless patience and skill. To hunt an animal successfully you must think like an animal, move like an animal, climb to the top of the mountain just to go down the other side, and always be watching, and waiting, and watching. To hunt well is to be at once the pursuer and the object of pursuit. The process is circular, and female somehow, like giving birth, or dancing. A hunt, at its best, ought to look from the air like a carefully choreographed ballet.

French psychoanalyst Jacques Lacan believed that men desire the object of their desire, while women desire the condition of desiring, and this gives women a greater capacity for relishing the hunt. I believe that is why, in so many ancient and contemporary societies, women have been the superior hunters. Good hunting is no more about killing an animal than good sex is about making babies or good writing is about publication. The excitement, even the fulfillment, is in the beauty of the search. While a man tends to be linear about achieving a goal, a woman can be circular and spatial. She can move in many directions at once, she can be many things at once, she can see an object from all sides, and, when it is required, she is able to wait.

Occasionally there is a man who can do these things (most of the male guides I knew were far better at them than I), and he is a pleasure to guide and to learn from. But the majority of my clients started out thinking that hunting is like war. They were impatient like a poor general, impatient like an earnest sergeant who thinks he should be the general, impatient for the sound of his own gun and impatient for the opposition to make a mistake.

But the sheep didn't often make mistakes, and they were as patient as stone. So it was my job to show the hunter that he would be required to choose a different metaphor. If hunting can be like war it can also be like opera, or like fine wine. It can be like out-of-body travel, it can be like the suspension of disbelief. Hunting can be all these things and more; like a woman, it won't sit down and be just one thing.

Collected in this anthology are forty-seven ways in which women writers have made the hunting metaphor their own. A few of these women are avid hunters, a few more stand in adamant and angry opposition to hunting and everything it means. Most of the women fall, like me, somewhere in between. For each of us, hunting has touched our lives in some way that ignited the place inside us that gives rise to story telling. Hunting, in this anthology, is neither a sport, nor a philosophical dilemma, as much as it is a metaphorical framework from which to tell a tale.

And speaking of metaphors:

I wore a necklace in my hunting days, a bear claw of Navajo silver. The man I was in love with, the hunting guide, had given it to me to make amends for one of our breakups, one of his affairs. He gave it to me in a tiny box, wrapped elaborately like a ring, and I shook it, heard it clunk, thought, Oh my God, Oh my God, he's really doing it. When I opened it, saw that it was not a ring but a pendant, I was not disappointed. I simply wore the pendant like a ring, confusing the symbolism of that pendant just enough to carry me back into the relationship, and back into hunting camp one last time.

It was late August and much too warm in the high mountains. I'd been dropped by airplane one hundred air miles from Tok with two bow hunters from Louisiana. We'd made a base camp and climbed from it, up the valley of the Tok River to the glacial headlands. The sheep would stay high in the warm weather, higher probably than we could climb. But we tried anyway, crossing glacial rivers normally small but now raging in the heat wave, knowing after each crossing that we wouldn't make it back across until the weather turned again and the water began to subside. We had our packs, of course, a tent, sleeping bags, a change of clothes, and enough food, if we didn't shoot anything, for a little better than three days.

When we got to the glacier at the head of the valley we hadn't seen any recent sheep sign, and this told us the sheep would be higher still, lying with their bellies in a snowfield, not even needing to eat until the weather cooled down. We were wet and tired, hot and hungry, but we dropped half our gear, the tents and bedding, and climbed higher up the rocky moraine that flanked the glacier. We climbed through tangled forests of alders that grew, it seemed, horizontally out of the rocks, climbed over the soggy mounds of tundra, squeezing into it with our boot tips and fingernails when it got too steep. Our socks got wetter, out breathing more labored, for hours we climbed, and still no sign of the sheep.

The hunters, I forget their names now, but let's just call them Larry and Moe, were nervous. We were all nervous. The packs were too heavy, the air was too thin, the sun was too hot— but we'd come too long and too far not to have seen any sign of

the sheep. We collapsed on the top of a rocky outcrop surrounded by tundra. Larry amused himself by shooting arrow after arrow at a ptarmigan (a fat bird with fuzzy white après-ski
boots on) who, as slow and stupid as that particular bird can be,
let the arrows whiz by its head. Larry couldn't hit it, and the
bird refused to fly away. Moe poked at a hole in the ground with
a long stick, worrying whatever was inside. I went into my pack
looking for food and found, buried between the cans of tuna
and dried apricots, a rock, quartz, I believe, weighing six or
seven pounds.

"You sons of bitches," I said to Larry and Moe, who had
been watching me, smirking.

That's when the ground hornets finally got angry enough
to come out of the hole in front of Moe. Maybe bees know who,
in a crowd, is allergic to them. These bees seemed to; four of
them, anyway, came straight for me and stung me on the hand.
The first-aid kit, the shots of epinephrine, had made it as far as
the mouth of the glacier and no farther, and that was at least
four hours away.

I sat quietly and listened to my heartbeat quicken, my
breathing accelerate into a frenzy. This is how it's all going to
end, I thought, bee stung, and trapped on the glacier with Larry
and Moe. Then self-preservation took over. I ordered Larry to
carry me on his back over to the glacier, ordered Moe to scout
ahead and find a place where the ice had melted and the water
had pooled. I tried to exert no energy as Larry climbed with me
across the moraine and onto the glacier. Moe whistled that he
had found a pool several inches deep, and Larry lay me in it,
while I did my best trying to breathe through the ever-smaller
opening that was my throat.

I lay in that glacial pool until I was so numb I wasn't even
sure I could feel my torso. Eventually, the adrenaline subsided
and my throat eased back open. My hand, my whole arm, was
swollen to five or six times its normal size. I wrapped myself up
in what remained of our dry clothes and tried to chew on a gra-

nola bar, but I had no appetite. The late Alaskan summer night was bending on into evening, the sun rolling sideways along the horizon and threatening to go below it. It would be cold soon and the night wind off the glacier would start. No one wanted to say what we all knew, that we had to get back down to the mouth of the glacier by nightfall, had to get to our sleeping bags before it turned cold. Larry couldn't carry me the whole way, and I wondered, if I couldn't make the climb back down through the tundra and rock and alders to where our gear lay, whether or not it would be the right thing for them simply to leave me behind.

"Let's give it a try," I said. "If we go now we can go slowly." This wasn't true, but I spoke with authority and the boys believed me. We'd be climbing back through those alders at the worst time of day. Our range of vision would be cut way down, the rocks and tree trunks would be slippery with dew, and the grizzly bears would be moving. "You guys sing real loud now," I told them, "let's give the bears the opportunity to do the right thing."

We moved across the tundra and back down into the alders. With every step, every tightening of muscle, my arm exploded in pain and my head swam. My pulse increased, my throat tightened, and I had to drop back a little and rest until it began to open again. Eventually the fall got so steep and the alders so thick that there was nothing to do but lower ourselves through the branches with our arms, like children on a jungle gym. The pain in my arm reached a certain level of excruciation, and then moved on into numbness, the way a blister will if you keep walking long hours after it has popped. We could hear animals moving near us in the alders, big animals, and every now and then we'd get a whiff of dark musk.

"Sing louder, goddammit!" I shouted ahead to the boys, who were scared into silence by the noises beside them and bent on getting back out in the open to the relative safety of the place on the glacier where we'd left the tent. They broke into a halfhearted round of "King of the Road," and I could tell by their voices they were moving much faster than I could and would soon leave me out of screaming range.

That's when the heavy chain on which I wore my bear claw caught on an alder branch, just as I bent my elbows and swung my legs down to the next lower set of branches, and my head snapped up and I was nearly hung there by the strength of that chain and the weakness of my arm and the force of gravity pulling me down. I gasped for breath but there was none, and so I lifted my one good arm up to the branch above me and did something I never could do in gym class—a one-handed chin-up—and repositioned my feet and unhooked my necklace from the alder branch.

I took the bear claw into the palm of my hand and felt the coolness of the silver. I felt my strong heart pumping, sending blood to every part of my body, including my misshapen arm, and I realized I'd had it wrong all along about the necklace. That I had relied on somebody else's set of metaphors to understand it. That it had nothing to do, finally, with an engagement ring or the man who gave it to me, that it had, finally, nothing whatsoever to do with a man. And that whatever role that man had played in taking me to the Alaskan wilderness in the first place, he had nothing to do with why I stayed, nothing to do with all the things my seasons with the hunters, with the animals, had taught me, nothing whatsoever to do with the strength and tenacity that was getting me, bee stung and frightened and freezing, down that near-dark Alaskan hill.

I wore the necklace differently after that. And years later, when the clasp on it wore paper-thin and the pendant fell one day into my accidentally open hand, I replaced it with a piece of eight from the seventeenth century that I found near a silver mine in Bolivia. I wait now to discover the meaning of this new/old silver I wear.

It's been four years since I've guided any hunters, though I have returned to the Alaskan wilderness every year—with a

camera or a kayak or a pair of cross-country skis. I am a far better outdoorsperson for my years guiding hunters, and even
more importantly, I have a much deeper understanding of my
animal self. I also have the blood of five fine and wild animals
on my hands and will never forget it. And this is perhaps why,
like the hunters, I need to keep telling my story, over and over
again.

Joyce Carol Oates
THE BUCK

This is such a terrible story. It's a story I have told a dozen times, never knowing *why*.

Why I can't forget it, I mean. Why it's lodged so deep in me . . . like an arrow through the neck.

Like that arrow I never saw—fifteen-inch, steel-tipped, razor-sharp—that penetrated the deer's neck and killed him, though not immediately. How many hours, I wonder, till he bled to death, till his body turned cold and grew heavier—they say the weight of Death is always heavier than that of life—how many hours, terrible hours, I don't know.

I was not a witness. The sole witness did not survive.

Each time I tell this story of the wounded buck, the hunter who pursued him, and the elderly woman who rescued him, or tried to rescue him, I think that maybe *this* telling will make a difference. *This* time a secret meaning will be revealed, as if without my volition, and I will be released.

But each telling is a subtle repudiation of a previous telling. So each telling is a new telling. Each telling a forgetting.

That arrow lodged ever more firmly, cruelly. In living flesh.

*   *   *

I'd take comfort in saying all this happened years ago, in some remote part of the country. *Once upon a time,* I'd begin, but in fact it happened within the past year, and no more than eight miles from where I live, in a small town called Bethany, New Jersey.

Which is in Saugatuck County, in the northwestern corner of the state, bordering the Delaware River.

A region that's mainly rural: farmland, hills, some of the hills large enough to be called mountains. There aren't many roads in this part of New Jersey, and the big interstate highways just slice through, gouge through the countryside, north and south, east and west. Strangers in a rush to get somewhere else.

The incident happened on the Snyder farm. A lonely place, no neighbors close by.

The name "Snyder" was always known in Saugatuck County even though, when I was growing up, the Snyders had sold off most of their land. In the family's prime, in the 1930s, they'd owned three hundred twenty acres, most of it rich farmland; in the 1950s they'd begun to sell, piecemeal, as if grudgingly, maybe with the idea of one day buying their land back. But they never did; they died out instead. Three brothers, all unmarried; and Melanie Snyder, the last of the family. Eighty-two years old when she was found dead in a room of the old farmhouse, last January.

In deer-hunting season. The season that had always frightened and outraged her.

She'd been vigilant for years. She'd acquired a local reputation. Her six acres of land—all that remained of the property—was scrupulously posted against hunters ("with gun, bow and arrow, dog") and trespassers. Before hunting with firearms was banned in Saugatuck County, Melanie Snyder patrolled her property in hunting season, on foot, fearless about moving in the direction of gunfire. "You! What are you doing here?" she would call out to hunters. "Don't you know this land is posted?" She was a lanky woman with a strong-boned face, skin that looked permanently wind-burnt, close-cropped starkly white hair. Her eyes were unusually dark and prominent; everyone commented on Melanie Snyder's eyes; she wasn't a woman any man, no matter his age, felt comfortable confronting, especially out in the woods.

She sent trespassers home, threatened to call the sheriff if they didn't leave. She'd stride through the woods clapping her hands to frighten off deer, pheasants, small game, send them panicked to safety.

White-tailed deer, or, as older generations called them, Virginia deer, were her favorites, "the most beautiful animals in creation." She hated it that state conservationists argued in favor of controlled hunting for the "good" of the deer themselves, to reduce their alarmingly fertile numbers.

She hated the idea of hunting with bow and arrow—as if it made any difference to a deer, how it died.

She hated the stealth and silence of the bow. With guns, you can at least hear the enemy.

* * *

His name was Wayne Kunz, "Woody" Kunz, part owner of a small auto parts store in Delaware Gap, New Jersey, known to his circle of male friends as a good guy. A good sport. You might say, a "character."

The way he dressed: his hunting gear, for instance.

A black simulated-leather jumpsuit, over it the regulation fluorescent-orange vest. A bright red cap, with earflaps. Boots to the knee, like a Nazi storm trooper's; mirror sunglasses hiding his pale lashless eyes. He had a large, round, singed-looking face, a small damp mouth: this big-bellied, quick-grinning fellow, the kind who keeps up a constant chatting murmur with himself, as if terrified of silence, of being finally *alone.*

He hadn't been able to talk any of his friends into coming with him, deer hunting with bow and arrow.

Even showing them his new Atlas bow, forty-eight inches, sleek blond fiberglass "wood," showing them the quill of arrows, synthetic-feathered, lightweight steel and steel-tipped and razor-sharp like no Indian's arrows had ever been—he'd been disappointed, disgusted with them, none of his friends wanting to come along, waking in the predawn dark, driving out in Saugatuck County to kill a few deer.

Woody Kunz. Forty years old, five feet ten inches, two hundred pounds. He'd been married, years ago, but the marriage hadn't worked out, and there were no children.

Crashing clumsily through the underbrush, in pursuit of deer.

Not wanting to think he was lost—*was* he lost?

Talking to himself, cursing and begging himself—"C'mon, Woody, for Christ's sake, Woody, move your fat *ass*"—half sobbing as, another time, a herd of deer broke and scattered before he could get into shooting range. Running and leaping through the woods, taunting him with their uplifted white tails, erect snowy-white tails like targets so he couldn't help but fire off an arrow—to fly into space, disappear.

"Fuck it, Woody! Fuck you, asshole!"

Later. He's tired. Even with the sunglasses his eyes are seared from the bright winter sun reflecting on the snow. Knowing he deserves better.

Another time the deer are too quick and smart for him,

must be they scented him downwind, breaking to run before he even saw them, only heard them, silent except for the sound of their crashing hooves. This time, he fires a shot knowing it won't strike any target, no warm living flesh. Must be he does it to make himself feel bad.

Playing the fool in the eyes of anybody watching and he can't help but think uneasily that somebody *is* watching—if only the unblinking eye of God.

And then: he sees the buck.

His buck, yes, suddenly. Oh, Jesus. His heart clenches, he *knows*.

He has surprised the beautiful dun-colored animal drinking from a fast-running stream; the stream is frozen except for a channel of black water at its center, the buck with its antlered head lowered. Woody Kunz stares, hardly able to believe his good luck, rapidly counting the points of the antlers—eight? ten?—as he fits an arrow into place with trembling fingers, lifts the bow, and sights along the arrow aiming for that point of the anatomy where neck and chest converge—it's a heart shot he hopes for—drawing back the arrow, feeling the power of the bow, releasing it; and seemingly in the same instant the buck leaps, the arrow has struck him in the neck, there's a shriek of animal terror and pain, and Woody Kunz shouts in ecstatic triumph.

But the buck isn't killed outright. To Woody's astonishment, and something like hurt, the buck turns and runs—flees.

* * *

Later he'd say he hadn't seen the NO TRESPASSING signs in the woods, he hadn't come by way of the road so he hadn't seen them there, the usual state-issued signs forbidding hunting, trapping, trespassing on private land, but Woody Kunz would claim he hadn't known it was private land exactly; he'd have to confess he might have been lost, tracking deer for hours moving more or less in a circle, not able to gauge where the center of the circle might be; and yes, he was excited, adrenaline rushing in his veins as he hadn't felt it in God knows how long, half a lifetime maybe, so he hadn't seen the signs posting the Snyder property or if he'd seen them they had not registered upon his consciousness or if they'd registered upon his consciousness he hadn't known what they were, so tattered and weatherworn.

That was Woody Kunz's defense, against a charge, if there was to be a charge, of unlawful trespassing and hunting on posted property.

* * *

Jesus is the most important person in all our lives!
Jesus abides in our hearts, no need to see Him!

These joyful pronouncements, or are they commandments, Melanie Snyder sometimes hears, rising out of the silence of the old house. The wind in the eaves, a shrieking of crows in the orchard, and this disembodied voice, the voice of her long-dead fiancé—waking her suddenly from one of her reveries, so she doesn't remember where she is, what year this is, what has happened to her, to have aged her so.

* * *

She'd fallen in love with her brothers, one by one. Her tall strong indifferent brothers.

Much later, to everyone's surprise and certainly to her own, she'd fallen in love with a young Lutheran preacher, just her age.

Standing just her height. Smiling at her shyly, his wire-rimmed glasses winking as if shyly too. Shaking her gloved hand. Hello, Miss Snyder. Like a brother who would at last see *her.*

Twenty-eight years old! She'd been fated to be a spinster,

of course. That plain, stubborn, sharp-tongued girl, eyes too large and stark and intelligent in her face to be "feminine," her body flat as a board.

In this place in which girls married as young as sixteen, began having their babies at seventeen, were valued and praised and loved for such qualities as they shared with brood mares and milking cows, you cultivated irony to save your soul—and your pride.

Except: she fell in love with the visiting preacher, introduced to him by family friends, the two "young people" urged together to speak stumblingly, clumsily to each other of—what? Decades later Melanie Snyder won't remember a syllable, but she remembers the young man's preaching voice, *Jesus! Jesus is our only salvation!* He'd gripped the edges of the pulpit of the Bethany church, God love shining in his face, white teeth bared like piano keys.

How it happened, how they became officially engaged—whether by their own decision or others'—they might not have been able to say. But it was time to marry, for both.

Plain, earnest, upright young people. Firm-believing Christians, of that there could be no doubt.

Did Melanie doubt? No, never!

She was prepared to be a Christian wife and to have her babies one by one. As God ordained.

There were passionate-seeming squeezes of her hand, there were chaste kisses, fluttery and insubstantial as a butterfly's wings. There were Sunday walks, in the afternoon. *Jesus is the most important person in my life, I feel Him close beside us—don't you, Melanie?*

The emptiness of the country lane, the silence of the sky, except for the crows' raucous jeering cries. Slow-spiraling hawks high overhead.

Oh, yes, certainly! Oh, yes.

Melanie Snyder's fiancé. The young just-graduated seminary student, with his hope to be a missionary. He was an energetic softball player, a pitcher of above-average ability; he led the Sunday school children on hikes, canoe trips. But he was most himself there in the pulpit of the Bethany church, elevated a few inches above the rapt congregation, where even his shy stammering rose to passion, a kind of sensual power. How strong the bones of his earnest, homely face, the fair-brown wings of hair brushed back neatly from his forehead! *Jesus, our redeemer. Jesus, our only salvation.* As if the God love shining in the young man's face were a beacon, a lighthouse beacon, flung out into the night, giving light yet unseeing, blind, in itself.

The engagement was never officially terminated. Always, there were sound reasons for postponing the wedding. Their families were disappointed but eager, on both sides, to comply. His letters came to her like clockwork, every two weeks, from North Carolina, where he was stationed as a chaplain in the U.S. Army. Dutiful letters, buoyant letters about his work, his "mission," his conviction that he was at last where God meant him to be.

Then the letters ceased. And they told Melanie he'd had an "accident" of some kind; there'd been a "misunderstanding" of some kind. He was discharged from his army post and reassigned to a Lutheran church in St. Louis, where he was to assist an older minister. But why? Melanie asked. Why, what has happened? Melanie demanded to know, but never was she told, never would a young woman be told such a thing, not for her ears, not for an ignorant virgin's ears; she'd wept and protested and mourned and lapsed finally into shame, not knowing what had happened to ruin her happiness but knowing it must constitute a rejection of her, a repudiation of the womanliness she'd tried so hard—ah, so shamefully hard!—to take on.

That feeling, that sense of unworthiness, she would retain for years. Studying her face in a mirror, plain, frank, unyielding, those eyes alit with irony, she realized she'd known all along— she was fated to be a spinster, never to be any man's wife.

And didn't that realization bring with it, in truth, relief?

Now, fifty years later, if those words *Jesus! Jesus abides in our hearts, no need to see Him!* ring out faintly in the silence of the old house, she turns aside, unhearing. For she's an old woman who has outlived such lies. Such subterfuge. She has taken revenge on Jesus Christ by ceasing to believe in Him—or in God, or in the Lutheran faith, or in such pieties as meekness, charity, love of one's enemies. Casting off her long-dead fiancé (who had not the courage even to write Melanie Snyder, finally, to release her from their engagement), she'd cast off his religion, as, drifting off from a friend, we lose the friends with whom he or she connected us, there being no deeper bond.

*　　*　　*

What is it?

She sees, in the lower pasture, almost out of the range of her vision, a movement of some kind: a swaying dun-colored shape, blurred by the frost on the aged glass. Standing in her kitchen, alert, aroused.

An animal of some kind? A large dog? A deer?

A wounded deer?

Melanie hurries to pull her sheepskin jacket from a peg; she's jamming her feet into boots, already angry, half knowing what she'll see.

Guns you could at least hear; now the slaughter is with bow and arrow. Grown men playing at Indians. Playing at killing.

The excuse is, the "excess" deer population in the county has to be kept down. White-tailed deer overbreeding, causing crop damage, auto accidents. As if men, the species of men who prowl the woods seeking innocent creatures to kill, need any excuse.

Melanie Snyder, who has known hunters all her life, including her own brothers, understands: to the hunter, killing an animal is just a substitute for killing another human being. Male, female. That's the forbidden fantasy.

She has never been frightened of accosting them, though, and she isn't now. Running outside into the gusty January air. A scowling wild-eyed old woman, sexless leathery face, white hair rising from her head in stiff tufts. She is wearing a soiled sheepskin jacket several sizes too large for her, a relic once belonging to one of her brothers; her boots are rubberized fishing boots, the castoffs of another, long-deceased brother.

Melanie is prepared for an ugly sight but this sight stuns her at first; she hears herself cry out, "Oh. Oh, God!"

A buck, full grown, beautiful, with handsome pointed antlers, is staggering in her direction, thrashing his head from side to side, desperate to dislodge an arrow that has penetrated his neck. His eyes roll in his head, his mouth is opening and closing spasmodically, blood flows bright and glistening from the wound; in fact it is two wounds, in the lower part of his neck near his left shoulder. Behind him, in the lower pasture, running clumsily after him, is the hunter, bow uplifted: a bizarre sight in black jumpsuit, bright orange vest, comical red hat. Like a robot or a spaceman, Melanie thinks, staring. She has never seen any hunter so costumed. Is this a man she should know? a face? a name? He's a hefty man with pale flushed skin, damp mouth, eyes hidden behind sunglasses with opaque mirrored lenses. His breath is steaming in the cold; he's clearly excited, agitated—dangerous. Fitting an arrow crookedly in his bow as if preparing, at this range, to shoot.

Melanie cries, "You! Get out of here!"

The hunter yells, "Lady, stand aside!"

"This land is posted! I'll call the sheriff!"

"Lady, you better gimme a clear shot!"

The buck is snorting, stamping his sharp-hooved feet in the snow. Deranged by terror and panic, he thrashes his antlered head from side to side, bleeding freely, bright-glistening blood underfoot, splattered onto Melanie Snyder's clothes as, instinctively, recklessly, she positions herself between the wounded animal and the hunter. She's pleading, angry. "Get off my land! Haven't you done enough evil? This poor creature! Let him alone!"

The hunter, panting, gaping at her, can't seem to believe what he sees: a white-haired woman in men's clothes, must be eighty years old, trying to shield a buck with an arrow through his neck. He advances to within a few yards of her, tries to circle around her. Saying incredulously, "That's my arrow, for Christ's sake, lady! That buck's a goner and he's *mine!*"

"Brute! Murderer! I'm telling you to get off my land or I'll call the sheriff and have you arrested!"

"Lady, that buck is goddamned dangerous—you better stand aside."

"*You* stand aside. Get off my property!"

"Lady, for Christ's sake—"

"You heard me: *get off my property!*"

So, for some minutes, there's an impasse.

Forever afterward Woody Kunz will remember, to his chagrin and shame: the beautiful white-tailed full-grown buck with the most amazing spread of antlers he'd ever seen—*his* buck, *his* kill, *his* arrow sticking through the animal's neck—the wounded buck snorting, thrashing his head, stamping the ground, blood everywhere, blood-tinged saliva hanging from his mouth in threads, and the crazy old woman shielding the buck with her body, refusing to surrender him to his rightful owner. And Woody Kunz is certain *he* is the rightful owner; he's shouting in the old woman's face, he's pleading with her, practically begging, finally; the fucking deer is *his*, he's earned it, he's been out tramping in the cold since seven this morning, God damn it if he's going to give up! Face blotched and hot, tears of rage and impotence stinging his eyes: oh, Jesus, he'd grab the old hag by the shoulders, lift her clear, and fire another arrow this time into the heart so there'd be no doubt—except, somehow, he doesn't do it, doesn't dare.

Instead, he backs off. Still with his bow upraised, his handsome brand-new Atlas bow from Sears, but the arrow droops useless in his fingers.

In a voice heavy with disgust, sarcasm, he says, "OK. OK, lady, you win."

The last glimpse Woody Kunz has of this spectacle, the old woman is trying clumsily to pull the arrow out of the buck's neck, and the buck is naturally putting up a struggle, swiping at her with his antlers, but weakly, sinking to his knees in the snow, then scrambling to his feet again; still the old woman persists; sure, she *is* crazy and deserves whatever happens to her, the front of her sheepskin jacket soaked in blood by now, blood even on her face, in her hair.

*   *   *

It isn't until late afternoon, hours later, that Woody Kunz returns home.

Having gotten lost in the countryside, wandered in circles in the woods, couldn't locate the road he'd parked his goddamned car on, muttering to himself, sick and furious and shamed, in a state of such agitation his head feels close to bursting, guts like a nest of tangled snakes. Never, *never*, is Woody Kunz going to live down this humiliation in his own eyes.

So he's decided not to tell anyone. Not even to fashion it into an anecdote to entertain his friends. Woody Kunz being cheated out of a twelve-point buck by an old lady? Shit, he'd rather die than have it known.

Sure, it crosses his mind he should maybe report the incident to the sheriff. Not to reiterate his claim of the deer—though the deer *is* his—but to report the old woman in case she's really in danger. Out there, seemingly alone, so old, in the middle of nowhere. A mortally wounded full-grown whitetail buck, crazed with pain and terror, like a visitation of God, in her care.

*   *   *

She's begging, desperate: "*Let* me help you, oh, please! Oh, please! Let me—"

Tugging at the terrible arrow, tugging forward, tugging back, her fingers slippery with blood. Woman and beast struggling, the one disdainful, even reckless, of her safety; the other dazed by trauma or loss of blood, not lashing out as ordinarily he would, to attack an enemy, with bared teeth, antlers, sharp hooves.

"Oh, please, you must not die, please—"

It's probable that Melanie Snyder has herself become deranged. All of the world having shrunk to the task at hand, to the forcible removal of this steel bar that has penetrated the buck's neck, fifteen-inch steel-glinting sharp-tipped arrow with white, synthetic quills—nothing matters but that *the arrow must be removed.*

The bulging eyes roll upward, there's bloody froth at the shuddering nostrils, she smells, tastes, the hot rank breath—then the antlers strike her in the chest, she's falling, crying out in surprise.

And the buck has pushed past her, fleeing on skidding hooves, on legs near buckling at the knees, so strangely—were she fully conscious she would realize, *so* strangely—into her father's house.

*   *   *

It won't be until three days later, at about this hour of the morning, that they'll discover her—or the body she has become. Melanie Snyder and the buck with the arrow through his neck.

But Melanie Snyder has no sense of what's coming, no cautionary fear. As if, this damp-gusty January morning, such a visitation, such urgency pressed upon her, has blotted out all anticipation of the future, let alone of danger.

In blind panic, voiding his bowels, the buck has run crashing into the old farmhouse, into the kitchen, through to the parlor; as Melanie Snyder sits dazed on the frozen ground beneath
her rear stoop he turns, furious, charges into a corner of the
room, collides with an upright piano, making a brief discordant
startled music, an explosion of muted notes; turns again, crashing into a table laden with family photographs, a lamp of stip-
pled milk glass with a fluted shade. A renewed rush of adrenaline empowers him; turning again, half rearing, hooves skidding
on the thin loose-lying Oriental carpet faded to near transpar-
ency, he charges his reflection in a mirror as, out back, Melanie
Snyder sits trying to summon her strength, trying to compre-
hend what has happened and what she must do.

She doesn't remember the buck having knocked her down,
thus can't believe he *has* attacked her.

She thinks, Without me, he is doomed.

She hears one of her brothers speaking harshly, scolding:
What is she doing there sitting on the ground?—*For the Lord's
sake, Melanie!*—but she ignores him, testing her right ankle, the
joint is livid with pain but not broken—she can shift her weight
to her other foot—a high-pitched ringing in her head as of
church bells, and where there should be terror there's determi-
nation, for Melanie Snyder is an independent woman, a woman
far too proud to accept, let alone solicit, her neighbors'
proffered aid since the death of the last of her brothers: she
wills herself not to succumb to weakness now, in this hour of
her trial.

Managing to get to her feet, moving with calculating slow-
ness. As if her bones are made of glass.

Overhead, an opaque January sky, yet beautiful. Like
slightly tarnished mother-of-pearl.

Except for the crows in their gathering place beyond the
barns, and the hoarse *uh-uh-uh* of her breathing: silence.

She enters the house. By painful inches, yet eagerly. Leaning heavily against the door frame.

She sees the fresh blood trail, sees and smells the moist animal droppings, so shocking, there on the kitchen floor she keeps clean with a pointless yet self-satisfying fanaticism, the aged linoleum worn nearly colorless, yes, but Melanie has a house owner's pride, and pride is all. The buck in his frenzy to escape the very confines he has plunged into is turning, rearing, snorting, crashing in the other room. Melanie calls, "I'm here! I will help you!"—blindly too entering the parlor with its etiolated light, tasseled shades drawn to cover three-quarters of the windows as, decades ago, Melanie Snyder's mother had so drawn them, to protect the furnishings against the sun. Surely she's a bizarre sight herself, drunk-swaying, staggering, her wrinkled face, hands glistening with blood, white hair in tufts as if she hasn't taken a brush to it in weeks, Melanie Snyder in the oversized sheepskin jacked she wears in town, driving a rusted Plymouth pickup truck with a useless muffler—everybody in Bethany knows Melanie Snyder though she doesn't know them, carelessly confuses sons with fathers, granddaughters with mothers, her own remote blood relations with total strangers—she's awkward in these rubberized boots many sizes too large for her shrunken feet, yet reaching out—unhesitantly, boldly—to the maddened buck who crouches in a corner facing her, his breath frothing in blood, in erratic shuddering waves, she is speaking softly, half begging, "I want to help you! Oh—" as the heavy head dips, the antlers rush at her—how astonishing the elegance of such male beauty, and the burden of it, God's design both playful and deadly shrewd, the strangeness of bone growing out of flesh, bone calcified and many-branched as a young apple tree—clumsily he charges this woman who is his enemy even as, with a look of startled concern, she opens her arms to him, the sharp antlers now striking her a second time in the chest and this time breaking her fragile collarbone as easily as one might break a chicken wishbone set to dry on a windowsill for days, and the momentum of his charge carries him helplessly forward, he falls, the arrow's quill brushing against

Melanie Snyder's face; as he scrambles in a frenzy to upright himself his sharp hooves catch her in the chest, belly, pelvis; he has fallen heavily, as if from a great height, as if flung down upon her, breath in wheezing shudders and the blood froth bubbling around his mouth, and Melanie Snyder lies pinned beneath the animal body, legs gone, lower part of her body gone, a void of numbness, not even pain, distant from her as something seen through the wrong end of a telescope, rapidly retreating.

* * *

How did it happen, how strange; they were of the same height now, or nearly: Melanie Snyder and her tall strong indifferent brothers. Never married, none of them, d'you know why? No woman was ever quite good enough for the Snyder boys, and the girl, Melanie—well, one look at her and you know: a born spinster.

It's more than thirty years after they informed her, guardedly, without much sympathy—for perhaps sympathy would have invited tears, and they were not a family comfortable with tears—that her fiancé had been discharged from the army, that Melanie dares to ask, shyly, without her customary aggressiveness, what had really happened, what the mysterious "accident," or was it a "misunderstanding," had been. And her brother, her elder by six years, an aged slope-shouldered man with a deeply creased face, sighs and passes his hand over his chin and says, in a tone of mild but unmistakable contempt, "Don't ask."

She lies there beneath the dying animal, then beneath the lifeless stiffening body, face no more than four inches from the great head, the empty eyes—how many hours she's conscious, she can't gauge.

At first calling, into the silence, "Help—help me! Help—"

There *is* a telephone in the kitchen; rarely does it ring, and when it rings Melanie Snyder frequently ignores it, doesn't want people inquiring after her, well-intentioned neighbors, good Lutherans from the church she hasn't set foot in, except for funerals, in twenty-odd years.

The dying animal, beautiful even in dying, bleeding to death, soaking Melanie Snyder's clothes with his blood, and isn't she bleeding too, from wounds in her throat and face, her hands?

And he's dead, she feels the life pass from him—"Oh, no, oh, *no*," sobbing and pushing at the body, warm sticky blood by degrees cooling and congealing—the wood-fire stove in the kitchen has gone out and cold eases in from out-of-doors; in fact the kitchen door must be open, creaking and banging in the wind. A void rises from the loose-fitting floorboards as from the lower part of Melanie's body; she's sobbing as if her heart is broken, she's furious, trying to lift the heavy body from her, clawing at the body, raking her torn nails and bleeding fingers against the buck's thick winter coat, a coarse-haired furry coat, but the buck's body will not budge.

The weight of Death, so much more powerful than life.

Later. She wakes moaning and delirious, a din as of sleet pellets against the windows, and the cold has congealed the buck's blood and her own, the numbness has moved higher, obliterating much of what she has known as "body" these eighty-odd years; she understands that she is dying—consciousness like a fragile bubble, or a skein of bubbles—yet she is able still to wish to summon her old strength, the bitter joy of her stubborn strength, pushing at the heavy animal body, dead furry weight, eyes sightless as glass and the arrow, the terrible arrow, the obscene arrow: "Let me *go*. Let me *free*."

Fainting and waking. Drifting in and out of consciousness.

Hearing that faint ringing voice in the eaves, as always subtly chiding, in righteous reproach of Melanie Snyder, mixed with the wind and that profound agelessness of wind as if blowing to us from the farthest reaches of time as well as space—

Jesus! Jesus is our only salvation! Jesus abides in our hearts!—
but in pride she turns aside unhearing; never has she begged,
nor will she beg now. Oh, never.

And does she regret her gesture, trying to save an innocent
beast? She does not.

And would she consent, even now, to having made a mistake, acted improvidently? She would not.

* * *

When after nearly seventy-two hours Woody Kunz over-
comes his manly embarrassment and notifies the Saugatuck
County sheriff's office of the "incident" on the Snyder farm and
they go out to investigate, they find eighty-two-year-old Melanie Snyder dead, pinned beneath the dead white-tail buck, in
the parlor of the old farmhouse in which no one outside the
Snyder family had stepped for many years. An astonishing sight:
human and animal bodies virtually locked together in the rigor
of death, their mingled blood so soaked into Melanie Snyder's
clothes, so frozen, it is possible to separate them only by force.

Margaret Atwood

DREAM 2: BRIAN THE STILL-HUNTER

The man I saw in the forest
used to come to our house
every morning, never said anything;
I learned from the neighbours later
he once tried to cut his throat.

I found him at the end of the path
sitting on a fallen tree
cleaning his gun.

There was no wind;
around us the leaves rustled.

He said to me:
I kill because I have to

but every time I aim, I feel
my skin grow fur
my head heavy with antlers
and during the stretched instant
the bullet glides on its thread of speed
my soul runs innocent as hooves.

Is God just to his creatures?

I die more often than many.

He looked up and I saw
the white scar made by the hunting knife
around his neck.

When I woke
I remembered: he has been gone
twenty years and not heard from.

Margaret Atwood
THE TRAPPERS

The trappers, trapped
between the steel jaws of their answerless
dilemma, their location,
follow, stop, stare down
at dead eyes
                    caught in fur

Each time there is a repetition
of red on white, the footprints, the inevitable

blood. The dead thing, the
almost-dead that must be
bludgeoned, the few they leave
alive to breed for next year's
traps. The chain, the
steel circles

The snow snaps in their faces;
the forest closes
behind them like a throat.
The branches have
cold blood

    Their following, the abstract hunger
    to trap and smash
    the creature, to crush
    the red sun at the centre

also the wish
to mark the snow with feral
knowledge, to enter the narrow
resonant skull, to make each
tree and season an owned
territory

    but then the recurring fear
    of warm fur, the puritan
    shunning of all summer

I can understand

the guilt they feel because
they are not animals
the guilt they feel
because they are

Louise Erdrich
THE WANDERING ROOM

My father taught me how to use my hands as tools, how to flex them, toughen them, how to keep them steady, how to work big, work fine, how to build arrows. We used a small wooden table in a cleared out corner of the basement. I sat beside Jack in a creaking chair, and kept his things in order, lined up his tubes of bonding cement in rows, kept jars of orange and yellow nocks sorted out, the vanes in rectangular boxes–green, gray, white, and red. We sat in the light of a little black adjustable lamp, just him and me, as he sighted down a light Serpent shaft and cut it to the right size for the draw weight on his bow. He carefully lifted a three-blade Broadhead from a special wooden container, and began to build. We'd work for hours in the little circle of intense light, and when we had half a dozen balanced shafts, all matched, all ready, all perfect, I handed them to him one by one and he fit those arrows into a rack high above the shelves of levels, just underneath the ceiling tiles, to dry where no one could accidentally touch and slice themselves upon the razor sharp and fitted blades.

Some people like to hunt on days of good weather only, but Jack liked threatening skies. He woke me one cold morning in November and we went out with the smell of grit in the air, the clouds low and sullen even in the ink-dark of 5 A.M. By seven the sun would glow behind them like a feeble bulb, the light would grow and spread until the cut fields, the roads, the sloughs, and land along the river exuded bands of chilly fog. Jack drove carefully, and I dozed beside him, strapped into the passenger's seat of the pickup. The seat belt was too big and in my dreams I felt my head roll against it, back and forth. The metallic belt landed on my mouth like tape again and again. Jack's army jacket, on the seat between us, had deep pockets full of candy bars, sandwiches, and apples, for me, and for the dog, Liver Snaps and two big Milk Bones. Candice had made us take Pepperboy along, and the dog curled on the floor of the truck. I could feel the tension running off its fur, and I was afraid to move or shift my feet.

Jack always started hunting on his dad's and uncle's land, a huge old farm that he had bought out from under them, gambling that someday it would be a prime development parcel. Along the eastern corner, through it, ran an oxbow of the river, and there was, in the tangle of brush and downed trees, enough shelter for a few deer to haunt the edges of the fields now and live off the missed corn and the wheat stubble. Jack wasn't a successful hunter, he used a left-handed Martin Recurve, a classic, and rarely got a clear shot, but there was an understanding between the two of us about hunting anyway. Since he had started using a bow, Jack had never shot a deer, said he didn't care all that much about whether or not he got one, anyway, because he felt that bow hunting made him superior to those who killed by looking through the sights of a powerful rifle. "What did they know," he had said to his girlfriend Candice once, "what intimacy did they feel with the animal?"

"Intimacy?" A wondering tone had lifted her voice. She hadn't said anything else, but Jack was positive she scorned his hobby and we were both sure, considering how careful she usually was with Pepperboy, that she had sent the dog along in order to scare off any deer that might stumble into his range. Jack knew how to fix that, of course, and he told me that he planned to tie the dog to the back of the pickup anyway and hunt far enough from its noise and scent so that it couldn't cause problems. Now, we turned down an almost unused section road, and steered for the river, lowering the front wheels gently into the deep washouts and ruts, calmly managing a few impossible spots where the road fell away entirely.

I woke the way I always did, popping to the surface of sleep, ready for what came next.

"Where are we?"

And then I looked at the twist of leafless box elders, eased my feet out from under the dog. I flipped the passenger's mirror down to slick my hair back, and smiled at myself, always anxious. My teeth were big and lopsided that year, and I kept hoping they would straighten out all by themselves.

"Did you see any?"

"No."

We got out of the truck. Jack took half a ham sandwich from his pocket and placed it on the step-up board. When Pepperboy snatched it, Jack grabbed his collar, tied him onto a piece of nylon rope, and secured it around the fender. Then Jack nudged at the dog with his foot, teasing, growled back when Pepperboy growled at him and lunged to the end of the tether. Jack turned away and took his bow from the quilted camouflage-printed case, bent it, strung it, and then took one arrow from the rack attached to the handle and carried it loosely along with the bow, the nock between his knuckles on the string.

"How come you're carrying that arrow out?" I said, mocking him.

"Always be prepared," Jack said. "That's my motto. What's yours?"

I didn't have one yet.

We started down the dwindled road, me following carefully, and didn't speak as we passed into the sudden growth of woods just past the plowed-under stubble of wheat. No branch rasped. It was just dawn, the light breaking in red streaks under a low inverted bowl of thick gray-blue clouds. The breeze was not yet up and every step and breath rang hollow. We followed a thinly worn trail into the deeper underbrush along the river, and when that petered out, and the river ran on, made an oxbow farther west, Jack headed for a copse of tall trees on its bank where I knew he had nailed a little stand last year.

The tree was just on the edge of a field of corn. The dried stalks were still neck high and now, as the light broadened, the wind gathered enough to blow the flat blades of the leaves against one another. The deep whisper of their noise was a relief. Jack leaned down, told me that he had an idea. We could hear, faintly, Pepperboy's barks, a low odd gurgling noise of complaint, from behind us. The tree where his stand was nailed up was across the field directly, and there were probably, we felt sure of it, deer even now stopped silently in the uncut cover, ears turning, gathering each sound. He stopped, and in a crouch, whispered my instructions.

He would double far around and reach his tree from the next field over, from behind, it would take him about half an hour. Jack put his watch on my wrist and marked the time. In exactly half an hour, then, I was to walk slowly through the cornfield toward the tree that he pointed out. I was to walk one step per second, One Mississippi, Two Mississippi, Three. I would put my hands out and brush the stalks as I went forward, not to make a lot of noise, but enough simply to move the deer. They wouldn't be driven. Jack said, but they might be coaxed, encouraged to move by the sound of the dog and my presence. They would only flow from one area of cover to another, preferably denser, and in that nearest place of cover he would wait.

I looked at the face of the heavy black diver's watch, my heart tapping regularly. He ticked the end of my nose with his finger and said, "Good boy."

"Good lady."

I punched at him.

"Now," he said in a low voice, "here I go." He touched his wrist to remind me of the watch, and walked sharply right to begin his wide circle. I watched him walk noiselessly as possible through a thick shelterbelt of wild plums and evergreens, melt along the sides of trees, avoid fallen branches, slide his feet carefully along the edges of the pits of brush and grass. I lost sight of him on the edge of the next field over, sunflowers, then saw him briefly as he took the edge and swiftly found his way through the back side of the strip of woods that faced onto the river. Then he disappeared. His tree, I remembered, was the second largest, with a big low limb to use as a step. He'd thread his bow and rack through the leafless twigs and make his way up to the sturdy little platform he'd built. All would be as he'd left it. Even the nail I'd banged in to hang his thermos of coffee by the strap would still be there, unrusted.

Now, I imagined, he'd find his posture, put his arrows in exact reach, prepare himself. He couldn't see me yet because I was still crouched out of sight, but I was wearing a bright pink jacket. He'd made me wear an orange cap, too, fluorescent, and so the moment that I stood that cap would be a beacon.

I still see myself, as if through his eyes, just as he'd pictured, the orange-pink dash wavering across the field into the furrow as I began walking, half hidden as I entered the nearest row. I couldn't hear the dog or see any deer at all yet. On one knee, balanced, ready and sighting along the margins of the field for the first nervous buck to step out, I knew Jack bated his breath and counted with me, stepping along with me, One Mississippi, Two. He kept me, brilliant, in the corner of his eye, and never lost me as he scanned the field for moving shadows. Gray as sand, sifting, soft as swept powder, they would appear without announcement, materializing almost, as if the air took shape. There, now, I saw two. Does, both of them. Another. It was a medium-sized buck, not bad at all, perfect. It had a small rack, its sides were filled out with corn. I coaxed it through the pale stalks, toward my father, who sighted above the stroke of the blade, nothing but air between him and it, watching it, waiting it out. My heart pumped. He would get it with one shot. Ours. I willed it closer, willed it to turn, heading toward the stand, as it must. It was recalcitrant, though, and moved slowly, suspiciously, unwilling to give up the restless leaves all around. Every so often, it stared testingly, hung back behind the does, froze and studied the air. Twenty Mississippi. Thirty. Forty. I stepped and halted. And then, tipping my face up carefully, I saw my father draw the bowstring. Quiet, even, slow, with all of his strength, he pulled back and poised.

I turned back to the back, and was watching so hard that I felt the tremble of its planted hooves. There was a long lazy moment before the shock, the sick wonder. Jack's arrow slammed into it light, pure light. I didn't see it happen. First the buck blew a huff of alarm, and then exploded upward in shock.

I thought I heard, impossibly, the animal laugh high in surprise, like a little child.

Then it flew, as high on springs, and bounced straight over my outflung body. I had thrown myself down and now I came up running. Toward Jack, safe. The buck, hit, bounded straight back into the corn cover.

Jack hadn't moved, his mouth was open, and his bow,

dropped from his shocked fingers, caught in a lower branch. I stood below the tree, looking up at him, right underneath the suspended rack of arrows, and I knew in one part of my mind that he hadn't known I was so close.

"Step back slowly, careful," Jack said to me in a calm voice.

When I had, he retrieved the bow and climbed down the tree and then put the bow down in the grass. He stood before me, but he couldn't look at me. My arms felt heavy, my face fat as the moon. I shook my head, dizzy, then shook it harder as if to scatter my thoughts. I took a deep breath, groaned, and again the weight of that shot creaked through that living body, squeezing my heart shut. Tears flushed behind my eyes, salting the edges of my lids, but I opened my eyes wide.

"Goddamn, come here." He knelt down and when I walked into his arms I buried my face against his neck, beneath his collar, for just an instant. I smelled cold grit from the field, the faintly sour wool of his scarf and mittens, a teasel breath of sweet soap. His arms closed tighter and my wild thoughts composed in sentence strings, together, balanced on wires. I wanted to speak, but I couldn't form a word, and somehow a moment later I was all right.

"I hit that buck," he was standing up, all business now, explaining, "so I have to go after it."

I patted my mittens together. "I'm going with you. Don't say no."

He didn't answer, just walked forward, bending down to the little trampled placed, me right behind him. He touched the edge of a leaf and walked a little farther down, rubbed his fingers in the sudden, dark rich blood.

"Paunched it, oh fuck."

I stepped behind him, alert and noiseless now, intent as he was on the trail of blood and deep split moons of hoofprints that led back through the field and into the gnarled swatch of trees and rigid tip-ups on the riverbank. He said that the thing to do would have been to wait for a couple of hours and let the deer go until it lay down and stiffened. But the wind had deepened, gone raw with that choking dust smell of oncoming snow, so we had to follow. A little sleet swirled out of the trees and down along the edges of the field. The buck was taking the riverbank and heading west, in deepest cover, toward an area that was well hunted and where Jack was sure that someone else would put a tag on his buck if he just left it. So he looked again at me, I stared right back at him. We kept on tracking.

Every so often, he bent down, put a finger into the side of a print, or showed me the blood sign. I was careful, spotted details, pointed out the waver in the side of the hoof that marked our buck from other deer tracks. Sometimes, I caught the trail where he had lost it and we went on, the snow swirling up at us now, a couple of inches deep, the dark blood unfrozen once, before the buck caught our scent and bolted across a field.

"We're going to find it, over there, dead," Jack told me, and we started across the field at a diagonal. He could feel me lagging, trying to keep up, slowing down and then galloping at him. The wind had gone past raw and stuck at freezing. It lay a burning hand on my brow and stiffened my cheeks. My fists had shut in my sleeves, wooden blocks, and Jack said that when we reached the trees we'd stop and build a fire to warm up before he dressed out the buck. Then he looked back more keenly, and met my eyes for a moment. I was blank, empty and stopped of will, except that I was bound not to quit. He paused, waited for me, and when he saw me close, cheeks slashed with white, his face changed. He sucked in his breath and stuck his bow upright in dirt.

"Remember where I put this," he said. As if we could, in snow that began to fall.

He lifted me against him, staggered as I molded to his chest, legs around his waist, arms under his and fists balled against his jacket, face at the opened zipper of his parka, taking in the warmth of his chest and scarf. The snow fell thicker, in waving bands that met, until the world was white around us and ghostly. We almost seemed not to be moving. We tried to test the air for direction, but lost bearings. Jack thought he had made it to the edge of the field, but there was no shelterbelt. He muttered, thought he'd turned, heading toward the highway, but the highway did not rise beneath his feet. There were no fences, no boundaries, no features in the landscape, just the whiteness that enclosed us in a wandering room.

* * *

When my father was pressed to the limit, he always made things come out all right, and he did that time, too. He didn't stop, he knew better than to stop. He didn't once put me down. You can say all you want to about him, but when I think back to who he really was, he was that man. He was that man in the whiteout who refused to put me down. He kept walking and made his way back along the river where the snow let up enough so that, eventually, he found his way back to the road and the pickup truck.

He bundled me right into the door, before the heater, took his parka off and packed it around me, then jumped in and turned the key in the ignition. The motor caught, and after a few moments he swung into reverse and decided that he could back down the road. Glancing over my shoulder, I looked straight into Pepperboy's contemptuous muzzle at the back window. We'd forgotten about the dog, but he was tied onto the tailgate's metal and the rope was long enough so he could sit on the pile of tarps next to the cab. As Jack eased the truck backwards, Pepperboy disappeared. I opened my mouth but said nothing.

"You okay?" said Jack.

"Yeah." My voice came from somewhere far away. I could feel myself shaking deep in his jacket.

"The heat should come on," Jack said.

He moved the wand to red and the roar of air filled the cab as we swung off the two-rut road onto the highway. There, the snow squall had finished and blown straight off the asphalt, dusting the ditches and fields. The sky came back in blowing patches of blue. Jack fished a sandwich from his pocket and ate it wolfishly. I threw myself across the seat and wrung my hands in the air while my toes and fingers thawed, stinging, but when I was warm I sat up, remarkably and suddenly all right, and I unwrapped a sandwich and began to eat with Jack. Perhaps because the heater roared so loud, filling our heads, or maybe because we were so intent on eating every bit of food we'd brought, neither one of us noticed that, when we stopped at the town's first light, Pepperboy jumped from the back of the pickup. Tied to the tailgate, the dog tumbled end over end, tried to skitter to his feet, got tossed down again, lunged once at the collar and the rope that held him. Then, for about a quarter of a mile, he gave up and went entirely limp as the truck dragged him to the next light.

We heard the car behind us honking, but the sound did not penetrate until the sudden frantic drumming on the back wall of the pickup box. A man's face appeared suddenly in his window, mouth open in a long shout. Jack opened the window, turned down the heater so he could hear, then turned off the engine. I jumped out the other side, and ran back to the dog. Limp, stretched long, legs folded and curled beneath, Pepperboy lay at the end of the chain, the collar bound tight beneath his ears. Jack bent down first, undid the collar with careful hands and gave the rope to me. I knelt and the dog's cold eye opened, blinked wide, fixed me in a flat beam of understanding. My father put his arms on my shoulder then, to spare me I suppose, to turn me away. But resisted. I would not let myself be turned.

Carol Frost
TO KILL A DEER

Into the changes of autumn brush
the doe walked, and the hide, head and ears
were the tinsel browns. They made her.
I could not see her. She reappeared, stuffed with apples,
and I shot her. Into the pines she ran,
and I ran after. I might have lost her,
seeing no sign of blood or scuffle,
but felt myself part of the woods,
a woman with a doe's ears, and heard her

dying, counted her last breaths like a song
of dying, and found her dying.
I shot her again because her eyes
were open, and her lungs rattled like castanets,
then poked her with the gun barrel
because her eyes were dusty and unreal.
I opened her belly and pushed the insides
like rotted fruit into a rabbit hole,
skinned her, broke her leg joints under my knee,
took the meat, smelled the half-digested smell
that was herself. Ah, I closed her eyes.
I left her refolded in some briars
with the last sun on her head
like a benediction, head tilted on its axis
of neck and barren bone; head bent
wordless over a death, though I heard
the night wind blowing through her fur,
heard riot in the emptied head.

Carol Frost

BALANCE

i s how you carry it, how it is; for example, the turkeys
   which seemed ordinary—grazing
through the piled brush for butternuts, all head and
      feathers, then taking the shot
because they didn't see you standing on a stump,
one dying outright, the other baffled, half rising in the
      brown light and batted
to the ground—how ungainly large they made the
      afternoon, heaping up out of slopes,

trees, torn pieces of clouds
an excitement. When you stopped running, you took
    them from under your jacket,
where they had kept shifting and threatening to slip out,
still with a bit of warmth in them, and grasped one in
    each hand
by its horned feet like handles to steady yourself, leaning
    into the
land's steepness and accord, growing used to them, their
    difference.

Annie Dillard

STALKING

I

Summer: I go down to the creek again, and lead a creek life. I watch and stalk.

*   *   *

The Eskimos' life changes in summer, too. The caribou flee from the inland tundra's mosquitos to the windy shores of the

Arctic Ocean, and coastal Eskimos hunt them there. In the old days before they had long-range rifles, the men had to approach the wary animals very closely for a kill. Sometimes, waiting for a favorable change of weather so they could rush in unseen and unscented, the Eskimos would have to follow the fleet herds on foot for days, sleepless.

Also in summer they dredge for herring with nets from shoreline camps. In the open water off the Mackenzie River delta, they hunt the white whale (the beluga) and bearded seal. They paddle their slender kayaks inland to fresh water and hunt muskrats, too, which they used to snare or beat with sticks.

To travel from camp to camp in summer, coastal Eskimos ply the open seas in big *umiaks* paddled by women. They eat fish, goose or duck eggs, fresh meat, and anything else they can get, including fresh "salad" of greens still raw in a killed caribou's stomach and dressed with the delicate acids of digestion.

On St. Lawrence Island, women and children are in charge of netting little birds. They have devised a cruel and ingenious method: after they net a few birds with great effort and after much stalking, they thread them alive and squawking through their beaks' nostrils, and fly them like living kites at the end of long lines. The birds fly frantically, trying to escape, but they cannot, and their flapping efforts attract others of their kind, curious—and the Eskimos easily net the others.

They used to make a kind of undershirt out of bird skins, which they wore under fur parkas in cold weather, and left on inside the igloos after they'd taken the parkas off. It was an elaborate undertaking, this making of a bird-skin shirt, requiring thousands of tiny stitches. For thread they had the stringy sinew found along a caribou's backbone. The sinew had to be dried, frayed, and twisted into a clumsy thread. Its only advantages were that it swelled in water, making seams more or less waterproof, and it generally contained a minute smear of fat, so if they were starving they could suck their sewing thread and add maybe five minutes to their lives. For needles they had shards of bone, which got thinner and shorter every time they pushed through tough skins, so that an old needle might be little more than a barely enclosed slit. When the Eskimos first met the advanced culture of the south, men and women alike admired it first and foremost for its sturdy sewing needles. For it is understood that without good clothing, you perish. A crewman from a whaler with a paper of needles in his pocket could save many lives, and was welcome everywhere as the rich and powerful always are.

I doubt that they made bird-skin shirts anymore, steel needles or no. They do not do many of the old things at all anymore, except in my mind, where they hunt and stitch well, with an animal skill, in silhouette always against white oceans of ice.

Down here, the heat is on. Even a bird-skin shirt would be too much. In the cool of the evening I take to the bridges over the creek. I am prying into secrets again, and taking my chances. I might see anything happen; I might see nothing but light on the water. I walk home exhilarated or becalmed, but always changed, alive. "It scatters and gathers," Heraclitus said, "it comes and goes." And I want to be in the way of its passage, and cooled by its invisible breath.

In summer, I stalk. Summer leaves obscure, heat dazzles, and creatures hide from the red-eyed sun, and me. I have to seek things out. The creatures I seek have several senses and free will; it becomes apparent that they do not wish to be seen. I can stalk them in either of two ways. The first is not what you think of as true stalking, but it is the *Via negativa*, and as fruitful as actual pursuit. When I stalk this way I take my stand on a bridge and wait, emptied. I put myself in the way of the creature's passage, like spring Eskimos at a seal's breathing hole. Something might come; something might go. I am Newton under the apple tree, Buddha under the bo. Stalking the other way, I forge my own passage seeking the creature. I wander the banks; what I find, I follow, doggedly, like Eskimos haunting the caribou herds. I am Wilson squinting after the traces of electrons in a cloud chamber; I am Jacob at Peniel wrestling with the angel.

* * *

Fish are hard to see either way. Although I spend most of the summer stalking muskrats, I think it is fish even more than muskrats that by their very mystery and hiddenness crystalize the quality of my summer life at the creek. A thick spawning of fish, a bedful of fish, is too much, horror; but I walk out of my way in hopes of glimpsing three bluegills bewitched in a pool's depth or rising to floating petals or bubbles.

The very act of trying to see fish makes them almost impossible to see. My eyes are awkward instruments whose casing is clumsily outsized. If I face the sun along a bank I cannot see into the water; instead of fish I see water striders, the reflected undersides of leaves, birds' bellies, clouds and blue sky. So I cross to the opposite bank and put the sun at my back. Then I can see into the water perfectly within the blue shadow made by my body; but as soon as that shadow looms across them, the fish vanish in a flurry of flashing tails.

Occasionally by waiting still on a bridge or by sneaking smoothly into the shade of a bankside tree, I see fish slowly materialize in the shallows, one by one, swimming around and around in a silent circle, each one washed in a blue like the sky's and all as tapered as tears. Or I see them suspended in a line in deep pools, parallel to the life-giving current, literally "streamlined." Because fish have swim bladders filled with gas that balances their weight in the water, they are actually hanging from their own bodies, as it were, as gondolas hang from balloons. They wait suspended and seemingly motionless in clear water; they look dead, under a spell, or captured in amber. They look like the expressionless parts hung in a mobile, which has apparently suggested itself to mobile designers. Fish! They manage to be so water-colored. Theirs is not the color of the bottom but the color of the light itself, the light dissolved like a powder in the water. They disappear and reappear as if by spontaneous generation: sleight of fish.

I am coming around to fish as spirit. The Greek acronym for some of the names of Christ yields *ichthys*, Christ as fish, and fish as Christ. The more I glimpse the fish in Tinker Creek, the more satisfying the coincidence becomes, the richer the symbol, not only for Christ but for the spirit as well. The people must live. Imagine for a Mediterranean people how much easier it is to haul up free, fed fish in nets than to pasture hungry herds on those bony hills and feed them through a winter. To say that holiness is a fish is a statement of the abundance of grace; it is the equivalent of affirming in a purely materialistic culture that money does indeed grow on trees. "Not as the world gives do I give to you;" these fish are spirit food. And revelation is a study in stalking: "Cast the net on the right side of the ship, and ye shall find."

Still—of course—there is a risk. More men in all of time have died at fishing than at any other human activity except perhaps the making of war. You go out so far . . . and you are blown, or stove, or swamped, and never seen again. Where are the fish? Out in the underwater gaps, out where the winds are, wary, adept, invisible. You can lure them, net them, troll for them, club them, clutch them, chase them up an inlet, stun them with plant juice, catch them in a wooden wheel that runs all night—and you still might starve. They are there, they are certainly there, free, food, and wholly fleeting. You can see them if you want to; catch them if you can.

It scatters and gathers; it comes and goes. I might see a monstrous carp heave out of the water and disappear in a smack of foam, I might see a trout emerge in a riffle under my dangling hand, or I might see only a flash of back parts fleeing. It is the same all summer long, all year long, no matter what I seek. Lately I have given myself over almost entirely to stalking muskrats—eye food. I found out the hard way that waiting is better than pursuing; now I usually sit on a narrow pedestrian bridge at a spot where the creek is shallow and wide. I sit alone and alert, but stilled in a special way, waiting and watching for a change in the water, for the tremulous ripples rising in intensity that signal the appearance of a living muskrat from the underwater entrance to its den. Muskrats are cautious. Many, many evenings I wait without seeing one. But sometimes it turns out that the focus of my waiting is misdirected, as if Buddha had been expecting the fall of an apple. For when the muskrats don't show, something else does.

* * *

I positively ruined the dinner of a green heron on the creek last week. It was fairly young and fairly determined not to fly away, but not to be too foolhardy, either. So it had to keep an eye on me. I watched it for half an hour, during which time it stalked about in the creek moodily, expanding and contracting its incredible, brown-streaked neck. It made only three lightning-quick stabs at strands of slime for food, and all three times occurred when my head was turned slightly away.

The heron was in calm shallows; the deepest water it walked in went two inches up its orange legs. It would go and get something from the cattails on the side, and, when it had eaten it—tossing up its beak and contracting its throat in great gulps—it would plod back to a dry sandbar in the center of the creek which seemed to serve as its observation tower. It wagged its stubby tail up and down; its tail was so short it did not extend beyond its folded wings.

Mostly it just watched me warily, as if I might shoot it, or steal its minnows for my own supper, if it did not stare me down. But my only weapon was stillness, and my only wish its continued presence before my eyes. I knew it would fly away if I made the least false move. In half an hour it got used to me—as though I were a bicycle somebody had abandoned on the bridge, or a branch left by high water. It even suffered me to turn my head slowly, and to stretch my aching legs very slowly. But finally, at the end, some least motion or thought set it off, and it rose, glancing at me with a cry, and winged slowly away upstream, around a bend, and out of sight.

*   *   *

I find it hard to see anything about a bird that it does not want seen. It demands my full attention. Several times waiting for muskrats, however, I have watched insects doing various special things who were, like the mantis laying her eggs, happily oblivious to my presence. Twice I was not certain what I had seen.

Once it was a dragonfly flying low over the creek in an unusual rhythm. I looked closely; it was dipping the tip of its abdomen in the water very quickly, over and over. It was flying in a series of tight circles, just touching the water at the very bottom arc of each circle. The only thing I could imagine it was doing was laying eggs, and this later proved to be the case. I actually saw this, I thought—I actually saw a dragonfly laying her eggs not five feet away.

It is this peculiar stitching motion of the dragonfly's abdomen that earned it the name "darning needle"—parents used to threaten their children by saying that, if the children told lies, dragonflies would hover over their faces as they slept and sew their lips together. Interestingly, I read that only the great speed at which the egg-laying female dragonfly flies over the water prevents her from being "caught by the surface tension and pulled down." And at that same great speed the dragonfly I saw that day whirred away, downstream: a drone, a dot, and then gone.

Another time I saw a water strider behaving oddly. When there is nothing whatsoever to see, I watch the water striders skate over the top of the water, and I watch the six dots of shade—made by their feet dimpling the water's surface—slide dreamily over the bottom silt. Their motion raises tiny ripples or wavelets ahead of them over the water's surface, and I had noticed that when they feel or see these ripples coming towards them, they tend to turn away from the ripples' source. In other words, they avoid each other. I figure this behavior has the effect of distributing them evenly over an area, giving them each a better chance at whatever it is they eat.

But one day I was staring idly at the water when something out of the ordinary triggered my attention. A strider was skating across the creek purposefully instead of randomly. Instead of heading away from ripples made by another insect, it was racing towards them. At the center of the ripples I saw that some sort of small fly had fallen into the water and was struggling to right itself. The strider acted extremely "interested;" it jerked after the fly's frantic efforts, following it across the creek and back again, inching closer and closer like Eskimos stalking caribou. The fly could not escape the surface tension. Its efforts were diminishing to an occasional buzz; it floated against the bank, and the strider pursued it there—but I could not see what happened, because overhanging grasses concealed the spot.

Again, only later did I learn what I had seen. I read that striders are attracted to any light. According to William H. Amos, "Often the attracting light turns out to be the reflections off the ripples set up by an insect trapped on the surface, and it is on such creatures that the striders feed." They suck them dry. Talk about living on jetsam! At any rate, it will be easy enough to watch for this again this summer. I especially want to see if the slow ripples set up by striders themselves reflect less light than the ripples set up by trapped insects—but it might be years before I happen to see another insect fall on the water among striders. I was lucky to have seen it once. Next time I will know what is happening, and if they want to play the last bloody act offstage, I will just part the curtain of grasses and hope I sleep through the night.

II

Learning to stalk muskrats took me several years.

I've always known there were muskrats in the creek. Sometimes when I drove late at night my headlights' beam on the water would catch the broad lines of ripples made by a swimming muskrat, a bow wave, converging across the water at the raised dark vee of its head. I would stop the car and get out: nothing. They eat corn and tomatoes from my neighbors' gardens, too, by night, so that my neighbors were always telling me that the creek was full of them. Around here, people call them "mushrats;" Thoreau called them "musquashes." They are not of course rats at all (let alone squashes). They are more like diminutive beavers, and, like beavers, they exude a scented oil from musk glands under the base of the tail—hence the name. I had read in several respectable sources that muskrats are so wary they are almost impossible to observe. One expert who made a full-time study of large populations, mainly by examining "sign" and performing autopsies on corpses, said he often went for weeks at a time without seeing a single living muskrat.

One hot evening three years ago, I was standing more or less *in* a bush. I was stock-still, looking deep into Tinker Creek from a spot on the bank opposite the house, watching a group of bluegills stare and hang motionless near the bottom of a deep, sunlit pool. I was focused for depth. I had long since lost myself, lost the creek, the day, lost everything but still amber depth. All at once I couldn't see. And then I could: a young muskrat had appeared on top of the water, floating on its back. Its forelegs were folded languorously across its chest; the sun shone on its upturned belly. Its youthfulness and rodent grin, coupled with its ridiculous method of locomotion, which consisted of a lazy wag of the tail assisted by an occasional dabble of a webbed hind foot, made it an enchanting picture of decadence, dissipation, and summer sloth. I forgot all about the fish.

But in my surprise at having the light come on so suddenly, and at having my consciousness returned to me all at once and bearing an inverted muskrat, I must have moved and betrayed myself. The kit—for I know now it was just a young kit—righted itself so that only its head was visible above water, and swam downstream, away from me. I extricated myself from the bush and foolishly pursued it. It dove sleekly, reemerged, and glided for the opposite bank. I ran along the bankside brush, trying to keep it in sight. It kept casting an alarmed look over its shoulder at me. Once again it dove, under a floating mat of brush lodged in the bank, and disappeared. I never saw it again. (Nor have I ever, despite all the muskrats I have seen, again seen a muskrat floating on its back.) But I did not know muskrats then; I waited panting, and watched the shadowed bank. Now I know that I cannot outwait a muskrat who knows I am there. The most I can do is get "there" quietly, while it is still in its hole, so that it never knows, and wait there until it emerges. But then all I knew was that I wanted to see more muskrats.

I began to look for them day and night. Sometimes I would see ripples suddenly start beating from the creek's side, but as I crouched to watch, the ripples would die. Now I know what this means, and have learned to stand perfectly still to make out the muskrat's small, pointed face hidden under overhanging bank vegetation, watching me. That summer I haunted the bridges, I walked up creeks and down, but no muskrats ever appeared. You must just have to be there, I thought. You must have to spend the rest of your life standing in bushes. It was a once-in-a-lifetime thing, and you've had your once.

Then one night I saw another, and my life changed. After that I knew where they were in numbers, and I knew when to look. It was late dusk; I was driving home from a visit with friends. Just on the off chance I parked quietly by the creek, walked out on the narrow bridge over the shallows, and looked

upstream. Someday, I had been telling myself for weeks, someday a muskrat is going to swim right through that channel in
the cattails, and I am going to see it. That is precisely what happened. I looked up into the channel for a muskrat, and there it
came, swimming right toward me. Knock; seek; ask. It seemed
to swim with a side-to-side, sculling motion of its vertically flattened tail. It looked bigger than the upside-down muskrat, and
its face more reddish. In its mouth it clasped a twig of tulip tree.
One thing amazed me: it swam right down the middle of the
creek. I thought it would hide in the brush along the edge; instead, it plied the waters as obviously as an aquaplane. I could
just look and look.

But I was standing on the bridge, not sitting, and it saw me.
It changed its course, veered towards the bank, and disappeared
behind an indentation in the rushy shoreline. I felt a rush of
such pure energy I thought I would not need to breathe for
days.

*   *   *

That innocence of mine is mostly gone now, although I felt
almost the same pure rush last night. I have seen many muskrats since I learned to look for them in that part of the creek.
But still I seek them out in the cool of the evening, and still I
hold my breath when rising ripples surge from under the
creek's bank. The great hurrah about wild animals is that they
exist at all, and the greater hurrah is the actual moment of seeing them. Because they have a nice dignity, and prefer to have
nothing to do with me, not even as the simple objects of my vision. They show me by their very wariness what a prize it is simply to open my eyes and behold.

Muskrats are the bread and butter of the carnivorous food
chain. They are like rabbits and mice: if you are big enough to
eat mammals, you eat them. Hawks and owls prey on them, and
foxes; so do otters. Minks are their special enemies; minks live
near large muskrat populations, slinking in and out of their

dens and generally hanging around like mantises outside a bee-
hive. Muskrats are also subject to a contagious blood disease
that wipes out whole colonies. Sometimes, however, their whole
populations explode, just like lemmings', which are their near
kin; and they either die by the hundreds or fan out across the
land migrating to new creeks and ponds.

Men kill them, too. One Eskimo who hunted muskrats for
a few weeks each year strictly as a sideline says that in fourteen
years he killed 30,739 muskrats. The pelts sell, and the price is
rising. Muskrats are the most important fur animal on the North
American continent. I don't know what they bring on the Mackenzie River delta these days, but around here, fur dealers, who
paid $2.90 in 1971, now pay $5.00 a pelt. They make the pelts
into coats, calling the fur anything but muskrat: "Hudson seal"
is typical. In the old days, after they had sold the skins, trappers
would sell the meat, too, calling it "marsh rabbit." Many people
still stew muskrat.

Keeping ahead of all this slaughter, a female might have as
many as five litters a year, and each litter contains six or seven
or more muskrats. The nest is high and dry under the bank;
only the entrance is under water, usually by several feet, to foil
enemies. Here the nests are marked by simple holes in a creek's
clay bank; in other parts of the country muskrats build floating,
conical winter lodges which are not only watertight, but edible
to muskrats.

The very young have a risky life. For one thing, even
snakes and raccoons eat them. For another, their mother is easily confused, and may abandon one or two of a big litter here or
there, forgetting as it were to count noses. The newborn hanging on their mother's teats may drop off if the mother has to
make a sudden dive into the water, and sometimes these drown.
The just-weaned young have a rough time, too, because new litters are coming along so hard and fast that they have to be
weaned before they really know how to survive. And if the just-
weaned young are near starving, they might eat the newborn—

if they can get to them. Adult muskrats, including their own mothers, often kill them if they approach too closely. But if they live through all these hazards, they can begin a life of swimming at twilight and munching cattail roots, clover, and an occasional crayfish. Paul Errington, a usually solemn authority, writes, "The muskrat nearing the end of its first month may be thought of as an independent enterprise in a very modest way."

*   *   *

The wonderful thing about muskrats in my book is that they cannot see very well, and are rather dim, to boot. They are extremely wary if they know I am there, and will outwait me every time. But with a modicum of skill and a minimum loss of human dignity, such as it is, I can be right "there," and the breathing fact of my presence will never penetrate their narrow skulls.

What happened last night was not only the ultimate in muskrat dimness, it was also the ultimate in human intrusion, the limit beyond which I am certain I cannot go. I would never have imagined I could go that far, actually to sit beside a feeding muskrat as beside a dinner partner at a crowded table.

What happened was this. Just in the past week I have been frequenting a different place, one of the creek's nameless feeder streams. It is mostly a shallow trickle joining several pools up to three feet deep. Over one of these pools is a tiny pedestrian bridge known locally, if at all, as the troll bridge. I was sitting on the troll bridge about an hour before sunset, looking upstream about eight feet to my right where I know the muskrats have a den. I had just lighted a cigarette when a pulse of ripples appeared at the mouth of the den, and a muskrat emerged. He swam straight towards me and headed under the bridge.

Now the moment a muskrat's eyes disappear from view under a bridge, I go into action. I have about five seconds to switch myself around so that I will be able to see him very well when he emerges on the other side of the bridge. I can easily hang my head over the other side of the bridge, so that when he appears from under me, I will be able to count his eyelashes if I want. The trouble with this maneuver is that, once his beady eyes appear again on the other side, I am stuck. If I move again, the show is over for the evening. I have to remain in whatever insane position I happen to be caught, for as long as I am in his sight, so that I stiffen all my muscles, bruise my ankles on the concrete, and burn my fingers on the cigarette. And if the muskrat goes out on a bank to feed, there I am with my face hanging a foot over the water, unable to see anything but crayfish. So I have learned to take it easy on these five-second flings.

When the muskrat went under the bridge, I moved so I could face downstream comfortably. He reappeared, and I had a good look at him. He was eight inches long in the body, and another six in the tail. Muskrat tails are black and scaled, flattened not horizontally, like beavers' tails, but vertically, like a belt stood on edge. In the winter, muskrats' tails sometimes freeze solid, and the animals chew off the frozen parts up to about an inch of the body. They must swim entirely with their hind feet, and have a terrible time steering. This one used his tail as a rudder and only occasionally as a propeller; mostly he swam with a pedaling motion of his hind feet, held very straight and moving down and around, "toeing down" like a bicycle racer. The soles of his hind feet were strangely pale; his toenails were pointed in long cones. He kept his forelegs still, tucked up to his chest.

The muskrat clambered out on the bank across the stream from me, and began feeding. He chomped down on a ten-inch weed, pushing it into his mouth steadily with both forepaws as a carpenter feeds a saw. I could hear his chewing; it sounded like somebody eating celery sticks. Then he slid back into the water with the weed still in his mouth, crossed under the bridge, and, instead of returning to his den, rose erect on a submerged rock and calmly polished off the rest of the weed. He was about four feet away from me. Immediately he swam under the bridge again, hauled himself out on the bank, and unerringly found the same spot on the grass, where he devoured the weed's stump.

All this time I was not only doing an elaborate about-face every time his eyes disappeared under the bridge, but I was also smoking a cigarette. He never noticed that the configuration of the bridge metamorphosed utterly every time he went under it. Many animals are the same way: they can't see a thing unless it's moving. Similarly, every time he turned his head away, I was free to smoke the cigarette, although of course I never knew when he would suddenly turn again and leave me caught in some wretched position. The galling thing was, he was downwind of me and my cigarette: was I really going through all this for a creature without any sense whatsoever?

After the weed stump was gone, the muskrat began ranging over the grass with a nervous motion, chewing off mouthfuls of grass and clover near the base. Soon he had gathered a huge, bushy mouthful; he pushed into the water, crossed under the bridge, swam towards his den, and dove.

When he launched himself again shortly, having apparently cached the grass, he repeated the same routine in a businesslike fashion, and returned with another shock of grass.

Out he came again. I lost him for a minute when he went under the bridge; he did not come out where I expected him. Suddenly to my utter disbelief he appeared on the bank next to me. The troll bridge itself is on a level with the low bank; there I was, and there he was, at my side. I could have touched him with the palm of my hand without straightening my elbow. He was ready to hand.

Foraging beside me he walked very humped up, maybe to save heat loss through evaporation. Generally, whenever he was out of water he assumed the shape of a shmoo; his shoulders were as slender as a kitten's. He used his forepaws to part clumps of grass extremely tidily; I could see the flex in his narrow wrists. He gathered mouthfuls of grass and clover less by actually gnawing than by biting hard near the ground, locking his neck muscles, and pushing up jerkily with his forelegs.

His jaw was underslung, his black eyes close set and glistening, his small ears pointed and furred. I will have to try and see if he can cock them. I could see the water-slicked long hairs of his coat, which gathered in rich brown strands that emphasized the smooth contours of his body, and which parted to reveal the paler, softer hair like rabbit fur underneath. Despite his closeness, I never saw his teeth or belly.

After several minutes of rummaging about in the grass at my side, he eased into the water under the bridge and paddled to his den with the jawful of grass held high, and that was the last I saw of him.

In the forty minutes I watched him, he never saw me, smelled me, or heard me at all. When he was in full view of course I never moved except to breathe. My eyes would move, too, following his, but he never noticed. I even swallowed a couple of times: nothing. The swallowing thing interested me because I had read that, when you are trying to hand-tame wild birds, if you inadvertently swallow, you ruin everything. The bird, according to this theory, thinks you are swallowing in anticipation, and off it goes. The muskrat never twitched. Only once, when he was feeding from the opposite bank about eight feet away from me, did he suddenly rise upright, all alert—and then he immediately resumed foraging. But he never knew I was there.

I never knew I was there, either. For that forty minutes last night I was as purely sensitive and mute as a photographic plate; I received impressions, but I did not print out captions. My own self-awareness had disappeared; it seems now almost as though, had I been wired with electrodes, my EEG would have been flat. I have done this sort of thing so often that I have lost self-consciousness about moving slowly and halting suddenly; it is second nature to me now. And I have often noticed that even a few minutes of this self-forgetfulness is tremendously invigorating. I wonder if we do not waste most of our energy just by spending every waking minute saying hello to ourselves. Martin Buber quotes an old Hasid master who said, "When you walk across the fields with your mind pure and holy, then from all the stones, and all growing things, and all animals, the sparks of their soul come out and cling to you, and then they are purified and become a holy fire in you." This is one way of describing the energy that comes, using the specialized Cabalistic vocabulary of Hasidism.

I have tried to show muskrats to other people, but it rarely works. No matter how quiet we are, the muskrats stay hidden. Maybe they sense the tense hum of consciousness, the buzz from two human beings who in the silence cannot help but be aware of each other, and so of themselves. Then too, the other people invariably suffer from a self-consciousness that prevents their stalking well. It used to bother me, too: I just could not bear to lose so much dignity that I would completely alter my whole way of being for a muskrat. So I would move or look around or scratch my nose, and no muskrats would show, leaving me alone with my dignity for days on end, until I decided that it was worth my while to learn—from the muskrats themselves—how to stalk.

* * *

The old, classic rule for stalking is, "Stop often 'n' set frequent." The rule cannot be improved upon, but muskrats will permit a little more. If a muskrat's eyes are out of sight, I can practically do a buck-and-wing on his tail, and he'll never notice. A few days ago I approached a muskrat feeding on a bank by the troll bridge simply by taking as many gliding steps towards him as possible while his head was turned. I spread my weight as evenly as I could, so that he wouldn't feel my coming through the ground, and so that no matter when I became visible to him, I could pause motionless until he turned away again without having to balance too awkwardly on one leg.

When I got within ten feet of him, I was sure he would flee, but he continued to browse nearsightedly among the mown clovers and grass. Since I had seen just about everything I was ever going to see, I continued approaching just to see when he would break. To my utter bafflement, he never broke. I broke first. When one of my feet was six inches from his back, I refused to press on. He could see me perfectly well, of course, but I was stock-still except when he lowered his head. There was nothing left to do but kick him. Finally he returned to the water, dove, and vanished. I do not know to this day if he would have permitted me to keep on walking right up his back.

It is not always so easy. Other times I have learned that the only way to approach a feeding muskrat for a good look is to commit myself to a procedure so ridiculous that only a total unselfconsciousness will permit me to live with myself. I have to ditch my hat, line up behind a low boulder, and lay on my belly to inch snake-fashion across twenty feet of bare field until I am behind the boulder itself and able to hazard a slow peek around it. If my head moves from around the boulder when the muskrat's head happens to be turned, then all is well. I can be fixed into position and still by the time he looks around. But if he sees me move my head, then he dives into the water, and the whole belly-crawl routine was in vain. There is no way to tell ahead of time; I just have to chance it and see.

I have read that in the unlikely event that you are caught in a stare-down with a grizzly bear, the best thing to do is talk to him softly and pleasantly. Your voice is supposed to have a soothing effect. I have not yet had occasion to test this out on grizzly bears, but I can attest that it does not work on muskrats. It scares them witless. I have tried time and again. Once I watched a muskrat feeding on a bank ten feet away from me; after I had looked my fill I had nothing to lose, so I offered a convivial greeting. Boom. The terrified muskrat flipped a hundred and eighty degrees in the air, nose-dived into the grass at his feet, and disappeared. The earth swallowed him; his tail shot straight up in the air and then vanished into the ground without a sound. Muskrats make several emergency escape holes along a bank for just this very purpose, and they don't like to feed too far away from them. The entire event was most impressive, and illustrates the relative power in nature of the word and the sneak.

* * *

Stalking is a pure form of skill, like pitching or playing chess. Rarely is luck involved. I do it right or I do it wrong; the muskrat will tell me, and that right early. Even more than baseball, stalking is a game played in the actual present. At every second, the muskrat comes, or stays, or goes, depending on my skill.

Can I stay still? How still? It is astonishing how many people cannot, or will not, hold still. I could not, or would not, hold still for thirty minutes inside, but at the creek I slow down, center down, empty. I am not excited; my breathing is slow and regular. In my brain I am not saying, Muskrat! Muskrat! There! I am saying nothing. If I must hold a position, I do not "freeze." If I freeze, locking my muscles, I will tire and break. Instead of going rigid, I go calm. I center down wherever I am; I find a balance and repose. I retreat—not inside myself, but outside myself, so that I am a tissue of senses. Whatever I see is plenty, abundance. I am the skin of water the wind plays over; I am petal, feather, stone.

III

Living this way by the creek, where the light appears and vanishes on the water, where muskrats surface and dive, and red-

wings scatter, I have come to know a special side of nature. I
look to the mountains, and the mountains still slumber, blue
and mute and rapt. I say, it gathers; the world abides. But I look
to the creek, and I say: it scatters, it comes and goes. When I
leave the house the sparrows flee and hush; on the banks of the
creek jays scream in alarm, squirrels race for cover, tadpoles
dive, frogs leap, snakes freeze, warblers vanish. Why do they
hide? I will not hurt them. They simply do not want to be seen.
"Nature," said Heraclitus, "is wont to hide herself." A fleeing
mockingbird unfurls for a second a dazzling array of white
fans . . . and disappears in the leaves. Shane! . . . Shane! Nature
flashes the old mighty glance—the come-hither look—drops the
handkerchief, turns tail, and is gone. The nature I know is old
touch-and-go.

I wonder whether what I see and seem to understand
about nature is merely one of the accidents of freedom, repeated by chance before my eyes, or whether it has any coun-
terpart in the worlds beyond Tinker Creek. I find in quantum
mechanics a world symbolically similar to my world at the
creek.

* * *

Many of us are still living in the universe of Newtonian
physics, and fondly imagine that real, hard scientists have no
use for these misty ramblings, dealing as scientists have no use
for these misty ramblings, dealing as scientists do with the mea-
surable and known. We think that at least the physical causes of
physical events are perfectly knowable, and that, as the results
of various experiments keep coming in, we gradually roll back
the cloud of unknowing. We remove the veils one by one, pains-
takingly, adding knowledge to knowledge and whisking away
veil after veil, until at last we reveal the nub of things, the sparkling equation from whom all blessings flow. Even wildman
Emerson accepted the truly pathetic fallacy of the old science

when he wrote grudgingly towards the end of his life, "When the microscope is improved, we shall have the cells analysed, and all will be electricity, or somewhat else." All we need to do is perfect our instruments and our methods, and we can collect enough data like birds on a string to predict physical events from physical causes.

But in 1927 Werner Heisenberg pulled out the rug, and our whole understanding of the universe toppled and collapsed. For some reason it has not yet trickled down to the man on the street that some physicists now are a bunch of wild-eyed, raving mystics. For they have perfected their instruments and methods just enough to whisk away the crucial veil, and what stands revealed is the Cheshire cat's grin.

The Principle of Indeterminacy, which saw the light in the summer of 1927, says in effect that you cannot know both a particle's velocity and position. You can guess statistically what any batch of electrons might do, but you cannot predict the career of any one particle. They seem to be as free as dragonflies. You can perfect your instruments and your methods till the cows come home, and you will never ever be able to measure this one basic thing. It cannot be done. The electron is a muskrat; it cannot be perfectly stalked. And nature is a fan dancer born with a fan; you can wrestle her down, throw her on the stage and grapple with her for the fan with all your might, but it will never quit her grip. She comes that way; the fan is attached.

It is not that we lack sufficient information to know both a particle's velocity and its position; that would have been a perfectly ordinary situation well within the understanding of classical physics. Rather, we know now for sure that there is no knowing. You can determine the position, and your figure for the velocity blurs into vagueness; or, you can determine the velocity, but whoops, there goes the position. The use of instruments and the very fact of an observer seem to bollix the observations; as a consequence, physicists are saying that they cannot study nature per se, but only their own investigation of nature.

And I can only see bluegills within my own blue shadow, from which they immediately flee.

The Principle of Indeterminacy turned science inside-out. Suddenly determinism goes, causality goes, and we are left with a universe composed of what Eddington calls, "mind-stuff." Listen to these physicists: Sir James Jeans, Eddington's successor, invokes "fate," saying that the future "may rest on the knees of whatever gods there be." Eddington says that "the physical world is entirely abstract and without 'actuality' apart from its linkage to consciousness." Heisenberg himself says, "method and object can no longer be separated. *The scientific world-view has ceased to be a scientific view in the true sense of the word.*" Jeans says that science can no longer remain opposed to the notion of free will. Heisenberg says, "there is a higher power, not influenced by our wishes, which finally decides and judges." Eddington says that our dropping causality as a result of the Principle of Indeterminacy "leaves us with no clear distinction between the Natural and the Supernatural." And so forth.

These physicists are once again mystics, as Kepler was, standing on a rarefied mountain pass, gazing transfixed into an abyss of freedom. And they got there by experimental method and a few wild leaps such as Einstein made. What a pretty pass!

* * *

All this means is that the physical world as we understand it now is more like the touch-and-go creek world I see than it is like the abiding world of which the mountains seem to speak. The physicists' particles whiz and shift like rotifers in and out of my microscope's field, and that this valley's ring of granite mountains is an airy haze of those same particles I must believe. The whole universe is a swarm of those wild, wary energies, the sun that glistens from the wet hairs on a muskrat's back and the stars which the mountains obscure on the horizon but which catch from on high in Tinker Creek. It is all touch and go. The heron flaps away; the dragonfly departs at thirty miles an hour; the water strider vanishes under a screen of grass; the muskrat dives, and the ripples roll from the bank, and flatten, and cease altogether.

*   *   *

Moses said to God, "I beseech thee, shew me thy glory." And God said, "Thou canst not see my face: for there shall no man see me, and live." But he added, "There is a place by me, and thou shalt stand upon a rock: and it shall come to pass, while my glory passeth by, that I will put thee in a clift of the rock, and will cover thee with my hand while I pass by: And I will take away mine hand, and thou shalt see my back parts: but my face shall not be seen." So Moses went up on Mount Sinai, waited still in a clift of the rock, and saw the back parts of God. Forty years later he went up on Mount Pisgah, and saw the promised land across the Jordan, which he was to die without ever being permitted to enter.

Just a glimpse, Moses: a clift in the rock here, a mountain-top there, and the rest is denial and longing. You have to stalk everything. Everything scatters and gathers; everything comes and goes like fish under a bridge. You have to stalk the spirit, too. You can wait forgetful anywhere, for anywhere is the way of his fleet passage, and hope to catch him by the tail and shout something in his ear before he wrests away. Or you can pursue him wherever you dare, risking the shrunken sinew in the hollow of the thigh; you can bang at the door all night till the innkeeper relents, if he ever relents; and you can wail till you're hoarse or worse the cry for incarnation always in John Knoepfle's poem: "and christ is red rover . . . and the children are calling/come over come over." I sit on a bridge as on Pisgah or Sinai, and I am both waiting becalmed in a clift of the rock and banging with all my will, calling like a child beating on a door: come on out! . . . I know you're there.

And then occasionally the mountains part. The tree with the lights in it appears, the mockingbird falls, and time unfurls across space like an oriflamme. Now we rejoice. The news, after all, is not that muskrats are wary, but that they can be seen. The hem of the robe was a Nobel Prize to Heisenberg; he did not go home in disgust. I wait on the bridges and stalk along banks for those moments I cannot predict, when a wave begins to surge under the water, and ripples strengthen and pulse high across the creek and back again in a texture that throbs. It is like the surfacing of an impulse, like the materialization of fish, this rising, this coming to a head, like the ripening of nutmeats still in their husks, ready to split open like buckeyes in a field, shining with newness. "Surely the Lord is in this place; and I knew it not." The fleeing shreds I see, the back parts, are a gift, an abundance. When Moses came down from the clift in Mount Sinai, the people were afraid of him: the very skin on his face shone.

Do the Eskimos' faces shine, too? I lie in bed alert: I am with the Eskimos on the tundra who are running after the click-footed caribou, running sleepless and dazed for days, running spread out in scraggling lines across the glacier-ground hummocks and reindeer moss, in sight of the ocean, under the long-shadowed pale sun, running silent all night long.

Rosellen Brown

THREE POEMS
FROM *CORA FRY*

One bad winter
my father poached
a deer and I died

thousands of hard
separate deaths
waiting for the

sheriff to come.
The blue light swung
across my wall

one snowbound night.
I stopped breathing.
I woke up Sam.

But it was just
the deputy,
fat Lloyd the tease,

coming to get
Daddy, his plow
and all, to pull

some foreign car
out of his field.
"Some kid got throwed

clear in a bank,
but he hit hard."
I clamored till

I got to come,
in Dad's army
blanket, shivering.

The boy was still
lying in blue
shadows, his arms

out like a snow
angel. He woke
after a while,

blood in his mouth,
swearing he had
only one beer.

The sheriff laughed
and winked at us.
Lloyd muttered "Bull . . . "

Quarter to four
on a moony
night in late March

I swallowed hard
and the deer went down.

Muskrat. Muskrat.
Trapped at the tooth-
pick ankle, when
you pull you are
raking yourself
to the soft dark
center. You gouge
your groin with what
edges you find—
can opener,
stone-lip, blunt flint,
what's the difference,
they're all like teeth.
You saw, you chew,
forward and back,

raising a smoke-
trail, hot, quiet,
over your head.
A snarl: come free
you roll, hobble,
you start a new
life on three legs.

Big game-hunters
Chip and Craig Fry,
checking the trap,
will pick your leg up,
shake it, bloody
knotted short string
trailing a rag
of web, and curse
you. "Double cross."
(Fry to his son,
angry. Chip pouts
to please his dad.)
Fry cracks your bone,
wishbone easy
in his tight fist.
The leg sails, lands
on leaves, becomes
a crooked twig,
or an inchworm.
They turn to lunch.

In my kitchen,
blotting water
stains off the forks,
the child-safe knives,
I can see you:

By now you are
under the cliff,
under the mountain,
eating your pain.

Coming home late from work,
I stopped the car one long thirsty minute
on the hilltop near my father's meadow.

Something plunged and tossed in the center
like a show animal in a lit ring.

He threw his head, he shook it free of air,
his legs flung whichway. There were the antlers,
a forest of spring twigs that rose and dived,
dancing. *Singing,* for all I knew, glassed in.

I rolled my window down
knowing I'd lose him, and I did: he ducked
into nowhere. But I had that one glimpse,

didn't I, of the animal deep in
the animal? Of his freedom flaring

only a quick blink of light? I think spring
must be a crazy water animals drink.

Melanie Rae Thon
WHAT SHE WANTS

I waited for you in the rain. My tongue hurt. I'd been telling lies all day. Lies to the four Christian teenagers who
thought they could save me. My first ride, Albany to Oneonta—
they sang the whole way. More lies to the jittery pink-skinned
man who offered tiny blue pills and fat black ones. He said: *It's
safe—don't worry—I'm a nurse.* He said: *I'll make you feel good.*

I think I had a sister once. Everywhere I go she's been
before me. There's no getting out of it.

When the pink nurse stopped to piss, my sister Clare

whispered: *Look at him—he'll kill you if he can.* I hid in the
woods by the lake full of stumps. I didn't move. I let the sky
pour through me. He called the name I'd said was mine. Sometimes I heard branches breaking. Sometimes only rain. Finally
he yelled at me, at who he thought I was. He said: *No more
games.* He said: *Fine, freeze your ass.* His voice cracked. I could
have chosen him instead of you, but Clare breathed on my
hands. She said: *He doesn't have anything you want.*

You were driving toward me already, still hours away. I
swear I knew you, your blue truck, your soft beard, how it
would be. But you never imagined us together. You never meant
to stop for me.

This I won't tell. This you'll never know. Mick says I'm
fourteen going on forty. I've got that dusty skin, dry, my eyes
kind of yellowish where they're supposed to be white. It's the
rum I drink, and maybe my kidneys never did work that well.
Mick, who is my mother's husband now, says I'll be living on the
street at sixteen, dead at twenty. He says this to me, when we're
alone. Once I paid $2, let Mama Rosa read my palm to see if he
was right, and she told me I was going to outlive everyone I love.

It's dark. Clare pulls me toward the gully. She wants me to
run down between the black trees and twisting vines. She wants
me to feel my way—she wants me to crawl.

I know I'm strange. I drift. Maybe I'm smoking a cigarette,
leaning on the bricks. Somebody's talking. Then I'm not there.
I'm a window breaking. I'm pieces of myself falling on the
ground. Later I wake up in my own body and my fingers are
burned.

Clare says: *Just stand up.*

She's careless, my sister. She gets drunk. She puts other
people's blood in her veins. Her skin's hot. She goes out in the
cold without her coat and waits for her lover to come. Wind
drives snow in her face. Ice needles her bare arms. Some night
she'll lie down in the woods and he won't find her. Some night
she'll lie down in the road.

It's November. I know because there are Halloween men rotting in all the yards, snagged on fences, skewered on poles. Pumpkin heads scooped hollow—they stink of their own spoiled selves. One boy's stuck in a tree. His head's a purple cabbage. You could peel him down to his brainless core.

I know some men downtown, Halloween men trying to walk on their stuffed legs. Rags on sticks, pants full of straw, foul wind blowing through them to scare the crows. I think they made themselves. They have those eyes. Carved. Candles guttering inside their soft skulls.

They live in a brick house you can't blow down—boards instead of windows, nails in the doors. They tell me: *Come alone.*

They have dusted joints and I have $7. They have pockets full of pills and I have pennies I found in the snow. I know how easy it is to go down the steps to the basement, to stand shivering against the wall. Nothing hurts me. Earl says: *Pain is just a feeling like any other feeling.* He should know. *Knife, slap, kiss, flame.* He says: *Forget their names and they pass through you.* Earl has wooden arms and metal hands. His left ear's a hole, his nose a bulb of flesh from somewhere else. He sits in the corner and smokes. He holds the joint in his silver claw. His long feet are always bare. When he whispers in his half-voice, everything stops.

No money and one of the Halloween men said: *Come with me.* He had pink hearts and poppers. He knew I'd need them. He said: *It's dangerous to sleep.* I looked at Earl. I thought his lips moved. I thought he said: *Nothing lasts too long.*

This speedboy was the whitest man I ever saw. When I closed my eyes he was a white dog bounding through streets of snow. I tried not to think of his skin, all of it, how bright it was, how his body exposed would blind me, how his white palms blazed against my hips. I thought of Earl instead, smooth arms, cool hands, Earl who only burned himself, hair flaming around soft ears, holy angel, face melting into bone.

Clare said: *Nobody will find you.*

The whiteman was in me, close enough to hear; he said: *Not even God.*

God doesn't like to watch little girls pressed against basement walls. God doesn't like little girls who swallow pills and drink rum. God's too old to get down on his hands and knees and peer through the slats of boards. Glass broken long ago but shards still on the ground. He might cut his palms. If he ever thinks of me, maybe he'll send his son.

I never slept with the whiteman.

I mean, I never lay down and closed my eyes.

Clare said: *There's no reason to go home.* She made me remember the trailer in December, a ring of Christmas lights blinking its outline, red and green and gold, the wet snow the first winter she was gone. She made me remember the white ruffled curtains on the windows and the three plastic swans in the yard. She said she hitched a hundred miles once to stand outside, to watch us inside, the fog of our breath on the glass. She said our mother had a new husband and two sons. She said we were nobody's daughters. She said: *They all want you to go.*

I had a dream once of your body, damp hair of your chest, my fingers in it. As soon as you stopped, I remembered the hunting cap on the seat between us, the rabbit fur inside your gloves.

I surprised you. I'm the living proof. Tall bony Nadine. Dark-eyed Nadine. Girl from the lake of stumps. Water swirling in a mother's dream. His face rising toward her. Shadow of a hand making the sign of the cross.

I pulled the blanket from my head and you saw the holes in my ear—you counted the tarnished hoops, nine, cartilage to lobe.

Later I'll show you: the holes in my ear never hurt like the hole in my tongue.

You were amazed by the space I filled—long legs, muddy boots—you had no reason to let the wet wool black hair smell of me into your warm truck. Unnecessary kindness. Moments before, I looked small and helpless, a child on the road, no bigger than your own daughter, ten years old, her impossibly thin arms, all her fragile breakable bones.

I closed my eyes so you wouldn't be afraid. I was just a girl again, alone, but the smell—it filled the cab—you breathed me—I was in your lungs. I was your boyself, the bad child, the one who ran away from you, the one you never found.

Later there was fog and dark, the rain, heavy. You didn't know where we were going. You didn't know where to stop. The lights of cars coming toward us exploded in mist, blinding you. I said: *Pull over.* I said: *We can wait it out.*

And it was there, in the fog, in the rain, in the terrifying light of cars still coming that I kissed you the first time. It was there parked on the soft gravel shoulder that I stuck my pierced tongue in your mouth and you put your hands under my shirt to feel my ribs, the first time. It was there that you said: *Careful, baby,* and you meant my tongue, the stud—it hurt you—and I thought of the handcuffs in my bag, stolen from the Halloween man, the last one, the white one—he was cursing me even now—I could have cuffed you to your wheel, left you to explain. I imagined myself in your coat, carrying your gun.

But I loved you.

I mean, I didn't want to go.

The rain slowed. The fog blew across the road. You drove. I wore your gloves, felt the fur of the animal around every finger. I stared at the lights till my eyes were holes.

You were tired. You were sorry. It was too late to throw me out. You said we'd stop at a motel. You said we'd sleep. You said: *What happened back there—don't worry.* You meant it wasn't going to go any further. You meant you thought it was your fault.

I disgusted you now. I saw that. Your tongue hurt. My sour breath was in your mouth. *Never,* you thought, *not with her.* Dirty Nadine. Nothing like her pretty sister. Pale half sister. Daughter of the father before my father. Not like Clare, lovely despite her filth, delicate Clare, thin as your daughter—you could hold her down. You could take her to any room. You could wash her. You could break her with one blow. You would never guess how dangerous she is. You can't see the shadows on her lungs, her hard veins, her brittle bones. You can't see the bloom of blood. Later I'll tell you about the handprints on all the doors of the disappeared. Later I'll explain the lines of her open palm.

Is she alive? Try to find her. Ask her yourself.

Never is the car door slamming. *Never* is the key in the lock, the Traveler's Rest Motel, the smell of disinfectant, the light we don't turn on. *Never* is the mattress so old you feel the coils against your back when you fall. My tongue's in your mouth. Your cock's hard against my thigh. *Never.*

Clare has a game. We strobe. She grabs my hand, sticks the wire in the socket. She dares me to hang on.

I'm a thief. It's true.

I turn you into a thief. It's necessary. You'll think of that forever, the sheet you had to steal to get out of the motel. You'll remember your bare legs in the truck, the cold vinyl through thin cloth, the white half-moon hanging in the morning sky, facedown.

Days now and hundreds of miles since I left you. You wear your orange vest, carry your oiled gun. You follow tracks in snow. I follow Clare to the road. She wants me to find her, to feel what she feels, to do everything she's done.

When you see the doe at last, you think of me. You're alone with me—there's no one you can tell about the girl on the road, her sore tongue in your mouth. *Never,* you said, *no* and *no,* but you twitched under her, blinded by the flickering in your skull. No one will understand. You thought her hands would turn you inside out, but you held on. There's no one you can tell about the wallet she opened, the cash and pictures, the pants she stole.

Careful, baby.

I've got your life now—your little girl smiling in my hand, dressed in her white fairy costume, waving her sparkling fairy wand; I hold your sad wife in her striped bathing suit. If I could feel, her chubby knees would break my heart. I've got you in my pocket—your driver's license, my proof. I'm in your pants. I belt them tight. I keep your coins in my boots for good luck. I wear your hat, earflaps down. I bought a silver knife with your $43. I carved your name in a cross on my thigh.

Today, I found a dump of jack-o'-lanterns in the ditch, the smashed faces of all the men I used to know. They grinned to show me the stones in their broken mouths. They've taken themselves apart. I'm looking for their unstuffed clothes, hoping they didn't empty their pockets before their skulls flamed out.

Today, a deer, only the head and legs, bits of hide, a smear of blood, five crows taking flight, wings hissing as they rose. Someone's accident butchered here, the stunned meat taken home. Before you fell asleep, I said: *Anyone can kill.*

She's in your sights. Nobody understands your fear, how you feel my hands even now, reaching for your wrists, slipping under your clothes. So many ways to do it, brutal or graceful, silent as the blood in my sister's veins or full of shattered light and sound. Kick to the shoulder, blast of the gun—she staggers, wounded—not killed all at once. There's snow on the ground, gold leaves going brown. There's light in the last trembling leaves but the sun is gone. You follow her trail, dark puddles spreading in snow, black into white, her blood.

You remember a farmer straddling his own sheep. *Will it be like this?* The knife, one slit, precise. *Pain is just a feeling like any other feeling.* She never struggled. He reached inside, grabbed something, squeezed hard. *I can't tell you what it was.*

She won't drop in time, won't give up. When you put your hands in front of you, you almost feel her there: hair, flesh, breath, blood. She wants only what you want: to survive one minute more.

What would you do if you found her now, if her ragged breathing stopped? Too far to drag her back to the truck, you'd have to open her in the sudden dark, pull her steaming entrails into the snow.

I wait for the next ride. Clare wants me to follow in her tracks, to find her before she falls, to touch her, to wash her blood clean in this snow, to put it back in her veins, to make her whole.

You walk in a circle. You wonder if you're lost. The doe's following you now, but at a distance. She's trying to forgive you. If she could speak, she might tell you the way home. She might say: *You can climb inside me, wear my body like a coat.*

You can't explain this to anyone. *Never, no.* You need me. I'm the only one alive who knows your fear, who understands how dangerous we are to each other in these woods, on this road.

Nance Van Winckel
She Who Hunts

1

She knows to wait in the thicket, to stoop
ready among its brambles, soundless as snow.

But first, like snow, she must gather herself,

a long inhaling for the long letting go, the breath
given up into freezing air. Slowly the earth,

the earth comes up to meet her. This meeting
the hunters call patience.

2

Hours in the thicket. Legs of thorns.
Briars up her dead calves. Her back
burrowing a nest there, its slow
sinking as she listens for deer, light

careful footsteps. With the surprise
and strength of her quiet, she calls them.

3

Days of snow. The thicket full, deep
around her. Only her eyes, blue blades,
cut through the wide white clearing
where the one who can
no longer resist her vigil
must come forward
and release her.

4

Or not. That no deer remain.
That she will wait for one more new moon
to open, or for the starlight of April alone
to melt her, return her
to her stiff little sac of flesh.
And that the earth will fall away
into mud, deepening rot,
and she in her thicket
with it. All that she considers.

5

Disentangling herself from the brambles,
she shakes off the white mantle and goes to him.
Her hand divides his body, empties him clean.

His eyes, the darker black of many nights
to come, watch as her knife goes down.

And the arrow in her hand again as if it had never
left. The weight of snow is a memory
on her shoulder, and the fear her arm
pulled back, pulled and pulled. How
had she let go? How had she sent
warm blood rushing into the trees?
And how long before she forgets
what she's done here, how she's done it.

Terry Tempest Williams
DEERSKIN

I remember, as a small girl, waking up one morning to the wild enthusiasm of my father and brothers. They were outside my bedroom window, and I could vaguely hear them talking about some sort of tracks they had found. Their voices conveyed a sense of awe as well as excitement. Not wanting to miss anything, I ran out to see.

The front door had been left open, and through it I could see all four of them crouching in the snow.

"Deer tracks . . ." my father said, touching them gently.

"Deer tracks," I said. "So?"

"Deer tracks," my brother restated emphatically.

"Deer tracks," I said again under my breath. No, something was missing when I said it. Feeling out of place and out of touch, I went back inside and shut the door. Through the glass I watched the passion that flowed between my father and brothers as they spoke of deer. Their words went beyond the occasion.

Many years have passed since that morning, but I often reflect on the relationship my brothers and father share with deer. Looking back and looking forward into the Navajo Way, I have come to realize the power of oral traditions, of stories, even in our own culture, and how they color our perceptions of the world around us.

Nowhere is this relationship of earth and story more poignant than in the Navajo perception of living things, *nanise*. The Diné have been told in their origin histories that they will receive knowledge from the Holy People, from plants and animals. As with other Indian peoples, the Navajo do not "rank-order" animals. Barry Lopez writes:

> Each creature, from deer mouse to meadowlark, is respected for the qualities it best seems to epitomize; when those particular qualities are desired by someone, then that animal is approached as one who knows much about the subject. . . .

And elsewhere:

> In the native view, each creature carried information about the order of the universe—both at a practical level (ravens might reveal the presence of caribou to hunters), and at the level of augury. Moreover, each creature had its own special kind of power, and a person who wished knowledge in those areas—of patience, of endurance, of humor—would be attentive to those animals who possessed these skills

Gregory Bateson points out in *Mind and Nature* that

" . . . the very word, 'animal,' means endowed with mind and spirit."

This idea of animal mentors is illustrated in the Navajo Deerhunting Way. The Deerhunting Way is a blessing rite, a formula for corresponding with deer in the appropriate manner. Traditionally, hunters would participate in this ritual as a means to a successful hunt and their own personal safety.

Claus Chee Sonny, a Navajo medicine man who lives in the Tunitcha Mountains near the Arizona–New Mexico border, tells the following story, which is part of the Deerhunting Way. He learned the Deerhunting Way from his father, who had obtained it from his father, who was instructed by his father– Claus Chee's grandfather–and the many teachers who preceded him. The First People who taught the Deerhunting Way were the Deer Gods themselves. The Deer supplied the first divine hunters with the knowledge that was necessary to hunt them. And so the story begins:

> There was a hunter who waited in ambush. Wind had told him, "This is where the tracks are. The deer will come marching through in single file." The hunter had four arrows: one was made from sheet lightning, one of zigzag lightning, one of sunlight roots, and one of rainbow.
>
> Then the first deer, a large buck with many antlers, came. The hunter got ready to shoot the buck. His arrow was already in place. But just as he was ready to shoot, the deer transformed himself into a mountain mahogany bush, *tsé ésdaazii*. After a while, a mature man stood up from behind the bush. He stood up and said, "Do not shoot! We are your neighbors. These are the things that will be in the future when human beings will have come into existence. This is the way you will eat us." And he told the hunter how to kill and eat the deer. So the hunter let the mature Deerman go for the price of his information. And the Deerman left.

Then the large doe, a shy doe, appeared behind the one who had left. The hunter was ready again to shoot the doe in the heart. But the doe turned into a cliffrose bush, *awééts'áál*. A while later a young woman stood up from the bush. The woman said, "Do not shoot! We are your neighbors. In the future, when man has been created, men will live because of us. Men will use us to live on." So then, for the price of her information, the hunter let the Doewoman go. And she left.

Then a young buck, a two-pointer, came along. And the hunter got ready to shoot. But the deer transformed himself into a dead tree, *tsin bisgá*. After a while, a young man stood up from behind the dead tree and said, "In the future, after man has been created, if you talk about us the wrong way we will cause trouble for you when you urinate, and we will trouble your eyes. We will also trouble your ears if we do not approve of what you say about us." And at the price of his information, the hunter let the young Deerman go.

Then the little fawn appeared. The hunter was ready to shoot the fawn, but she turned into a lichen-spotted rock, *tsé dláád*. After a while, a young girl stood up from the rock and spoke: "In the future all this will happen if we approve, and whatever we shall disapprove shall all be up to me. I am in charge of all the other Deer People. If you talk badly about us, and if we disapprove of what you say, I am the one who will respond with killing you. I will kill you with what I am. If you hear the cry of my voice, you will know that trouble is in store for you. If you do not make use of us properly, even in times when we are numerous, you will not see us anymore. We are the four deer who have transformed themselves into different kinds of things. Into these four kinds of things can we transform ourselves. Moreover, we can assume the form of all the different kinds of plants. Then when you look, you will not see us. In the future, only those of whom we approve shall eat the mighty deer. If, when you hunt, you come across four deer, you will not kill all of them. You may kill three and leave one. But if you kill all of us, it is not good.

"These are the things which will bring you happiness. When you kill a deer, you will lay him with the head toward your house. You will cover the earth with plants or with branches of trees lengthwise, with the growing tips of the plants pointing the direction of the deer's head, toward your house. So it shall be made into a thick padding, and the deer shall be laid on that. Then you will take us home to your house and eat of us. You will place our bones under any of the things whose form we can assume—mountain mahogany, cliffrose, dead tree, lichen-spotted rock, spruce, pine, or under any of the other good plants. At these places you may put our bones. You will sprinkle the place with yellow pollen. Once. Twice. Then you lay the bones. And then you sprinkle yellow pollen on top of the bones. This is for the protection of the game animals. In this manner they will live on; their bones can live again and live a lasting life."

This is what the little fawn told the hunter. "You will be able to use the entire body of the deer, even the skin. And we belong to Talking-god. We belong to Black-god. We are in his hands. And he is able to make us deaf and blind. Those among you, of whom he approves, are the good people. They will hunt with success and will be able to kill us. According to his own decisions he will surrender us to the people. The Black-god is Crow. But when you hunt you do not refer to him as Crow but as Black-god."

Then, referring to what the fawn had said, the other three deer said, "This is what will be. And this is what will be. And this is how it is."

So these are the four who gave information; the large

buck, the doe, the two-pointer, and the fawn. Man was created later. All these events happened among the Gods, prior to the creation of man. All animals were like human beings then; they were able to speak. Thus, this story was not made up by old Navajo men. These events were brought about by Black-god. Then, after having obtained all this information, the hunter let the four deer go.

As final hunting instructions, Claus Chee Sonny shares the Deer People's knowledge:

> You will not throw the bones away just anywhere. Everything of which we are made, such as our skin, meat, bones, is to be used. . . . Anything that we hold onto, such as the earth from the four sacred mountains, the rainbow, the jewels, the corn, all the plants we eat, will be in us. Our bodies contain all these. And because of this we are very useful. . . . Needles can be made from the bones of the front and hind legs. This is what we use to stitch buckskin together. . . . A deer not killed by a weapon shall be used in the sacred ceremonies. All the meat is very useful. You can put deer meat as medicine on sheep, on horses, and on other domestic animals. All livestock lives because of deer.
>
> The usefulness of the deer is the foundation which has been laid. It serves as an example for other things. This is what is meant when we say that the deer are first in all things.

Through the Deerhunting Way one can see many connections, many circles. It becomes a model for ecological thought expressed through mythological language. The cyclic nature of the four deers' advice to the hunter is, in fact, good ecological sense. Out of the earth spring forth plants on which the animals feed. The animal, in time, surrenders its life so that another may live, and as its body parts are returned to earth, new life will emerge and be strengthened once again. Do not be greedy. Do not be wasteful. Remember gratitude and humility for all forms of life. Because they are here, we are here. They are the posterity of Earth.

It is this kind of oral tradition that gives the Navajo a balanced structure to live in. It provides continuity between the past and the future. They know how to behave. Stories channel energy into a form that can heal as well as instruct. This kind of cosmology enables a person to do what is appropriate and respect the rights of others. N. Scott Momaday tells the following story:

> There was a man living in a remote place on the Navajo reservation who had lost his job and was having a difficult time making ends meet. He had a wife and several children. As a matter of fact, his wife was expecting another child. One day a friend came to visit him and perceived that his situation was bad. The friend said to him, "Look, I see you are in tight straits. I see you have many mouths to feed, and that you have no wood and that there is very little food in your larder. But one thing puzzles me. I know you are a hunter, and I know, too, there are deer in the mountains very close at hand. Tell me, why don't you kill a deer so that you and your family might have fresh meat to eat?" And after a time the man replied, "No, it is inappropriate that I should take life just now when I am expecting the gift of life."

True freedom is having *no* choice. In this case, the man knew exactly what he had to do with respect to the land. Behavior became gesture. "It isn't a matter of intellection. It is respect for the understanding of one's heritage. It is a kind of racial memory, and it has its origin beyond any sort of historical experience. It reaches back to the dawn of time."

My thoughts return to that winter morning—to the deer tracks—and then to a crisp day in October when finally, at the age of sixteen, my father invited me to go deer hunting with him in the Dolores Triangle of Colorado. We participated in the rituals associated with the season, clothing ourselves in yellow sweatshirts, fluorescent orange vests, and red caps. We polished our boots with mink oil and rubbed Cutter's insect repellent all over our bodies, so as not to be bothered by remaining insects. We rose before the sun, and stalked west ridges to catch the last of day's light. Finally, around the campfire, I listened to the stories my father told until the stars had changed positions many times.

It was only then that I realized a small fraction of what my father knew, of what my brothers knew about deer. My brothers had been nurtured on such tales, and for the first time I saw the context they had been told in. My education was limited because I had missed years, layers of stories.

Walk lightly, walk slowly,
look straight ahead
with the corners of your eyes open.
Stay alert, be swift.
Hunt wisely
in the manner of deer.

I walked with reverence behind my father, trying to see what he saw. All at once he stopped, put his index finger to his mouth, and motioned me to come ahead. Kneeling down among the scrub oak, he carefully brushed aside some fallen leaves. "Deer tracks," he said.

"Deer tracks," I whispered.

Joanne Allred

To Bring Back the Deer

The deer is medicine. It is a healer.
—*Mary Crow Dog*, Lakota Woman

My blue moon rose deer love so much is budding,
one full bloom already blazing, shirred leaves
starred with blisters of dew, undisturbed.

It has been weeks since I've seen them shifting
along the tree line coming from the creek at dawn or
    spotted
twin petal hoofprints sprouting from the pond's mud
    ring.

I hike the hills tracking black pine-nut droppings
but find only a slope of yellow daisies
bent by the wind's hand and, hidden in thickets

swarming leaf shadows fringe, my own fear
that more wildness has been poached from my life.
I'm afraid to let a callus thicken over this absence

like those on thumbs of the old sheep rancher who gelds
his month-old lambs with rusty shears complaining the
tractor's carburetor needs cleaning. The stab of their cries

scabs more slowly than the wounds trailing red skeins
when they wobble to the fence mad ewes
watching butt, but he seems not even to hear them.

Isn't most history a scar marking what's been
lost? The green gap between poppies where antelope
grazed makes the old urge of spring sting

more like longing than desire. The first white men
who camped in the canyon, trapping beaver Butte Creek
no longer harbors, in a month killed four hundred elk

and a hundred fifty deer—*game* John Work wrote in his
     journal,
counting as wins what he destroyed. And John Bidwell's
     vision
a few years later—sixteen grizzlies fishing in this stream—

only fired his blood lust. He didn't think he tracked
their extinction or that the valley he claimed from the
     wild ridge
would tame him. He was a man blinded by his last
     miraculous sight.

Earth allows for our blindness with startling colors, but
    fear
is a passion for death that beads all life as target. Last
fall a young buck, torso burnished the shade of dried
    thistles

by the season's first rain, picked his way along the fence
camouflaged even at midday by the clever disguise
of light. Perhaps the deer are near but unseen,

bedding with new fawns in bramble-choked gullies.
Deer, return with your power
over fences supposed to seclude my garden

where you nip squash sprouts, prune rosebuds, then
vanish through gaps in the fence wires I can't even see.
Let these words be the song of a deer-toe rattle praying
    you back.

Alison Baker
THE HEAVEN OF ANIMALS

When I was eight years old I walked off the deck of the *Nautilus*, the world's first atomic-powered submarine, and dropped thirty feet into the harbor.

I hung there for a moment, like a cartoon dog suspended in air, before I began to fall. I could see the park at the edge of the harbor, and the people on the benches who'd been watching the waves, and the way their mouths opened into long, silent "Ohhhh!"s as I fell past.

I saw the pier at the edge of the water, and the barnacles on the black, wet pilings of the dock, and, as my feet smacked the water, I saw a Dixie cup floating on the surface.

The water was rock hard and it took my breath away. I thought I had broken my back. I kept my eyes wide open, because I always swam with my eyes open, even though my mother told me, "Taffy, you'll ruin your eyes that way." My mother thought I would ruin my eyes no matter what—reading with insufficient light, sitting too close to the television, shooting rubber bands. But try as I might, I couldn't keep my eyes closed underwater. It made me feel helpless, as if I might swim into a rock, or open them just in time to see an octopus looming up before me, about to seize me in its tentacles.

So I kept my eyes open, and I saw a school of fish gape at me in surprise and then dart away, and I saw light green bubbles springing up around me as if I was a Fizzy. A Fizzy! I laughed out loud, and that was the only mistake I made, because I laughed out all the air I'd been holding in, and when I automatically tried to breathe, I took in water through my nose, and I thought I was going to drown.

I started to flail, and then my eyes did close, and when something grabbed me around the waist I knew it was the octopus, and I gasped in fear, and I swallowed more water, and my heart hurt, and I knew I was dead. And the octopus squeezed like crazy around my waist, and then suddenly my head popped out of the water and I took a great gulp of air and began to cry, and the octopus said, "There, there," and it was a wet sailor with white scalp showing through the bristles of his crewcut.

All around me in the water bobbed the heads of wet sailors. I couldn't stop crying, and I was furious, because the one who had grabbed me wouldn't let go.

"I can swim," I said, but talking made me cough.

"Just relax," he said, and he pulled me through the water to where another sailor knelt on the floating dock. I felt myself handed from one sailor to another, pushed from behind and pulled from above, and I rose out of the water with no effort of my own.

"I can *walk*," I said with great irritation, but the sailor lifted me like a damsel in distress and carried me up the gang-plank to where my father was waiting on the pier.

"Oh, Taffy," my father said, and the sailor handed me over to him.

"Put me *down*," I said, and he did, because he was not as strong as the sailors. Someone draped a blanket over me, and my father stood there holding it around me and patting my back. Then I realized that people were cheering. I looked up; all the tourists who had been touring the *Nautilus*, and other people who were standing around on the pier, and the sailors who were climbing onto the dock, were all clapping. I had never been so embarrassed in my life.

"I turned around and you were gone!" my father was shouting at me.

"I was watching a seagull," I said, and I left it at that, because it seemed the simplest thing to do.

In fact, I had seen a different world. But later I couldn't remember it. I remembered the fall, the barnacles, the sailors. But I had bobbed to the surface too fast to get a good look at where I'd been.

It was troubling, like the words to a song just at the tip of my brain, or a memory of life before birth. I thought I'd been given a sign, some sort of evidence of another world.

* * *

I walk through the aviary on my way to work.

"Free us," whispers the Stanley Crane, sidling up to the fence. "Free us."

I stop and watch Stanley Crane, and Stanley Crane watches me, his beady gray eyes unblinking. He steps toward me, each footstep pulling his body along behind him, so that he bobs in very slow motion. "Free us," he whispers, and he hums softly, deep in his very long throat.

I look around to see who else has heard. The other birds

are moving toward me, nodding, their eyes fixed on me, on my hands, their beaks curved down, moving toward the fences of their private and shared enclosures.

"Free us," they whisper and hiss. Hubbard squashes and pumpkins have grown in the pens, giant flat leaves with sudden globes shining out from beneath them.

I look at the sign on the fence. Beside his name—STANLEY CRANE—there's a blank silhouette of the African continent, with an arrow pointing from nowhere into the heart of what is probably Kenya. I close my eyes for a moment and picture acres and acres of Stanley cranes, rising in a single motion from a vast wetlands, singing out in joy and lust as they lose sight of the earth under the canopy of their own wings.

"Free us," Stanley Crane whispers, but I shake my head.

"You would be lost in the wild now," I tell him, and I step back from his cage.

He follows me to the corner of his pen as I move down the sidewalk. "Free us!" he says, and watches me walk away. "If not freedom, food!"

* * *

My mother named me after her dog. "He was the sweetest little taffy-colored cocker," my mother would say, dreamily picturing her idyllic Hoosier childhood. Then she'd look at me and frown slightly, as if she was surprised that her daughter had turned out to have brown hair.

"Ruff, ruff," I said, letting my tongue hang out and panting. "Ruff."

My mother's frown deepened. "Whatever happened to him, I wonder," she said.

* * *

I leave the aviary and go down to the building where I work, and I step inside. The building is always filled with the smell of bear, a strong, rank, ragged odor, and I breathe deep. It smells like hope to me.

This is the headquarters of the Bear Restoration Project—BRP. I've been in on it from the start—during the blue-sky days, then the planning, then the raising of funds. Now we're in the second year of implementation, and this year I am in charge of Buster and Gladly, two orphaned cubs a hunter brought us in early spring.

Last year I tried to avoid the pain of anthropomorphism by just numbering the cubs, but it didn't work. They still spoke through my friend Billings.

"HI, TAFFY," he'd say, in Ten's deep voice.

"Hey look, Taffy's here!" he squeaked in Eleven's falsetto.

This year I went back to names, and the same thing happens.

"HI, TAFFY," Buster growls when I walk into the building.

"Oh boy, it's Taffy!" Gladly squeaks.

Buster and Gladly have gained over eighty pounds each this summer. They pay little or no attention to the fact that I'm here: it's a good sign. They've never taken food directly from us, never been caressed by human hands. They roll around in the straw, playing silently. When one of them's in a bad mood—usually it's Gladly—they make growly, squeaky noises.

"You'd love me if I were a bear," my friend Billings has said to me, and he's probably right. "Is it my upper body under-development? Would you like it if I lifted weights?"

"Billings, you are fine the way you are," I say time and again. "I wouldn't want you any other way." And that's true too.

To tell you the truth, I'm not looking for romantic entanglements. To tell you the truth, I'm still looking for evidence of other worlds.

* * *

"More talking animals?" my brother Daniel said, grabbing my book. " 'Stickytoes the Tree Toad,' " he read. "Just like you. Big flat stinky toes."

"Give it here," I said.

"Gladly," he said.

"Gladly the cross I'd bear," our mother sang, walking past in the hall.

"Listen, Taff," Daniel said. He read aloud from his own book. " 'The Great Auk could be herded right across gangplanks and onto boats.' " He looked up at me. "Once, that was how life was on earth."

"Who was the Great Auk?" I said.

"They're all dead," Daniel said. "They were the original penguins, and sailors used to bash them on the head for fun."

"I don't understand you," I said. "They marched them onto their boats and bashed them on the head?"

Daniel smiled at me. "Yes," he said. "Then they ate them."

"I thought sailors were kind." I said.

"You're in outer space," Daniel said.

* * *

I listen carefully when my friends talk about their experiences.

"There I was, hovering a few feet above my body, watching the fireman give me the kiss of life. I didn't *want* to live," Amy says. "I floated up a long shaft of light, and at the top it was bright, and welcoming, and I knew I belonged there."

"Heaven," I say.

Amy shrugs. "I don't know," she says. "All of a sudden there was my father, at the top of this shaft of light, and I was so glad to see him. But he said, 'Go back. It's not your time.' And I thought, he's rejecting me again."

* * *

More than once my mother told me, "You're as bad as your father."

"Earth to Taffy, Earth to Taffy, come in Taffy," Daniel whined into his fist.

"Don't encourage her," said our mother.

"What's the matter with Daddy?" I said.

"His head's in the clouds," my mother said. "He's in a different world."

I pictured my father's head at the end of a very long neck, like a giraffe's neck. I drifted up there among the clouds, as he glided along the earth.

"Taffy, you'd lose your head if it wasn't tied on," said my mother. But I'd heard her say it: there was another place to be, a different world.

*   *   *

"I can't believe you don't know what channeling is," says my friend Lorraine. "Don't you read the papers?"

"Well, no," I have to say. "Nothing about channeling, anyway."

"A spirit selects someone," Lorraine says. "And then speaks through that person. It's just a method of communicating."

"Oh, I see," I say, and I do. It's just like Buster and Gladly, speaking through Billings.

*   *   *

When I was eleven years old, I was sitting one day at the kitchen table eating a late breakfast and reading *Dr. Dolittle on the Moon* when I happened to look idly out the window, just as my mother, shaking the extra water out of one of Daniel's white socks, suddenly knelt in the leaves under the clothesline, and then lay down on the ground. I was surprised at his unexpected performance by my sensible mother, but not alarmed, until a man in a bright orange vest came out of the woods a few feet away, and stood at the edge of the yard, looking around.

I expected my mother to get up and ask the man if he needed some help. Instead, the man walked over to where my mother lay in the leaves. He put down his gun and knelt down beside her, not touching her; and then, still on his knees, he looked wildly toward the house, and right in at me.

"Call an ambulance!" he shouted, and although I couldn't hear him through the triple-paned thermal glass, I knew what he said.

It was the first day of hunting season.

*　　*　　*

I pay attention; and sometimes I do get hints, and messages.

"Allied horses have begun moving north," says the radio; and I watch the south for days, looking for the clouds of dust they'll be kicking up as they come, the Clydesdales, the Shetlands, the pure Arabian quarterhorses.

TOADS UNDER EIGHTEEN INCHES LONG WILL BE UNDETECTED says a sign on an overpass; and if I weren't traveling at seventy miles per hour I'd look over my shoulder into the bed of my truck, where hundreds of toads must be huddled together, hitching a ride undetected, each of them under eighteen inches long.

"In winter, snowshoe hares gather in great herds," says the February page of the calendar. And sure enough, in the backyard the snow has been trampled, flattened by hundreds of long four-toed feet, and here and there is a half-chewed carrot top, or a withered piece of iceberg lettuce.

*　　*　　*

After my mother died, Daniel and my father and I fled west, to a state where the word *wilderness* still appeared here and there on the map. As we drove across miles and miles of flat gray countryside, I dreamed of the land we were approaching: towering mountains teeming with wolves; dark, uncharted forests heavy with herds of buffalo. I'd read about the west: grizzly bears came right out on the road and looked in your car window. You could give them peanut butter, and scratch their ears.

But we moved to a city, into a house on a hill overlooking the city zoo.

"This will be nice for you, Taffy," my father said, as we stood in the backyard looking down into an enclosure where a golden eagle was perched on a log.

Someone had tied a live chicken on top of a stump for him; as we watched from our new deck, the eagle spread his one remaining wing, leaped down toward the chicken, and fell over. He scrambled around on his side in a circle, trying to stand up, the same way the chicken was scrambling around on the stump; and finally he hobbled over and began pecking at the chicken's neck.

"Oh, great," Daniel said. "A gimp eagle."

I burst into tears.

* * *

I grew up in the zoo, cleaning out cages, chopping head after head of cabbage in half, hurling unwanted Easter chicks in the pen of Walter, the one-winged eagle, and learning to watch as he tore at them until they died.

I worked my way up from cleaning cages to bottle-feeding the newborn orangutans to handling Maizy the corn snake in the visits to schoolchildren. After I got my college degree, I went from being a volunteer to being a paid staff member; and after I got a master's degree, I became Curator of Canids.

And now I am head of the Bear Restoration Project—BRP.

* * *

My father still lives in the house overlooking the zoo. At noon I walk up the street and have lunch with him, and take him to the grocery store, the dry cleaner's, the library, wherever he needs to go.

A clot of librarians is looking out the window at the parking lot. "The poor thing," says one.

"I bet he has Alzheimer's," says another.

I catch the attention of one librarian, who comes to check my books out. "I wonder if we should do something?" the librarian says over her shoulder to her colleagues.

"And it looks like rain, too," another one says, shaking her head.

I pick up my books. "He's a physicist," I say. "He used to design submarines."

I go out to the car. "Daddy," I say, "could you try to look more purposeful?"

"What, dear?" he says, still gazing up at the clouds. "Look, cumulonimbus. We're going to get that storm after all."

*　*　*

This spring we cleaned out the duck pond at the zoo and dredged up everything that had accumulated there since a rich bird lover donated it half a century ago.

There was everything you'd expect: oak leaves, bird feathers, peanut shells, potato chip bags, a sneaker. Plenty of bird excrement, in various stages of decomposition. A child's doll, a plastic pinwheel that still spun when a workman blew on it, and a brassiere. An entire layer of garbage, where someone had dumped a year's accumulation: milk bottles, aluminum foil, a tea kettle with a hole in the bottom.

The deeper the workmen dug, the better preserved everything was. Comic books, with the balloons above the characters' heads still legible. A foot, later identified as that of a trumpeter swan, perfectly preserved. A nest, complete with half a dozen eggs, that looked as if it had been carefully filled with silicone and then buried in silt.

And a little girl. *She* was not perfectly preserved; only her skeleton was left. One of the workmen lifted a thick layer of black leaves and there she was, as if nothing had disturbed her for thirty years. The police thought she may have been placed there, but she could have slipped on some wet stones. She might have been watching a seagull, and stepped off the edge, and sunk to the bottom of the pond.

She sat on the mud, surrounded by eelgrass, and, looking up toward the light, she saw dozens of paddling duckfeet; as she watched, ducks plunged their heads underwater to look at the girl who was sitting in their pond. She smiled politely. Most of them looked as if they were smiling back. Small fish came out from under the overhanging banks of the pond, darting toward her shyly and quickly, ready to zip away if she reached for them. A couple of snakes wriggled through the water and slid around her, tapping against her so softly with their noses and with the sides of their ropey bodies that she thought they were kissing her.

She kept her eyes open and saw waterbugs and spiders, newts and tadpoles, and turtles, their legs waving slowly through the water. She saw the thin stick legs of a great blue heron walking slowly along near the shore, and she saw the tip of his yellow beak as he lowered his head far enough to get a glimpse of her. She saw that part of the light overhead was obscured by lilypads, and by huge black clouds of watercress, and blooms of algae on the surface.

As if she were watching a different world, she saw other girls, and their brothers, leaning over the water, and laughing, and pointing at some of the ducks who were looking down at her. There was a sudden pocking of the surface, and she knew that the people were throwing crumbs of bread into the pond for the ducks to eat.

She imagined reaching her hand up from the bottom of

the pond and helping herself to a few crumbs. And at that thought she laughed, and let out the air she'd been holding for heaven knows how long, and she breathed in the dank green water of the pond and lay back in the eelgrass and looked at the light that had been the sky.

* * *

Until we dug up the girl in the pond, it had never occurred to me that worlds can be ours for the choosing.

Suppose I had stayed in the first other world I saw, down in the harbor in the shadow of the *Nautilus*. I might be there still, embedded in sand, no longer noticed by the cormorants, the harbor seals, the sea turtles who found me so startling in the beginning. I might be covered with barnacles. I could have been swallowed whole by a shark.

It might have changed everything. The sailors would have failed, my father would have looked for me in vain, Daniel would have been an only child, my mother would have had less laundry to do. I would have made it a different world for everyone.

* * *

This year I found a good place in the woods, about halfway up Raven's Hill on the west side of Mt. Umbo, under the roots of a big old spruce. I checked it out, looking out at the view to the south, lying for a while in the sun. When I decided it would do, I worked on it for days, digging the narrow entrance, then hollowing out a sleeping chamber farther in. Now it's big enough to curl up and spend the winter in. I spread dry leaves on the floor, and covered the entrance with logs and pine boughs.

Buster and Gladly have fallen asleep right on schedule. To-morrow Billings and I and the other members of the Bear Restoration Project—BRP—will sedate them, pull them out of their pen, and fit them with radio collars. Then we'll load the sleeping bears into a wooden crate and set off for Mt. Umbo.

Mt. Umbo is covered with snow. We'll drive in as far as we can in the Wildlife Service truck, and then we'll pull the bears out of their crate and stuff them into heavy canvas sacks. We'll have to go the rest of the way on snowshoes—four people, hauling bags full of bear. It will take a couple of hours to reach the den that I dug out last summer, and that we cleared the snow away from last week.

We'll empty Buster and Gladly out of the bags, check one last time for regular heartbeats and steady breathing, and then stuff them into the den, along with the straw they've been sleeping in. This is the hardest part: scratching their stubby ears for the last and only time, sniffing their bear odor, saying good-bye.

Then we'll pull the pine boughs back over the entrance, and shovel on a load of snow for insulation, and head back down the hill.

I'm not fooling myself that I'm helping to save the world, or the animal kingdom, or even a certain species of black bear. The project really has nothing to do with all that. It's only Buster and Gladly I'm thinking of.

*   *   *

Sometimes I dream of the *Nautilus*, of climbing out through the hatch and stepping off the deck into nothing. I relive every second and inch of that fall into cold green water. I go through it all in the dream, up to the second that the octopus grabs me and I struggle in vain toward the surface. I wake up with a start, gasping for air.

To calm myself, I close my eyes again, to see it as my mother might have seen it from the shore.

"There went Daddy," she would say, "stumbling along with his head in the clouds. And there came you, right behind him, just the same way. But you kept going straight, and you dropped right over the edge, and my heart stopped."

Here my mother's eyes would open wide with remembered horror, and she would reach out to touch my hair. "But before you even hit the water, every sailor on the deck of the *Nautilus* had jumped overboard. And it looked like a storm of pure white birds, or angels, falling into the sea to save your life."

*   *   *

I like to believe my mother got into the heaven of animals by mistake.

"Taffy's mother? That's not the information I was given," St. Peter says, frowning down at his list. "It says here 'Whitetail deer, eight-point buck, first day of hunting season.'"

"Oh, no," my mother says. "That was me, hanging out laundry. It was just Daniel's sock."

St. Peter shakes his head. "Sorry, but the rules are the rules."

My mother turns away; and, neatly sidestepping my father's head, she bounds across the clouds, and trots up the gangplank to the other gate.

"We've been waiting!" says a Great Auk. "But where are your antlers?"

"I guess I'm a doe," my mother says.

The Great Auk shakes his head. "Mistakes have been made," he says, and a sailor with great white wings opens the gate, and my mother goes in.

The last I see of her, she's walking slowly through the clouds, holding her head low, and a golden-haired cocker spaniel, who has been waiting for a long time, leaps about, yipping happily, nipping at her ears.

It's the heaven I'll choose, if I get the chance.

*   *   *

With luck, Buster and Gladly will sleep till spring. When they wake up, they won't be scared, because they'll have each other, and they'll have the same old straw they went to sleep with, smelling of bear, mostly, but with just a hint of their old friend Taffy. They'll snorkel around, stretching, yawning, and then push their way out of the den into a different world.

Of course, it's not really a different world. It's their old world, the one they belong in; it's just that now they'll be here without their mother. And after a while, they'll separate, probably without so much as a farewell. Buster will be on his hind feet somewhere, reaching for some berries, and Gladly will wander off over the top of the hill; and that will be that. They'll be alone.

And that, of course, is how they would have ended up anyway.

Mary TallMountain
GOOD GREASE

The hunters went out with guns
at dawn.
We had no meat in the village,
no food for tribe and dogs.
No caribou in the caches.

All day we waited.
At last!
When darkness hung at the river

we children saw them far away.
Yes, they were carrying caribou!
We jumped and shouted!

By the fires that night
we feasted.
The Old Ones clucked,
sucking and smacking,
sopping the juices with sourdough bread.
The grease would warm us
when hungry winter howled.

Grease was beautiful—
oozing,
dripping and running down our chins,
brown hands shining with grease.
We talk of it,
when we see each other
far from home.

Remember the marrow
sweet in the bones?
We grabbed for them like candy.
Good.
Gooooood.

Good grease.

Tess Gallagher

Although I've Never Carried a Gun: Some Notes on Women and Hunting in the Northwest

Considering their often peripheral relationship to hunting, I think the attitude of women in the Northwest toward it is quite diverse and vocal behind the scenes. Women even hold a complicitousness sometimes with hunting, as it contributes to an aspect of manhood that has been perhaps oversimplified. The word macho is a kind of pejorative shorthand, which doesn't allow for the true complexity of what hunting does supply for some of these men and the women they live with.

As someone born and raised in the Northwest, I have gradually come to both appreciate and question aspects of hunting as they relate to women's lives. Although I've never carried a gun, I have gone into the woods with hunters and been in hunting camps, but my reluctance to kill any creature has kept me in the spectator's box. I do have poems about hunting, and even about calamities that happen to hunters. Since hunting is a part of the Northwest life-style, there were always dire stories about members of families accidentally shooting each other, and also of seeming accidents which could have been score settlings.

Northwest women are especially conscious of their household boundaries extending into the forest zone of possible dangers from cougars or gunshot wounds or those who simply get lost. We always know when it's hunting season even if we don't venture out to hunt ourselves. Our couches are full of interlopers, and meals for two become meals for six. A lot of story telling occurs in episodic late-night bursts. And for my part, this is the best of hunting—the stories of happenings and mishaps, of fears and near misses, of human greed and carelessness, the wide spectrum of masculine display before the feminine, of boyishness and prowess—a wilderness of subsistence mentality which for the past one hundred years has supported a "meat on the table and racks on the wall" way of life.

Since I grew up in a time when the "meat on the table" aspect of hunting was a matter of true family survival, my first feelings about hunting had to do with a sense of necessity. And in some families in the Northwest, in these continuing hard times, "meat on the table" is still a necessity, strange as it may sound to a vegetarian-prone, baby-boomer, yuppified generation. The Northwest, despite the strong influence of its urban Asian population, has not yet converted to tofu.

Initiations

Part of the resilience of hunting in the Northwest life-style has to do with the Northwest tradition of initiation of sons by their fathers into hunting. I'm sure that since I was the first child, my father would have been glad to teach me to shoot had I been interested. I did go into the woods with him many times as a young girl. We would sit on stumps in the raw light of mountain clearings and wait for the deer to come to us. I also remember on one occasion going with my father to look for a deer he had shot, following the blood trail through the woods, then finding the deer and watching him quarter it for the pack out. It's a kind of meeting with mortality one never forgets.

As an adult one feels very torn about the initiation process that goes on for the boys in the family. These boys are having an intimate experience of being in the woods with their fathers, intent upon the objective of getting game, but along the way they are also learning those things about survival one can only learn from being in the unknown. There is a wildness and a freedom from the domestic life and life in the community that these young boys experience. I guess my own feeling has been that I wish they took cameras as often as they took guns into the woods.

At present I am a woman who mostly hears about hunting and from what I hear, I feel there is now a lot of male anger and wrongheadedness and escapism involved in what was once an activity that had solemnity, purpose, and even respect for the animal. I don't really accept the word *sport* when it's attached to hunting. I don't, for instance, condone the shooting of bobcats, which is regarded as a houndsman's sport in this neck of the woods. In fact I've said recently to my nephew that one can only get so many pelts on the wall before it's pretty much a redundancy. He looked at me like I was speaking Greek. His mother seems to be in my camp, but keeps her distance, allowing a male province here.

There is a certain amount of resentment from Northwest women, perhaps, in that hunting still involves a drawing away of their men from domestic life. Many of the houndsmen I've met have been young men with young families who are on the escape from their wives and children. They don't show moderation in how they conduct their hunting activities and go at it in such an impassioned way that they often alienate the women who support them, both in their livelihood and in the home.

Refusing the Waiting Game

Some of the younger women who are attached to houndsmen and hunters here in the Northwest have devised a way of handling the obsessive hunter in their lives by refusing to play the waiting game. They do their own things. But there is still that brand of woman who is perpetually watching the clock, wondering when her hunting husband and sons are coming home, worrying about their safety and delaying her own activities. As my sister-in-law says, "The clock is entirely different when you're married to a hunter."

Some Northwest women perhaps allow their men further limits of freedom than other women whose husbands don't hunt, but they do so in order to secure their own freedom. There's a kind of interlocking independence. There is also a dual wish from the women for more moderation from their men in their pursuit of game, and at the same time the honest desire for these men to have this passionate experience. Some women voice a not-so-subterranean view that hunting curbs more destructive impulses by men to womanize or to drink or gamble.

The main complaint from women attached to hunters is that there is little or no balance. Divorces happen because men disappear into the hunting season, neglecting their families and neglecting their jobs and responsibilities. The challenge of the chase can be a kind of drug, and the repercussions for family life in the Northwest can, in fact, be very similar.

My Mother's Hunting

In talking with my eighty-year-old mother, who worked as a choker setter with my father in Northwest logging from 1940 into the 1950s, I learned that she believed herself to be one of the few women who actually carried a rifle and hunted by herself on trips with my father. She talked about really enjoying being in the forest by herself, the great peacefulness of the quiet there, the stillness and mystery and light filtering down through the hemlocks and firs. She said she never killed a deer, but shot at one once and did know how to shoot. She had intended to kill the deer, but was off mark that day. She said as far as she knew there was only one other woman on this part of the Olympic Peninsula who went out hunting in deer season at that time in the early 1940s. Still, she didn't treat her own hunting as anything extraordinary, only some matter-of-fact happening. She had just quite naturally gone out.

I asked her how she had learned to shoot a gun and she said she had had a sweetheart once in Springfield, Missouri, who taught her to shoot game birds. She'd been a good shot, yet the only thing she had killed since the bird hunting when she was a young woman had been raccoons. A family of raccoons had been climbing at night into her fruit trees to shake down cherries and apples. When the Forest Service refused to help her control the raccoons, she stayed up nights until she had thinned the population herself, shooting with accuracy into the trees in the dark. This happened after my father's death, and I think emotionally it had something to do with the loss of him. He had planted every tree in the orchard. My mother had seemingly attacked the raccoons as some invasive presence that had forced her security in her recent widowhood.

I don't think I understood at the time why my mother had become so obsessed with ridding herself of the raccoons. I would go and come from the house those days and notice her lack of sleep and notice the 4-10 shotgun propped near the door. Several years later, at age seventy-nine, she climbed into the fruit trees and pruned all twelve of them. Single-handedly. It was in character that she didn't depend on either her sons or her son-in-law to help her. The tone of her mind was geared to self-sufficiency, and she prided herself in knowing what and how to do things and on not asking advice or permission.

My Mother's Regard for Guns as Attached to Presences

My mother had a great protectiveness over the hunting rifles left by my father and also over her own rifle. Although she would lend my father's gun after his death to my nephew during hunting season, she would not let him keep it. After each hunting season she would ask for it back, and if it wasn't returned promptly, she would make a trip down to my brother's and take it back herself. It seemed as if the necessity of keeping my father's gun at her house had something to do with continuing on with those things that had meant so much to him, hunting having been one of his primary pleasures. Also, she seemed to fear that someone might steal the gun at my brother's and that the loss of it that way would be a kind of trespass she would regret out of all proportion. Going to reclaim the gun was insurance against that.

These last things I've described are not actually about hunting itself, but connected to its meaning, for at least one woman. I tell them as an emblem, perhaps, of women we don't hear from in my mother's generation (those born around 1914) who found themselves with men who hunted, and who joined them for some period. Women who, if they didn't participate at the same frenzied level, at least took part in hunting enough to more than condone, and even to appreciate, what there was in the act of hunting that could draw a person out to do it in those days before the environmental clamor had soured and accused that remnant of early living off the land from which both my mother and father had come in their mid-South youths to the far Northwest where I was born.

Tess Gallagher
BIRTHMARK

Water on all sides as invitation to memory,
especially the deeply unspoken—or so I think
when, fishing eight miles out from the Elwha,
Stub begins to tell how his son Jimmy died, shot
like any wild thing on a hillside in Idaho, wearing
fluorescent vest and red hat he'd just bought him,
making sure Lyle, Jimmy's friend, wouldn't sight
on the moving elk-man against the hillside.
"They knew where he was," Stub says. "Knew
he'd staked out exactly there."

He's back in that instant of choice a boy had
before his bullet pierces friend, father, mother,
brothers, sisters, then zings fifteen years forward into
this boat so the blood of the fish we've caught
congeals along his right wrist,
and he can lift his son this time
as he couldn't then—laid up in the hospital
with appendicitis, telling his son, "Sure, take the pickup,"
which benediction reverberates as the shot
before the shot, the one this father wants to
call back, the good father's
permissiveness that strikes at his own heart
with regret so profound it can never be
assuaged. "It's only recently
I could even talk about it," he says.

The milky blue of years swells out from our boat.
It doesn't matter if the fish bite.
My brother and I let the story's silences gentle him
absently and receive a little more
those who are held past any clear way of mourning
because some sorrows are the amber
and, unresolved, cast us into water
that is only water. Gaps

in the story then, and the son's best girl
marrying Lyle a year after the death. A child born
to them and hardly a year before
divorce, the girl—someone said—just sorry
for him. My brother then, having heard the story
from Larri Ann, asks about the child. Was it so, did it
have a birthmark where his son was shot?
"I never heard that," Stub says,
and seems, considering it, near dissolving
like the pale, thin crescent above the mountains

at daybreak, a half-moon trying to dwindle
between glances into a trace, a scar
of moon, passed on. As this is passed on
for its quality of fading not quite out,
like a father's love tempted quietly
into flesh again—ours. Though no one has said
whether temple or cheek
took the bullet.

So the wound must shine
outside our bodies. Not to illumine, but to chasten
our witnessing, until it takes the force of omen—
something so ahead of us as dread
we know at last
there is nothing we could have done for that boy
except what is done for him now in the father.
So we sit with him on water
in the clear morning light, helping the cold thing
come true.

Francine Prose
FROM *PRIMITIVE PEOPLE*

*S*imone, *a young Haitian woman, has come to New York's Hudson Valley and found work as an au pair, taking care of Rosemary Porter's children, George and Maisie. Among Simone's new friends is Kenny, who runs Short Eyes, a hair salon for children*

* * *

That fall it snowed in October and all the leaves dropped at once. For a few hours it was beautiful, white frosting the scarlet maples, but by afternoon the world had turned snail-slime brown and jagged tree limbs littered the ground. Rosemary paced from window to window, monitoring the wreckage.

She said, "Simone, your first snowfall! What a historic event! It never snows in October, you *do* realize that. Freak storms are just the beginning. It's the death rattle of the planet. My personal calculation is that we're about six months from Armageddon."

Simone turned her back and crossed herself. From where she stood Rosemary would see just the appropriate shudder.

Rosemary said, "Those branches will have to be carted away. And those teenage hunks who mow the lawn are surely back in seventh grade. You see I am deteriorating about the housekeeping situation. It's gotten to where I don't give a hoot if a dish ever gets washed. Believe me, I wasn't always this way, but this is my present incarnation. The decision you have to make is how much disorder you can stand."

Rosemary often mentioned the house's messy state. Was she hinting that she wished the place were cleaner? But why then did she always insist that it was Simone's decision? Simone did her own and the children's laundry and what simple cooking there was. George and Maisie helped with the dishes and with keeping the kitchen and bathroom on the acceptable side of disgusting. How sad—children so heartened by being asked to sponge out the tub! The halls and public rooms of the house seemed dauntingly fragile, like a rusty book that might crumble to powder if you turned its pages.

For some reason the debris from the storm was proving hard for Simone to live with; perhaps because the fallen branches represented new, not preexisting, damage. For a few days Simone studied them through the windows or slowly drifted around the yard, contemplating the larger branches; then, overwhelmed by the size of the job, she'd give up and go back in. Then one foggy morning she went out and dragged all but the heaviest limbs into a series of brushy piles, far from the house at the edge of the lawn where it rolled up against the forest.

Simone hesitated at the tree line, gazing in at the fog and trees: white gauze shot through with black stitches. She filled her lungs and walked in to see how the woods looked from inside.

She could hardly see ahead of her and kept checking over her shoulder. She would not let herself lose sight of the house—before that she would go back.

And so she was trying to see the house when she backed into something furry. First she registered its fuzziness, then its revolting slippery wetness. Her skin and her nerves knew more or less what it was before she turned her head and saw.

A dead sheep, an enormous dead ram, hung upside down from a tree. Its curls were a nicotine yellow except where caked blood had dyed its pelt brown. The sheep's mouth and eyes were wide open and its head flopped off to one side.

A twig raked Simone's forehead as she ran through the woods. She kept scraping her face on the branches, bleating with terror and rage. Her heart raced around in her chest as if it were trying to escape.

At last she reached the edge of the woods and broke free into open space and ran up the lawn to the mansion. She ran upstairs to Rosemary's studio, where she had never been but found easily now by following the music from Rosemary's stereo, the same four notes repeating an insistent, maddening rhythm.

Several small rooms had been broken through and combined to make the studio. Bare patches of plaster where walls were knocked out reminded Simone of Haiti. Rosemary wore goggles, a long-snouted mask, white coveralls, and her fur coat.

"Hit the floor," Rosemary's voice bubbled from inside her mask. "This is a toxic event." She stepped back from a sculpture she had been spraying from a tank and scrutinized it so raptly that Simone had to look, too. It was a female torso with a pendulous belly and a dozen globular breasts that appeared to have been slathered on with a spatula dipped in rubber.

"My Goddess Series," Rosemary explained. "This one's a Demeter figure, very Earth Goddess–Great Mother with an edge of the Willendorf Venus. The irony is that it's made out of the deadliest space-age fiberglass resin. I think I'll have her holding a broken mirror or some kind of primitive votive object. This Phillip Glass tape can just flip me right into a shamanistic trance state in which for minutes at a time I forget that the whole thing totally misses. Because there is no going back to the time when the art object was pure magic. Primitive people knew things about art that we have forgotten. They knew what images were so powerful you could hardly bear to behold them, what could make your heart stop and congeal on the spot. The Assyrians and the Mayans and the Kwakiutl people—one look at those idols and you just drop straight down to your knees."

Simone's gaze had drifted to the paintings on the walls: prodigiously ugly canvases sharing a feather motif, muddy-colored peacocks' fans scrubbed into the canvas, as if the main artistic intent was to make a little paint go a long way. But if economy was the point, why was so much paint spilled on the floor?

"Two dimensions," Rosemary was saying. "Such obvious limitations. Goodness, Simone! You look like death! Whatever is the matter?"

Simone said, "I saw something in the woods. An animal hung from a tree."

Rosemary put down her brushes. "Oh, dear. What was it this time? Not another horse!"

"It was a sheep," Simone replied dully. A sheep seemed like nothing now.

"That's our neighbor up the Hudson. The Count. You don't want to know what goes on at the Count's house. I gather that underage children are the least of it. Believe me, we have complained and complained. George and Maisie found the dead horse. But six hundred riverfront acres buys some privacy up here—as it does everywhere, I suppose, the Amazon included. And decadent Bavarian royalty gets cut a certain amount of slack.

"Anyway, you weren't walking in the woods? What a suicidal idea! The story of Little Red Riding Hood is hardly about nothing. Once hunting season starts here they'll bag you like a quail. Last fall I thought I heard the mail lady, I was walking down the driveway, smiling, still in my nightgown. But it wasn't the mail lady, it was a mustard-colored Buick with four guys in Rambo suits eyeballing me through the windshield. At first they looked a little glum but when they saw me they sucked in their chests. Never have I had such a sense of what kind of morning the deer were having. I dressed and took the first train to the city. I thought, crackheads may kill me but I'm sure they won't tie me to the roof of their car. Well, *pretty* sure, is what I thought. It's all so neolithic . . . "

* * *

Maisie and George introduced Simone to the addictive pleasure of butternuts, small wild nuts with the vein of sweet meat you had to dig out with a needle. Partly it was the labor itself, the miniscule reward, the disproportionate joy of prying loose a slightly larger crumb—it kept you hungry and desirous in ways a bag of shelled walnuts could never. How wasteful that the difficult should seem so much more precious, so that the practically unattainable was valued most of all. In that way shelling butternuts was like being in love, Simone thought.

Simone and the children spent evenings at the kitchen table, picking at the butternuts with catatonic concentration. Their lives took on a squirrel motif that persisted to bedtime, when Maisie insisted Simone read aloud from a book in which talking squirrels discoursed tediously about the acorn supply. Simone and the children were hoarding, too, stockpiling nuts for the winter whose approach they felt in the wet chill wind already slapping at them from the Hudson. They had grocery bags full of nuts stored up—but suppose they ran out, and snow fell, and they couldn't find more? This seemed, as the autumn wound down, an unendurable prospect.

One afternoon the children came home from school and the sky was so blue and bright that it tricked Simone into forgetting how short the days had grown. She and the children decided to hunt for butternuts in the woods, and as they crossed the lawn Simone said, "Look up. What do you see?"

"Clouds," George said.

"What do you see in the clouds?" Simone asked.

Maisie was wearing large, heart-shaped sunglasses she'd got as a present from Shelly and now she tilted them forward to better see the sky.

"Seafood," George said finally. "An octopus and a lobster."

"A horse's head," said Maisie.

They walked on in silence until they reached the trees. Maisie said, "I can make clouds move by concentrating on them."

"Sure you can," said George.

"Let's talk about our fears," Maisie said.

"Let's not," said George. "She always wants to talk about her fears."

Ordinarily Simone might be curious about what Maisie was afraid of, but it was the last thing she wished to discuss, walking through the woods with the children. She had been frightened of the forest since she found the dead sheep.

"My worst fear is horses," Maisie said.

"We found a dead horse," George said.

Before Simone could decide whether or not to pursue this subject, Maisie said, "I mean live horses. The most beautiful thing in the world. I wish Mom would let me take riding lessons. I would be scared that I'd get trampled. But that would be a good way to die. Not like the guinea pig baby at school where the guinea pig mother ate it."

"Hamster," said George. "Don't you know *anything?*"

"Guinea pig," said Maisie.

"Hush," said Simone. Absurdly she was seized with fear that Maisie's talking about horses would somehow cause them to find another dead one dangling from a tree. She looked around for the shaggy bark that would mean nuts had fallen nearby.

"A lot of times I'm afraid of old people," said George. "Sometimes you don't know what they're going to say and—"

Just then something whistled past and smacked Simone on the side of the head. In fact it had not hit her, just hit the air near her face, hit the air with the violent crack of a diver cannonballing into water. It felt like someone blowing into her ear through a long, thin metal pipe. Pressure galloped in her skull and swelled inside her throat. Then something struck a birch tree, and splinters exploded off the bark.

The last yellow leaves showered down like a hail of coins. Afterwards the tree kept shaking for a very long time.

"What that a gun?" asked George.

The answer was a crackle of gunfire, the delicate pop of a shot. Simone threw the children to the ground and covered them with her body.

"What's going to happen?" said George.

"Nothing's going to happen," snapped Simone. Another bullet streaked overhead. Maisie buried her head in Simone's shoulder and began to cry.

A minute passed, then another. There were no more shots. "Stay down," said Simone. "Stay down until I tell you to get up."

"What's going to happen?" repeated George.

"Nothing. Nothing," answered Simone, and this time nothing did. In a while they lifted their heads and looked at each other. They squirmed around till they lay with their heads together, their legs like the spokes of a wheel. All three of them could have been children, playing in the dead leaves.

"Are we allowed to talk?" George whispered.

Simone said, "I guess. Don't move."

"There's this kid?" said George. "In our school? His dad grew up around here? And one year when his dad was in high school there was this squirrel population explosion and kids got paid fifteen cents for every dead squirrel they brought in?"

"Cheap," said Maisie.

"So this kid's dad took his gun and popped fifty squirrels and took them home in a bag? But his dad, I mean, the dad's dad got mad and made the mom skin the squirrels and put them in the freezer? The mom—the dad's mom—had to figure out all different ways to cook them? The kid's dad still eats squirrel. He takes the squirrel legs to work and cooks them in the microwave."

"Gross," pronounced Maisie. Then she said, "Maybe butternuts have feelings. Maybe God was punishing us for eating them."

"Yeah, sure," said George.

Maisie whispered, "The shooting stopped."

"Who was that, anyway?" asked George. "Who was shooting at us?"

"I don't know," said Simone. Why did the children think she had answers? "Not *at* us. Just *near* us. Maybe it was a hunter."

Maisie said, "Hunting season starts Monday. It's all Mom's talked about for weeks."

"Or a serial killer?" suggested George.

"What's that?" Maisie asked, and then said quickly, "I don't want to hear."

"They go around killing people?" said George. "It's what they do on vacation? They'll stab somebody in Florida and then take a car ride up the coast and strangle somebody in Maine?"

"Kids, too?" Maisie said.

"Some specialize in kids," said George. "I think they're called something else. Did you hear about that kid whose dad set him on fire with a can of gasoline?"

Simone tried to listen through their talk to the sounds of the forest. She felt somehow that they were alone, that the danger had passed, though before the shooting started she hadn't felt anything special, either.

"Be quiet for five minutes," she said. "Then we will very quietly and slowly get up and go home."

Maisie said, "I don't think we should go home. I don't think we should tell Mom."

* * *

Some instinct signaled Simone and the children: Rosemary must not be told. If she found out she might forbid them to leave the house ever again, or she might even fire Simone for having put George and Maisie at risk. Alternatively, perhaps more likely, Rosemary might not react at all. Then Simone and the children would feel cheated of their experience, with no excuse for the tremors that still shook their legs and shocked them into functioning as one creature with three heads and a single brain that knew they needed to get away—go somewhere and tell someone.

"Let's go see Kenny," Maisie said, and they piled into the car. Simone had never driven at dusk, and the prospect was unnerving. But whatever spared them this afternoon would just have to save them again.

Everything about driving to Short Eyes tested the limits of Simone's courage. She could never have managed if she hadn't so recently been so afraid. The only route she knew was the one she took that first day, small roads into larger roads and finally onto Route 9. She wondered if she would always have to recapitulate the beginning; in Port-au-Prince there was a crazy woman who used to get stalled on the street and had to go all the way back to her house to get herself going again.

Kenny seemed genuinely happy to see them, which in itself moved Simone. She always felt so indebted when a man registered her presence.

A little boy sat in Kenny's chair—a tiny, dark-haired prince.

"*Modified* spike," his mother was saying. "Modified is the operative word."

Kenny abandoned his victim when Simone and the children walked in, a reprieve for which the little boy dazzled them with a smile.

"You know that kid?" George asked Maisie.

"No," whispered Maisie. "Do you?"

"Hola!" said Kenny. "Bonjour! Yo!"

George said, "Yo!"

Maisie said, "Kenny! Bonjour!" The children seemed more cheerful already.

"Someone shot at us," said George. "We were walking in the woods near our house and someone shot at us. I think it was a 357 magnum? You should have seen what it did to our tree."

"A 357? I doubt it," said Kenny. He looked at Simone for corroboration.

"Someone shot at us," said Simone.

Kenny laughed. "The Count, I'll bet. Your neighbor to the south."

"Really?" said George. Kenny's salutary effect on the children evaporated in a flash.

"Joke," said Kenny. "The Count is a criminal and a freak but not a murderer. Or anyway, not of humans. Listen to Uncle Kenny. This is hunting season. You are considered a nine-point buck until you are proven human. Only the desperate or deeply impaired venture off the blacktop. After two six-packs you guys look like Bambi's mom and two Bambis. Simone, didn't Rosemary warn you? Some years she can't talk about anything else."

Simone was trying to remember the story Rosemary told about seeing a car full of hunters and fleeing to the city. Where were George and Maisie then? That had not been clear. It was often hard to tell from Rosemary's stories when they'd happened or who they'd happened to, or what exactly they meant.

Abruptly, the little boy's mother said, "I saw the most adorable item. Two doors down they're selling these darling Red Riding Hood capes, cute and warm and made for kids who have to go anywhere near the forest during the annual bloodbath the locals call deer season. The capes made me wish all over again that I'd had a girl. But I'm not having another child, not even to get a daughter. She *did* have these terrific red baseball caps. I got one for Max."

"Two doors down from *here?*" said Kenny.

"Good Witch of the East," said the woman. "Where did you think I meant?"

"Oh, Glenda's place," said Kenny. "Glenda's my buddy. Far out. Another total fuzzball with a blue-chip business sense."

He finished cutting the little boy's hair. The boy and his mother left.

"Button up," Kenny told George and Maisie. "Let's hit it. We're out of here. Uncle Kenny is going to treat you guys to one red cape and one red hat. Each."

Shooing Simone and the children out, Kenny said, "Hey, dig it. Over there's the jingling cash register, and I'm leaving the joint unlocked."

He led them several doors down to a store with a crowded, dusty window and a sign that said, in swirling letters, Good Witch of the East. Zither music played on a stereo, crystalline and frantic. The air smelled of potpourri, like the soap shop under Geoffrey's office but with a faint insecticide edge.

Guarding the door, large, sinister, wooden frogs affected debonair poses. On a table were drinks trays made from butterfly wings. A large stone cherub pouted, unappreciative of having been rescued from somebody's tombstone and set down among the painted hatboxes full of rolls of watered-silk ribbons, soft-sculpture bedroom slippers representing Nancy and Ronald Reagan in bed, and brightly colored, overdesigned toys that failed to catch the children's attention except for one tiny, expensive set of doll's woodworking tools. Simone wondered what principle of selection had gathered these items together.

"Good taste and magic." A trilling voice rang out in answer to Simone's unspoken question. A stout, sweet-looking woman swayed in from the back of the shop in a two-piece outfit ingeniously knotted from many flowered silk scarves. "I'm Glenda," she said. "Simple introductions are not Kenny's strong suit."

"Eat shit," said Kenny genially. "Simone, Maisie, and Big George. Glenda, what it *is*, babe?"

"Same old," said Glenda, and a lovely smile glorified her doughy face. It was always instructive to see what women turned into around Kenny. "The usual schnorrers and kleptos. Did I tell you about that old Native American guy the Sweat Lodge Church flew in from Utah and dumped. He came in trying to sell me some kind of animal pelt. He put it down on the counter and it was crawling with maggots! Little white blind grubby things wriggling down the display case. I started screaming, I made him take it away. Then I went next door and bought a six-pack of Black Flag. Very unorganic. Can you smell it?"

"Yuck," Maisie agreed.

Glenda turned to Maisie. "Whooo are yooou?"

"The caterpillar!" said Maisie. "In *Alice in Wonderland*."

"Exactly," Glenda told her. "I love your look. I could *sell* you in here."

"Yeah," said George. "Give her away!" This aspect of George troubled Simone, more even than his sadness: how quickly he allied himself with whoever was on the offensive, especially when it was at the expense of his sister or his mother.

Glenda said, "What about *you*, Simone?"

Simone replied, "I take care of the children."

"Simone takes care of the children," said Kenny, "while she reconnoiters and marshals her forces to take New York City by storm. She could be a model or an actress like Cicely Tyson's niece. Look at her, Glenda. Don't you think Simone could be a movie star?"

"Absolutely," Glenda answered.

The children were appraising Simone with new interest and

concern. They had never considered that they might be a way station on her road to success. That this disturbed them pleased Simone, though she knew it was wrong of her to want the children to worry more or feel less secure than they already did.

Maisie prompted Kenny, "Are we getting the cape?"

"How old are you, dear?" said Glenda. Simone, without thinking, put her arm around George.

"Six," Maisie replied.

"Six going on thirty-six," Glenda said. "The perfect Victorian mini-adult. Kenny, did I tell you this ugly story? A woman came into the shop this week, you know that survivalist couple, Vietnam vet, they live in that camouflage station wagon? He waits for her out in the car—"

"Check," said Kenny. "The one with the bowie knife in her belt. Half a dozen ratty children."

"Exactly. And one of the children glommed on to an egg"— Glenda pointed to a straw basket full of marbleized stone eggs— "and simply would not let go. The mother's prying its fingers loose, and by now the baby's howling and the poor woman asks if I take food stamps."

"Do you?" said Kenny. "I get asked all the time."

"The hell you do," said Glenda. "The question was: Did I want to give the child a malachite egg from Oaxaca? The answer was: No, I did not. So I make all sorts of lame little jokes. No, I'm sorry, I can't. But when the mother finally drags the kid out, I am totaled by guilt, thinking about how this woman can't buy anything pretty for her kids, and next week some rich witch will Mastercharge a two-hundred-dollar doll-carpentry set for a grandchild whose name she can't remember. I could have given the kid that egg. It cost me four bucks wholesale."

Kenny said, "You thought this after she left the store or you thought this after her car left the parking lot?"

"All right," Glenda said. "Anyway, I decided I wanted to do something for kids in general. And I remembered that poor little girl last year who was blown away by hunters on her backyard swing set. It was inspiration—Little Red Riding Hood! I *saw* these little capes in which kids would be visible and safe. Then I came up with red baseball caps, not to gender discriminate."

"Fuckin-A not to," said Kenny.

Simone stared at Glenda. She wished there were some way of asking about the little girl shot in her yard without alarming George and Maisie.

"How much?" Kenny asked.

"Seventeen ninety-five for the capes," said Glenda. "Eight ninety-five for the caps. Reasonable, no?"

"Outrageous," Kenny said. "I'll take one of each. Actually they are reasonable when what we're buying is protection."

"Protective magic," said Glenda. She handed Kenny a cape and a hat, and he passed them along to the children, saying, "Wear them in good health, kids. Don't get killed." Glenda led the children to look at themselves in a mirror in back of the shop.

"I left my wallet at the salon!" Kenny yelled to Glenda.

Glenda called back, "I trust you."

"She shouldn't," Kenny told Simone. "Others have made that mistake."

Maisie wore her cape home and George kept on his baseball cap. Rosemary said, "What is this? I thought we *did* Halloween. Or have the children joined some kind of cult or team?"

"It's a present from Kenny," Maisie said. "So hunters won't think we're deer and shoot us."

"I'm amazed Kenny knows what month it is," Rosemary said. "Let alone that a slip of paper allows our neighbors to use helpless children for target practice when they run out of mailboxes."

Simone and George and Maisie eyed each other and said nothing.

Pattiann Rogers
THE SUCCESS OF THE HUNT

There was a white hart that lived in that forest, and if anyone killed
it, he would be hanged. . . .

—*Willa Cather*, My Antonia

He was sighted once in a clearing at dusk, the gold
Grass up to his shoulders and he standing like a
    pillar
Of salt staring back; seen again from a high ledge,
A motionless dot of white curled like a bloom
In the green below; surprised along a lake shore
At night, taken for an irregular reflection
Of the moon on the surf.

Some looked only for his red eyes, believing
The body could be too easily hidden
By the translucent green of lighted leaves,
That it could sink blue below the water
Or become boundless against the snow, almost invisible,
That it was not white at night.

Some who followed what was presumed to be his trail
Found the purple toadflax said to grow only
From his hoof marks, and some became engulfed
By cecropia moths thought to spring from his urine.
Others testified to the impassable white cliffs
Alleged to be an accumulated battery of his shadows.

Those who lost their way were forced to rediscover
The edible buds of the winter spruce, and to use
The fronds of the cycas for warmth, to repeat again
To themselves the directional details of moss,
And part the pampas grasses clear to the earth,
To smell their way east.

But those who followed furthest with the most detail,
Who actually saw the water rising in his hoof prints
And touched the trees still moist where their bark
Had been stripped, those who recognized at the last
        moment
The prongs of his antlers disappearing over the edge

Of their vision, they were the ones who learned to tell
By the imbalance of their feet on the earth where it was
He slept at night and by their own vertigo how it was he
        rose
To nip the dogwood twigs above his head. They learned
        to smell
His odor in their bedclothes and to waken suddenly at
        night

To the silence of his haunches rubbing on the ash.
Even now they can find the spot where he walked
From the water dripping and trace on their palms
The path of his winter migration. They can isolate
From any direction the eight lighted points
Of his antlers imprinted in the night sky.
And these, who were methodical with the most success,
Always meant to do more than murder.

Diane Ackerman

FROM *THE MOON BY WHALE LIGHT*

We say dawn breaks, as if something were shattering, but what we mean is that waves of light crest over the earth. The next morning, rinsed by those light waves, I walked along the beach, beside overhanging cliffs, and realized what an ancient place the camp was based on. The cliffs were almost solid fossil—uplifted prehistoric seabeds. Fossil oysters large enough to have held more than a pound of meat jutted out from the top, and fossil sand dollars perhaps seventy million years old lay at the base. Fossil sea lions, crabs, and whales littered the beach. There was an array of dead penguins and other birds on the beach, too. In the tide wrack were feathers, flippers, mummified animals, and countless shells. Dunes of stones led down to the water. One thing the ocean does exceptionally well is sort according to size. There were fields of large stones, then ridges of medium-size ones, then areas of even smaller stones. Looking out at the water, I saw a mother and baby whale lolling in the shallows. When had they arrived? Rolling on her side, the mother whale swung her flippers up and nursed the baby. When a pack of seas appeared, and began playfully to pester them, the baby snuggled up to its mother and cupped its flipper around her. The whales appeared to have stopped in the water, but the faster I walked toward them, the more they seemed to be just another yard ahead of me. Finally, I left them and headed for breakfast at the Peludo Palace.

After coffee, cheese, and cereal-crackers, Roger, Judy, and I climbed into a car with Rubén, the pilot, and set out for the airstrip half an hour away. Roger pushed the windshield-washer button, but nothing happened. "No skunks," he said in Spanish to Rubén. Patagonians call the squirting washers "skunks." As a car passed us from the opposite direction, its driver put a hand against the front window. Roger did the same. In Argentina, car windows are made to shatter utterly on impact, so that someone thrown through the window in an accident won't get slashed by glass. Unfortunately, a sharp flying stone can shatter the glass, too, so locals mistakenly think they can hold the windshield together with one hand. Whenever they pass an oncoming car, they prop a hand against the windshield.

Rubén's Cessna 182 was hangared at a nearby *estancia*, next to a long dirt airstrip. Each year Rubén flies Roger and other camp people out over the bays, to photograph whales. Because the plane's tail letters are LV-JCY, Roger's children used to call it Love Juicy. We climbed aboard and headed for the southern bay, which was said to be packed with whales. Rubén spotted whales in the water, flew straight to them, and did steep

turns around them at three hundred feet, while Roger knelt and
shot pictures of each animal. On an outline of the peninsula, I
penciled in ♀ + ♀ + (two females, with one calf each) at our ap-
proximate position and, a little farther along, another ♀ +. As
Roger finished each roll of film, I handed him a fresh one and
marked the number of the roll and the date on the used one.
After an hour of steep turns, we headed back to the airstrip.
Rubén rolled out a yellow drum of gas and attached a green
hand pump to it that looked like a coffee grinder. Judy pumped
gas from it into a hose, which Rubén fed into a can topped with
chamois (to filter out contaminating water), and pumped the gas
from the can into the wing. It was a lengthy process. Then
Rubén and Judy climbed aboard and in a moment we were air-
borne again, flying over the great flat deserts. Sheep trails con-
verged and overlapped at the far-flung water tanks. In a few
minutes, Rubén landed on a dirt road, paused just long enough
for me to get out, turned the plane around, and took off to
spend the day photographing whales. Three kilometers from
camp, at the spot where the camp road meets the main one, I
began walking down roads that resembled gutted riverbeds. A
heard of ten guanacos took flight when they saw me. Two mares
("rabbits with white miniskirts," Roger called them) scampered
away as I passed, and lizards swaggered under bushes. In an
hour, I stood on the rise overlooking camp. Two boat trails leading from the boathouse to the water told me that the chicos
were already out at work. When I got to the house, I was struck
by the stillness and silence. Everyone was gone. Climbing up to
my hut, I took off my jacket and walked out to the cliff hut, a
little less than a mile away. An icy morning had turned into a
torrid noon, which would no doubt drop to near freezing by
nightfall. From the cliff hut, I saw below in the water the same
mother and baby I had seen earlier. She had a large, distinctive
wound on one flank, and the callosities on her snout formed a
sort of parenthesis. To some earlier observer, they resembled
fangs, and thus she was named Fang. Her new calf nestled be-

side her. They had spent all morning close to camp. The sun-light made a glittering path over the water. Each time the whales surfaced, drops of water sparkled around them.

Fang and her calf were close below me, but the whole bay was a waltz of mother and baby whales. Right whales are preg-nant for only about a year, which seems like a short time. After all, an elephant calf gestates for twenty-two months, and a whale is larger than an elephant. When an elephant calf is born it has to scramble up onto its legs, but a whale calf can go straight from the amniotic fluid of its mother's womb into the womb of the ocean. It doesn't have to support itself. Whales, be-ing warm-blooded mammals, which breathe as we do, could, in principle, live on land, but if a whale were on land, its organs would be crushed under its own weight. It needs the water to support its massive size, which is one of the reasons stranded whales fare so poorly. Because a whale baby doesn't have to stand up, its bones are so flexible that you could take the rib bone of a baby whale and bend it back and forth as if it were made of hard rubber. Baby whales are virtually weightless. It's as though they were flying. Another lovely thing about whale mothers and babies is that a mother whale is herself 97 percent water. When she speaks, the sound she makes travels directly through the water, through her body and her womb, and her baby hears it. But because there is no air in the womb, the baby can't speak back. The baby must wait in the mother's womb for a year, listening, until it's born into a world where it can finally answer.

A newborn whale calf does not leave its mother's side but often swims along eye to eye with her. Sometimes the mother whale swims so that with every downstroke of her tail, she touches the calf. Sometimes the calf gets obstreperous and bangs into its mother, or even breaches onto its mother's back. Finally, she will lose her patience and punish it by rolling over quickly onto her back as the calf is ready to ram her for, say, the fifteenth time. Then she catches it by the small of its tail and holds it underwater so that it begins spluttering, wheezing, sneezing, coughing. In a little while she lets it go. After that, the calf resumes its eye-to-eye position and is careful not to act up again. Hungry calves will butt their mothers, climb all over them, and slide off them, trying to get their mothers to roll over and let them nurse. Occasionally, a mother will calm a hyperactive calf by sliding underneath it and turning over to pick it up out of the water and balance it on her chest, holding it between her flippers. Every now and then, with a flipper the size of a wall, a mother reaches over and pats the calf sweetly.

For hours, I sat quietly and watched the busy nursery bay. Fang rolled onto her weighty side, and her baby nursed. Then the baby got rambunctious and strayed a little too far. Mother lowed to it in a combination of foghorn and moo, calling it back within eyeshot. From time to time, Fang submerged slowly, her tail hanging limp and loose, trailing one tip of a fluke in the water. She made burpy sounds, with occasional moans, and I think she may have been napping.

When a whale sleeps, it slowly tumbles in an any-old-crazy, end-over-end, sideways fashion, and may even bonk its head on the bottom. Or it just lies quietly, looking like a corpse. When it rises again to breathe in the midst of its sleep, it comes up as slow as a dream, breaks the surface, breathes a few times and, without even diving, falls again slowly toward the bottom. Right whales sometimes sleep in the mornings on calm days in Argentina, and some of them seem to be head-heavy, with light tails. The result is that they fall forward and their tails rise out of the water. Humpbacks are rarely visible when they're sleeping, because they're less buoyant and usually sink fast. But the behavior of right whales is easy to study, because they're at-the-surface whales. They're so fat that they float when relaxed, and they spend a lot of time with their backs in the air. When they're asleep at the surface, their breathing rate drops tremendously, they don't close their nostrils completely between breaths, and so sometimes they snore. In fact they make marvelous, rude, after-dinner noises as they sleep. When they wake, they stretch their backs, open their mouths, and yawn. Sometimes they lift their tails up and shake them, and then they go about their business. Often they sleep at the surface so long on calm days that their backs get sunburned; and then they peel the same way humans do, but on a big, whale-size scale. The loose skin from their backs falls into the water and becomes food for birds. When they breach, they shed a lot of loose skin as they hit the water, and seagulls, realizing this, fly out fast to a breaching whale. Not much skin sheds from the tail. The gulls know that, and when a whale is merely hitting its tail on the water, they don't bother with it.

A gull swept down, pulled a piece of skin from Fang's back, and Fang, in obvious pain, shook her head and tail simultaneously, flexed almost in half, then dove underwater. The gull flew to another pair of whales nearby, attacked them, and went off. A bizarre habit had developed among the gulls in this bay. Instead of waiting for the whales to shed skin, they landed on the backs of whales and carved the skin and blubber off. Two species of gulls—the brown-headed gulls and the kelp gulls—yanked off long strips of skin and set up feeding territories on the backs of their own particular whales. When Roger first started studying right whales at Valdés Peninsula, he noticed that only brown-headed gulls were peeling the skin off the backs of sleeping, sunburned whales. Soon, however, the kelp gulls not only learned this technique but also began carving holes in backs. The result was that whales like Fang were pitted with craters made by gulls. When a gull landed on a whale's back, the whale panicked. This year there were fewer whales in the bay, and Roger thought the kelp gulls might have been chasing them away, to bays where kelp gulls don't yet know the tricks.

Juan appeared at the edge of camp, on foot, apparently hiking in from a walk to a neighboring bay. By the time I got back to the main house, he was just arriving, wearing shorts, a T-shirt, and a knitted hat.

"Tired?" I asked with an inflection that said, I *really hope you aren't.* "Want to go find some whales?"

He grinned. "Just let me get a Coke, then *vamos.*"

I put on a leotard and tights and began crawling into a half-inch-thick wetsuit that included Farmer John overalls, a beaver-tail jacket, boots, gloves, and a hood. There was so much neoprene in the suit, trapping air, that I'd need to wear weights around my waist to keep from bobbing on the surface.

Sitting on the porch whale skull, John watched me suit up. He looked anxious. "Be careful," he said. "This morning, I was out in a boat with Tom collecting breath samples and the calf of that mother over there"—he pointed to Fang and her baby, just around the curve of the beach—"rocked the boat with its flipper and gave us a scare."

To tell the truth, if I was going swimming I'd have felt much safer with Roger on board, but I had been waiting all week for the water to calm down and all afternoon for Roger to get back from flying. It was already past four, and I very much doubted that he intended to return before sunset. So, some of my caution evaporated, and I knew it was now or never.

Juan returned from the Peludo Palace and tugged on a thin wetsuit and boots, and we went down to the beach, where Minolo joined us in the Zodiac. As we pulled out, I saw John and Tom on the porch, standing next to the sighting scopes. Heading north along the bay, we came upon two mothers and calves, but the mothers were naturally protective of their calves and hurried them away. We wanted to find a young adult. Juan had been collecting loose skin for Judy and then going into the water to photograph the heads of the whales it came from in order to identify them. I hoped to join him. We searched for an hour but found none in the mood to be approached. Finally, we headed back toward camp and, coming around a bend, discovered Fang and her calf still playing. We cut the motor about two hundred yards from the whales. Juan and I slipped over the side of the boat and began to swim toward them, approaching as quietly as possible, so that they wouldn't construe any of our movements as aggressive. In a few minutes, we were only yards from the mother's head. Looking down, I saw the three-month-old baby beside her underwater, its callosities bright in the murky green water. Slowly, Juan and I swam all the way around them, getting closer and closer. The long wound on Fang's flank looked red and angry. When her large tail lifted out of the water, its beauty stunned me for a moment, and then I yanked Juan's hand, to draw his attention, and we pulled back. At fifty feet long, weighing about fifty tons, all she would have needed to do was hit us with a flipper to crush us, or swat us with her tail to kill us instantly. But she was moving her tail gently, slowly, without malice. It would be as if a human being, walking across a meadow, had come upon a strange new animal. Our instinct wouldn't be to kill it but to get closer and have a look, perhaps touch it. Right whales are grazers, which have baleen plates, not teeth. We did not look like lunch. She swung her head around so that her mouth was within two feet of me, then turned her head on edge to reveal a large white patch and, under that, an eye shaped much like a human eye. I looked directly into her eye, and she looked directly back at me, as we hung in the water, studying each other.

I wish you well, I thought, applying all the weight of my concentration, in case it was possible for her to sense my mood. I did not imagine she could decipher the words, but many animals can sense fear in humans. Perhaps they can also sense other emotions.

Her dark, plumlike eye fixed me and we stared deeply at one another for some time. The curve of her mouth gave her a Mona Lisa smile, but that was just a felicity of her anatomy. The only emotion I sensed was her curiosity. That shone through her watchfulness, her repeated turning toward us, her extreme passivity, her caution with flippers and tail. Apparently, she was doing what we were—swimming close to a strange, fascinating life-form, taking care not to frighten or hurt it. Perhaps, seeing us slip over the side of the Zodiac, she thought it had given birth and we were its young. In that case, she might have been thinking how little we resembled our parent. Or perhaps she understood only too well that we were intelligent beasts who lived in the strange, dangerous world of the land, where whales can get stranded, lose their bearings and equilibrium, and die. Perhaps she knew somehow that we live in that desert beyond the waves from which whales rarely return, a kingdom we rule, where we thrive. A whale's glimpse of us is almost as rare as our glimpse of a whale. They have never seen us mating, they have rarely if at all seen us feeding, they have never seen us give birth, suckle our young, die of old age. They have never observed our society, our normal habits. They would not know how to tell our sex, since we hide our reproductive organs. Perhaps they know that human males tend to have more facial hair than females, just as we know that male right whales tend to have more callosities on their faces than females. But they would still find it hard to distinguish between a clothed, short-haired, clean-shaven man and a clothed, short-haired woman.

When Fang had first seen us in the Zodiac, we were wearing large smoked plastic eyes. Now we had small eyes shaped like hers—but two on the front of the head, like a flounder or a seal, not an eye on either side, like a fish or a whale. In the water, our eyes were encased in a glass jar, our mouths stretched around a rubber tube, and our feet were flippers. Instead of diving like marine mammals, we floated on the surface. To Fang, I must have looked spastic and octopuslike, with my thin limbs dangling. Human beings possess such immense powers that few animals cause us to feel truly humble. A whale does, swimming beside you, as big as a reclining building, its eye carefully observing you. It could easily devastate you with a twitch, and yet it doesn't. Still, although it lives in a gliding, quiet, investigate-it-first realm, it is not as benign as a Zen monk. Aggression plays a big role in its life, especially during courtship. Whales have weapons that are equal in their effects to our pointing a gun at somebody, squeezing a finger, and blowing him away. When they strike each other with their flukes in battles, they hit flat, but they sometimes slash the water with the edge. That fluke edge could break a person in two instantly. But such an attack has never happened in the times people have been known to swim with whales. On rare occasions, unprovoked whales have struck boats with their flukes, perhaps by accident, on at least one occasion killing a man. And there are three reported instances of a whale breaching onto a boat, again resulting in deaths. But they don't attack swimmers. In many of our science-fiction stories, aliens appear on earth and terrible fights ensue, with everyone shooting weapons that burn, sting, or blow others up. To us, what is alien is treacherous and evil. Whales do not visualize aliens in that way. So although it was frightening to float beside an animal as immense and powerful as a whale, I knew that if I showed her where I was and what I was and that I meant her no harm, she would return the courtesy.

Suddenly, Juan pulled me back a few feet and, turning, I saw the calf swimming around to our side, though staying close to its mother. Big as an elephant, it still looked like a baby. Only a few months old, it was a frisky pup and rampantly curious. It swam right up, turned one eye at us, took a good look, then wheeled its head around to look at us with the other eye. When it turned, it swung its mouth right up to my chest, and I reached out to touch it, but Juan pulled my hand back. I looked at him and nodded. A touch could have startled the baby, which might not have known its own strength yet. In a reflex, its flipper or tail could have swatted us. It might not have known that if humans are held underwater—by a playful flipper, say—they can drown. Its flippers hung in the water by its sides, and its small callosities looked like a crop of fieldstones. When it rolled, it revealed a patch of white on its belly and an anal slit. Swimming forward, it fanned its tail, and the water suddenly felt chillier as it stirred up cold from the bottom. The mother was swimming forward to keep up with it, and we followed, hanging quietly in

the water, trying to breathe slowly and kick our flippers as little
as possible. Curving back around, Fang turned on her side so
that she could see us, and waited as we swam up close again.
Below me, her flipper hovered large as a freight elevator. Tilt-
ing it very gently in place, she appeared to be sculling; her tail,
too, was barely moving. Each time she and the baby blew, a fine
mist sprayed into the air, accompanied by a *whumping* sound,
as of a pedal organ. Both mother and calf made no sudden
moves around us, no acts of aggression.

We did not have their insulation of blubber to warm us in
such frigid waters and, growing cold at last after an hour of traveling slowly along the bay with them, we began to swim back toward the beach. To save energy, we rolled onto our backs and
kicked with our fins. When we were a few hundred yards away
from her, Fang put her head up in a spy hop. Then she dove,
rolled, lifted a flipper high into the air like a black rubber sail,
and waved it back and forth. The calf did the same. Juan and I
laughed. They were not waving at us, only rolling and playing
now that we were out of the way. But it was so human a gesture
that we automatically waved our arms overhead in reply. Then
we turned back onto our faces again. Spears of sunlight cut
through the thick green water and disappeared into the depths,
a bottom soon revealed itself as tawny brown about thirty feet
below us, and then the sand grew visible, along with occasional
shells, and then the riot of shells near shore, and finally the
pebbles of the shallows. Taking off our fins, we stepped from
one liquid realm to another, from the whale road, as the Anglo-
Saxons called the ocean, back onto the land of humans.

Jane Hirshfield

Studying Wu Wei, Muir Beach

There are days when you go
out into the bright spring fields
with the blue halter, the thick length
of rope with its sky-and-cloud braiding,
even the bucket of grain—
all corn-and-molasses sweetness,
the maraca sound of shaken seduction—
and the one you have gone for simply will not be caught.
It could be that the grass that day is too ripe.

It could be the mare who comes over, jutting her body
between his and yours. It could be
the wild-anise breeze that wanders in and out of his
    mane.
He might nip at the smallest mouthful,
but your hands' slightest rising—no matter how slow,
how cautious—breaks him away.
He doesn't have to run, though he knows he could.
Knows he is faster, stronger, less tied.
He knows he can take you or leave you in the dust.
But set aside purpose, leave the buckles and clasps
of intention draped over the fence, come forward
with both hands fully exposed, and he greedily eats.
Allows you to fondle his ears, scratch his neck, pull out
the broken half-carrot his whiskered lips accept
tenderly from your palm. The mare edges close, and he
lays back one ear; the other stays pricked toward you,
in utmost attention. Whatever you came for,
this is what you will get: at best, a tempered affection
while red-tails circle and lupine shifts in the wind.
It is hard not to want to coerce a world that
takes what it pleases and walks away, but *Do not-doing*,
proposed Lao-tsu—and this horse. Today the world is
    tired.
It wants to lie down in green grass and stain its gray
    shoulders.
It wants to be left to study the nonhuman field,
to hold its own hungers, not yours, between its teeth.
Not words, but the sweetness of fennel. Not thought,
but the placid rituals of horse dung and flies.
Nuzzling the festive altars from plantain to mustard,
from budded thistle to bent-stemmed rye. Feasting and
    flowering
and sleeping in every muscle, every muzzle, every bone
    it has.

Antonya Nelson
FAIR HUNT:
IN THE LAND OF MEN

James had never killed an animal before. There were other facts he could have been wrestling but this one found him on his back porch at twilight, head at a thoughtful angle, thumbnail between his teeth. His hands smelled of the soap he'd used at the hospital, of the paper greens he'd worn, of the mask, smelled of the essence of illness itself, which he believed to be fear, and not at all of his wife. Surely he'd struck an animal on the road? For he'd driven countless vehicles, in the country and without caution, for over thirteen years. But nothing came to him, no jackrabbit, no snake, not one worthless grackle, a bird he might have killed without remorse.

He'd never hunted either and yet, as of this afternoon, he owned a gun. Driving home from the airport, he had stopped at the garish turquoise building whose excited sign—GUNS! AMMO! BEER!—had become so familiar to him that he nearly drove by when searching it out. The proprietor had been held up and shot with one of his own hand guns not too long ago, a bullet through the lung, he told James. Just made him mad. But he kept his eye on James, possibly thinking James's complete ignorance in the line of firearms suspicious. It was rural New Mexico, after all, and men owned guns.

Another thing, James thought, removed from the porch, past the can-opening routine that marked his recent meal-making, now eating his dinner in front of the television: he'd never fired a gun. He had studied the act, indirectly and repeatedly, via TV, but had never, to his knowledge, taken a gun in his hands, wrapped his finger around a trigger. His parents were pacifists; he'd been ten years too young for Vietnam. He hesitated, holding his soup spoon above the bowl, cocking his head and staring upward and to his right, the same pose he'd assumed earlier on the porch, the one his wife had told him all people take when trying to remember the past. This was something about Dee: her ability to make him self-conscious, like a hidden camera. She studied him and then fed him her findings. He was, she let him know, curious though worthy material. James stared purposefully down into the floating debris of his soup. There was no gun he could recall.

The secondhand shotgun lay, for lack of a better place, on the couch beside him. He had tossed it there trying to make it appear natural in his home, like a sweaty hat. Dee hated guns, had not long ago planted a homemade anti-NRA signboard in the front yard which had been promptly shot full of holes. Now the bravest of her stray toms suddenly jumped to a cushion, startling James, and sniffed along the instrument that tomorrow would be used to kill him.

"What do you think, Cat?" James squeaked and so had to clear his throat and repeat the question calmly. He'd never been in the habit of talking to the animals, either, another aberration Dee would have pointed out to him if she'd been home.

*   *   *

They were bad farmers, not really farmers at all, their garden eaten by rabbits, their chickens overrunning the outbuildings because Dee had declared herself, and James, extreme vegetarians, unwilling to consume animals or their by-products. So eggs were permitted to hatch. Coyotes, perhaps hawks, served to thin the group. James and Dee had come to the country first generation, both raised in suburban Houston, where crows and giant cockroaches constituted wildlife. They had bought a small cotton and pecan farm and allowed the meager acreage to take its own course. Tumbleweeds now filled the untilled cotton fields, the pecan trees bloomed and dropped their husky nuts and spread their summer canopy without interference. The county provided irrigation water which James could not remember to take advantage of. Both he and Dee worked in El Paso, across the New Mexico state line thirty miles south. They were happy enough to come home at night to the country, which was filled with the noises James had always associated with longing—coyotes, the relentless wind, train whistles and the accompanying clack of wheels—except, could it be longing, if he was here? Their animals accumulated as strays will, sent packing by intolerant adjoining farms, adopted by Dee, who turned each into a character, comical, harmless. Soon they owned a self-destructive goat who ate not only feed dishes and barbed wire but her own fur as well, her rump as bare and smooth as a human's, prone to eczema. She would ram her head into a wall until she passed out. From the litters of skinny cats in the fields, Dee fed kittens who became older and less wild, who soon moved under the house and then in, never somehow forsaking their outdoor habit of pissing wherever they happened to be standing. The chickens had begun with a single hen who'd walked up their washboard road one morning ("Like some old white-trash church lady," Dee laughed), fat and insolent, and had stayed, content by herself in the tin outbuilding, wandering only often enough to produce fertile eggs, busy creating her own quick empire of chicks.

The peacocks, two arrogant fellows who lived to outshine one another, had been won in a small-town raffle. Dee had a habit of winning prizes. They strutted, they preened, they presented their butts as if withholding the superior beauty of their plumage. Dee exalted in their cockiness, their purely natural conceit.

But she loved them all, without favorites, like children, loved to create their tales and salve their infections. It was her nature to rescue things, James came to understand. She kept a cardboard box of veterinary supplies beneath the bathroom sink, and more than once he had heard her through the closed bathroom door, convincing an unwilling animal to let her render aid.

* * *

In the morning it was the goat James decided to sacrifice first. She was a loud nervous beast, large enough to make James uncomfortable at the prospect of her watching him slaughter the rest. He led her into the pecan grove, over the cracked topsoil, ducking under low limbs. It was a windy spring morning, the kind of day Dee would have announced by saying, "I hate the wind." The trees' shadows, bending, frightened the goat; she balked at his lead. Or perhaps he put off some odor of desperation. James certainly felt desperate, and he was sweating heavily, the hand holding the shotgun slick.

Dee had been away so long now that James had grown used to mourning her absence; it was practice for her death, which was coming, a heavy blanket worn over his shoulders. At first, it had been worse, more sharp and random, prodding him when he was most vulnerable. But now loss simply characterized him. He was thin and unhappy; his house seemed sinister, the landscape malevolent. Moving from morning to night, he felt his own will tested. Dee would die, he knew that, though no one would say as much. A sterile home would prolong her passing. She came to him in small, tenuous images. Dee lying submerged in a tub of cloudy bathwater, islands of her pink flesh, breasts and belly and splayed knees. Dee disparaging the local newspaper. Dee sitting against the south side of the house, sunbathing, her face held up to the light, and afterward, sunburned, James tamping pungent Noxzema over her shoulders while she winced.

Superimposed over these images, however, was the more concrete one of Dee in a hospital bed. It seemed to James that merely being there had made her twice as sick. From nowhere and for no good reason, she'd begun fainting, exhaustion coming on her so quickly she sometimes could not make it to a chair or bed. She'd always had headaches but she started suffering migraines, spent hours at a time weeping with pain. Between attacks were whole days she walked delicately through the house, her neck held as if her head might tumble off. Then she would be subsumed once more. Pain had turned her ugly, impatient. The peacocks' noise made her shriek in fury. James once found her lying on the bed slapping her own forehead and cheeks, fighting what hurt her. The next day she'd had two black eyes.

They had loved their quaint and endearing rural life, treating it ironically and with good humor, but James suddenly felt enraged with local doctors and the slow resignation they offered as assessment of her complaints. Dee, afraid of the worst, pretended for a time to believe them, that she needed rest more than anything.

Eventually a hematologist was consulted, and then an oncologist in El Paso, who sent her to Albuquerque and then Phoenix. James had just returned from seeing her, yet felt as distant as ever. Each transfer had taken her farther away from him, from their marriage, their home, from health. She'd even left her friendly name behind, was now called Dierdre. What remained of her seemed to grow transparent, like a healing burn.

James tethered the goat to a tree at the far end of the grove. The Rio Grande passed not far from where he stood; he could smell the swampy water, and its mosquitoes kept landing on his neck. He lifted the shotgun awkwardly under his armpit, elbow cocked in a clumsy position, and aimed at the goat's head, which was lowered as she tried busily to pull free of the rope. She was stirring up dust, braying, and James decided to just kill her fast. "I'm sorry," he told her, though she paid no attention to him, "but you're dirty." He fired and fell on his ass. The goat's first reaction was to sit on her bare haunches, too, as if to join him on the ground. Then she dropped her head, which hung unnaturally stretched and slack over the rope. Her front legs had not buckled, still stood rigid. James began crying when her eyes blinked open. He aimed again but the gun's trigger would not budge. He hammered the safety with his palm, whacked the barrel on a tree, then aimed once more, this time at the exposed patch of her brown chest, and pressed the trigger, missing the goat, who, during James's panic, had died, still sitting up.

*   *   *

He had not thought about what to do with her body. Or any of the bodies, he realized, walking back to the house. He was hot and sickened but also exhilarated from adrenaline, from his sense of making progress. When he'd asked Dee's doctor what he could do, he was told to sanitize her home environment. She would be susceptible to any passing illness. Immediately James pictured germs the precise size of ticks and mites and fleas, the animals' combined stench, alone, enough to kill her. It was this image that had fortified him to shoot the goat, to take the first step. But it had not occurred to him how to get rid of the goat's large body. He was proceeding without any practicality, he realized, like walking blindfolded. It was Dee, six months older than he, who had set the tone of their married life, established in its three short years a policy of taking what came their way without prolonged deliberation.

After lunch he drove his car around the perimeter of the grove to where the goat still sat, head dangling as if hanged. Flies swarmed at the entrance points of the spray of pellets and at her open eyes. James put his hand to his turning stomach. He could not guess how to continue. Dig a hole? But it would have to be six feet long, probably six feet deep, and the earth, unwatered, would not give in easily to a shovel. He considered renting a backhoe, but operating one was another in an ever-growing list of things he'd never before done. For a second, genuine despair overtook him: he was ill-prepared for what he had to endure! It was not fair, to be so completely unqualified!

Again he smelled the foul Rio Grande. Behind the seat in his car he had brought his shotgun, as if he might have cause to defend himself. He stood until the sight of the goat did not nauseate him, until his necessary maturity caught up with him, then hit upon a solution.

He returned to the house for rope, and, finding none, settled on three leather belts from his closet. Back at the dead goat, he cut her from the tree, fashioned a kind of harness with the belts around her front legs and chest, then tied the lead rope to his small bumper. Across the empty field south of his grove he dragged the animal, careful to move so slowly there would be no chance of the rope's breaking or the car's high centering. He longed now for a rugged truck instead of his old 280Z, the one Dee called The Penis Car. He watched the goat in the rearview mirror, on her side, front legs erect with rigor mortis. Beyond her, behind the car perhaps two miles, diesels passed on the interstate, big shiny rectangles moving neatly across the desert to El Paso. James stopped at the river and wondered what he would say if someone came upon him.

He slammed the car door and surveyed the water, which
was now at its highest level, though it moved like lava, slow and
brown and hot. He hauled the goat himself, dragged her across
the broken beer bottles and desert scrub down to the muddy
bank. There she stuck and James lost a shoe pulling his own
feet from the slog. Tumbleweeds floated by, soda pop and motor oil cans. The water at the bank was shallow enough that
James had to push the goat's body away, lying prone in the water himself until the current finally caught her.

*   *   *

At home the peacocks rested on the porch railing like decoys, eyes in slits. This was the last he would see of them. James
showered. Afterward he found coarse white goat hairs in the
tub's drain screen which he flushed down the toilet. Instead of
getting on with the chore, James sat in the living room smoking
pot. He'd given this up more than a year ago, when Dee had,
but now he couldn't imagine what else would stop the shaking
in his hands. The stash he'd kept in the freezer was stale and
tasted like burning oregano. He got high anyway and watched
the dying sunlight turn the room a sentimental yellow. Pot
made him melancholy and hungry. He wished to be in a scene
of ordinary past, Dee slicing tomatoes and peppers and onions,
crying from the odors, he poking the bobbing ears of corn into
boiling water. Dee's oaky hair had been long and too thin,
hanging down her back in a fringey V, reaching just to the two
dimples of her extremely wide hips. She was flat-chested and
big-bottomed, called most of her life the Gourd by her brothers.
She wore sundresses and went braless, her big strong calves rippling where her hemline stopped. Eye makeup was the only
concession she made toward modifying herself, blue mascara,
blue eyeliner, blue eyeshadow, the rest of her face freckled and
ruddy, her eyes, she was convinced, too small.

James thought of her breasts, little more than big nipples

on either side of her bony rib cage, an areola of pale downy hair around each. The only good thing about pregnancy, Dee had supposed meditatively to James one evening after sex, was that it might give some bust to her bust. But there had been no children, and now there never would be. It was possible she would die before the year finished, before they both turned twenty-nine.

Sometimes he gave in, weakened by the effort of keeping his thoughts pure, to the fantasy of another woman, a healthy woman. When he'd married Dee, his sister told him he'd made a mistake, that Dee was cold, dedicated to negativity. She'd predicted that it wouldn't work out and now, when James looked into the future, he thought of his sister's words as prophetic, saw himself with his next wife, the true wife, a woman he would know more profoundly than Dee, having lived with her longer, among children, no doubt. She might be beautiful; she might wonder about the tragic character Dee would become. He indulged this fantasy with only half his mind, the other half experiencing acute shame. There was some relief in imagining that Dee had been nothing more than a detour, that the future lay ahead, refreshingly far from the way he felt now. But he always came back, always came crashing head-first to the here and now.

Just as James passed into the dreamless sleep he'd smoked himself toward, he remembered he'd left the shotgun in the Z, the doors of both the car and the house unlocked, lights blazing. Come and get me, he thought.

*   *   *

The smell of cat urine woke him. Sunday. Overhead a light burned palely in the sunshine from the east window. Birds twittered. On the cookie sheet on the coffee table the remaining marijuana bud looked like a scorpion. She would be home Tuesday, flown from Phoenix to El Paso, driven to her house by medical personnel. James had dredged up some lost bit of politeness and thanked the doctor in Arizona for providing curb service. "Actually, it's self-protection," the man had admitted. "Once she's out of our hands, there's nothing you can hold us responsible for." The tom Dee had named Opie licked himself sullenly at James's feet. He was orange and nearly always had, somewhere, a pus-filled infection from fights. Dee liked to open such wounds, using a sterile razor. An ear had been torn halfway off in a terrible scramble just a few months ago, giving Opie the lopsided look of a brain-damaged boxer. The urine smell propelled James from the couch and to the car, where he picked up the gun without taking time to feel its cool, dewy metal bulk in his hands. The cat had followed him as far as the porch door, and James took the opportunity to fire, recognizing the error of this instantly.

His ears rang with the gun's report, and he walked up the porch steps with a sense of unreality. The birds had hushed. He'd hit the animal's heart, just at the point where his front legs tapered down. One leg had been blown off, on the same side of the body as the torn ear, James noted. He stood sweating over the carnage, fur and blood and the leg's bone. It was seeing the concentric cross section of layers—fur, flesh, muscle, bone, and, finally, the small inner spore of marrow—that gave him stomach enough to clean the mess. He soaked the porch with water, then let the hose run into a patch of dry ground behind the chicken shed. When the earth was saturated, he dug a hole in the mud and, using a broad-ended shovel, brought the shattered cat to his grave.

*　*　*

Wiser, he soaked the ground and dug another hole, larger than the first, and put a makeshift barricade around it using sawhorses and blankets. Into this he threw all the chickens but Church Lady, who would not let him near her. The peacocks had disappeared, either smarter or more cowardly than the other fowl. James found himself both disappointed and relieved that he would not have a chance to blast their plucky, impertinent beauty.

He fired at the pit of chickens to shut them up, their hysteria shrill and childlike, fired until all movement ceased, removed the sawhorses and threw on dirt, stomped over it until the mound was solid. He shot the remaining hen on the run, down the road she'd arrived on. Too weak to dig another hole, he dropped her in a pile of old tires, covered her with a hill of rocks, and left her beside the driveway.

He realized one death made the next one easier, one killing leading more easily to another—shooting the chickens had reminded him of a carnival game—this massacre having given him the stamina to find the last cats, the three who had hidden after Opie's death. Their mistrust of him, their unwillingness to be coerced from the cool crawl space beneath the house, built his sense of its being a fair hunt, the hours it took to lure and trap them justification. He killed them without pity, one shot each, killed them and felt Dee that much closer to coming home.

*   *   *

James had gone gratefully to work on Monday, had purchased Clorox and Comet and industrial-sized sponges afterward and headed to the farm for the much simpler task of washing down the house. He was just outside the small town of Anthony, smiling to himself, remembering Dee's constant argument that he never helped with housekeeping, when a black-and-white dog dashed from the road's shoulder and was under James's front wheels before he realized it. He felt the animal pass under his feet, like a lump beneath a rug, then saw it land on the opposite shoulder. He lurched to a stop, the engine dying, and watched in the rearview. The dog did not move. Dee had never brought home a dog, a fact for which James felt sudden enormous gratitude. Could he have intentionally killed a dog? On the highway shoulder he waited for someone to come claim the one he'd killed accidentally, a young sobbing child to come running from the poor adobe house in the distance. But nothing stirred except the wind. He let loose the steering wheel and looked at his hands as if for blood.

When Dee phoned from Phoenix he was high again. Immediately he understood she could not discover this.

"So," he said, "everything friendly?"

Dee had acute myeloblastic leukemia, which had entered the bone marrow and turned it black. Or so James pictured it. The disease itself sounded like a weapon from a comic book. "Imagine little ray guns in your blood," he had suggested when the doctors encouraged Dee to use visualization. "Myeloblasters."

"I hate guns," was her response.

She'd had chemotherapy just to prepare her for the more difficult procedure of a marrow transplant. This new fluid, from her terrified younger brother, might save her but only if her body were completely amenable to hosting it.

"Not exactly unfriendly," she said tonight, "though I have a fever and everyone keeps whispering 'not pneumonia' like a prayer. I'm supposed to picture beautiful butterflies helping the transplant, I guess the same ones that were supposed to eat the leukemia cells. Not like they did such a great job of that, either. I think my imagination fell out with my hair."

James stood at the kitchen phone taking note of all he had to do. This dirt, like the animals, had come to equal Dee's disease, something to be forced from his life, the more thoroughly—the more violently—the better. "I guess I'm going to start cleaning up a little," James told her. "Scrape off the sheets and erase the plates. Ha, ha."

Dee snorted. "I'm so sick of this fucking place," she said suddenly. "I'm so sick of being sick, I could die."

He worked that night like a man possessed, first trying to vacuum the rug, running the Hoover over and over, later simply ripping up the yellow shag carpeting and, using a serrated bread knife, hacking it into chunks small enough to burn in the metal trash cans. After midnight, he stood overseeing the fire he'd filled with his and Dee's unsanitary belongings, the smoke laced with the smell of the rug's rubber backing. He'd returned to the Rio Grande and tossed in the gun, followed with the left-over ammunition. It was primitive, this purging and burning and washing, but he believed it would free him. He even threw into the fire his aged marijuana and did not inhale the smoke. The house smelled so strongly of chlorine bleach, its stark cleanliness was so daunting, he'd decided to sleep outside. He lay in a sleeping bag watching the flames die. Some last bit of burning cloth floated in the hot air, a little brilliant chink against the night, light and languid. Watching it until it landed on the ground, safely extinguished, James saw the red eyes of a small wild animal, cat or possum or, possibly, peacock, hidden down in the shadows of the overgrown cotton field, looking at him.

* * *

She came home in a private ambulance, sterile all the way, deposited with care by two young men whose responsibility for her well-being ended at her own front door. They approached, one at each of her elbows, masks beneath their noses. James wore his, his wife hers, as well as a white turban wrapped round her bald head. It would have been a scene from a movie about the future, when the air is poisonous and resourceful humans have erected clear bubbles over their plots of life-sustaining land.

"Easy," he said to her, steering her to the porch swing.

"Home," she said, crying suddenly. "I'd rather die than leave here again." Of course, she could only pretend she had this option. Her chance of survival had been eaten away like a deficit pie: within the sixty percent leukemia presented, twenty percent had to be cut, and then only for five years, if they were lucky. James had never been good at fractions, or at numbers at all. There wasn't much he was good at. He thought he'd been a pretty fair husband. Now he made his wife sit in the swing while he stood behind her and gently pushed. She was no longer Dee, he thought, her hair and heft gone, her gait timid and trembling, her insides radiated, expunged, replaced—and perhaps he would not have her long enough to discover who she had become.

James watched the ambulance roll slowly down the dirt road, sensing that its disappearance also marked the end of the lifeline, monitored night and day, that had kept his wife, himself, tied to procedure and authority. It was not until the vehicle's brake lights flashed one final time at the intersection of their driveway and the county road—a startling blast of red—that James realized his mistake of the last few days. Behind his mask his mouth went dry as dirt. Dee's shoulders swung toward him and he squeezed them as he pushed her.

Unbidden, the faces of a dozen people came to him, people who might have taken a neurotic goat, wild cats, chickens. The names of his neighbors reached him as if sung by an angel, McNeil, Tuft, Gutierrez, Gerard.

Stunned, he met Dee's eyes—so unnaturally, radiantly blue, housed as they were between the screaming white of her mask and turban—as she turned to face him. Just before she asked him, "Where are the animals?" he understood he might not ever convince her, he might not ever understand, himself, truthfully. He would live longer than she, and so have the opportunity to wonder at it for many years; he would never view peacocks without a certain unease. He'd killed her animals. But never once, until this moment, did it occur to him there was any other way. He had only done what he knew he had to.

Heather McHugh
NUMBERLESS

... composed that monstrous animal, a husband and wife.

—Henry Fielding

By law of rod and cone, the closer
it gets, the darker it looks. You look
benighted. I can hardly make out
elbow, lobe or nape, and once we go
into the whole conundrum, it's by blind
feel, slowly summing something's curve, or
multiplying verbs to come, toward where

our things have gone—the lamp shade, doorknob, chair—
    they've
gone inside: they've faded into
eyelid, nipple, hip;
it isn't long
before the room
and roof, the world at large is gone
inside us, into humming, thumping, damp, and then
    there's only
inside left to lose, and then it too
is lost, all's
lost, in a
drench, a
din of downfall . . .

(Voltage pours away in brilliant

paralyzing pulse . . .)

*

Four walls and seven
windows reappear. Our shoes
show up, right where we left them.
Glasses poised beside the bed, the innocence
that led us into such an indistinction. Now
the eight-limbed animal begins
to pull apart, into

the two of us. There's ticking,
there's a cooling off. I see,
upon a pillow, seven
inches from my face,

the watched wrists fallen
side by side: and yours
is a remming of fast-asleep
silvers. The other must be mine:

it's wide awake, it's strapped with hide.

Pam Houston

DALL

I am not a violent person. I don't shoot animals and I hate cold weather, so maybe I had no business following Boone to the Alaska Range for a season of Dall sheep hunting. But right from the beginning, my love for Boone was a little less like contentment and a little more like sickness, so when he said he needed an assistant guide I bought a down coat and packed my bags. I had an idea about Alaska: that the wildness of the place would enlarge my range of possibility. The northern lights, for example, were something I wanted to see.

After the first week in Alaska I began to realize that the object of sheep hunting was to intentionally deprive yourself of all the comforts of normal life. We would get up at 3 A.M., and leave the cabin, knowing it would be nearly twenty-four hours, if not several days, before we would return. Everything depended upon the sheep, where they were and how far we could chase them. Boone was a hunter of the everything-has-to-be-hard-and-painful-to-be-good variety, and there was nothing he liked better than a six- or seven-hour belly crawl through the soggy green tundra.

The weather was almost always bad. If it wasn't raining, it was sleeting or snowing. If the sun came out, the wind started to blow. We carried heavy packs full of dry and warm clothing, but if we saw some sheep and started stalking them, we had to leave our packs behind so that we'd be less conspicuous, and often we didn't return to them until after dark. We got our feet wet very early in the day. We carried only enough water so that we were always on the edge of real thirst. We ate Spam for lunch every day, even though smoked baby clams and dried fruit would have weighed considerably less in our backpacks. It seemed important, in fact, not to eat any fruits and vegetables, to climb up and down the steepest part of every mountain, and to nearly always get caught out after dark.

Boone and I were a good team, except when we fell into one of our fights, which was infrequent but spectacular. In Alaska we seemed to fight every time we had a minute alone, and those minutes were rare with a series of hunters who were scared of the bears and half in love with Boone's macho besides.

When Boone got really mad at me, when his face puffed up and his temples bulged out and he talked through his teeth and little flecks of spit splattered my face, it was so comic and so different from his guidely calm that I was always waiting for him to laugh, like it was all a big joke that I hadn't quite gotten. And when he grabbed me so hard he made me yell or threw me on the bed or kicked my legs out from under me it always felt less like violence and more like a pratfall. Like we were acting out a scene, waiting for some signal from the audience that the absurdity of Boone's actions had been properly conveyed.

Several times in my life I've sat with women, friends of mine, who reveal, sometimes shyly, sometimes proudly, bruises of one kind or another, and I know I've said, "If it happens one time, leave him." I've said, "It doesn't matter how much you love him. Leave him if it happens one time." And I've said it with utter confidence, as if I knew what the hell I was talking about, as if violence was something that could be easily defined.

It was never that clear-cut with Boone and me. For all the shoving around he did, he never hit me, never hurt me really. I'm big and strong and always tan, so I don't bruise easily. And I was always touched, in some strange way, by the ambivalence of his violent acts; they were at once aggressive and protective, as if he wanted not to hurt me but just to contain me, as if he wanted not to break me but just to shut me off.

*   *   *

We took four hunters out that season, one at a time for fourteen days each, and gave them the workout of their lives. We hiked on an average of fifteen miles a day, with a vertical gain of between four and five thousand feet; roughly equivalent to hiking in and out of the Grand Canyon every day for two months. At first confused by my presence and ability, the hunters would learn fast that I was their only ally, the one who would slip them extra candy bars, the one they could whine to.

"Aren't you hungry?" they'd whisper to me when Boone was out of earshot.

And I'd say, "How about a little lunch, Boone?" and Boone would look at me exasperated.

"We're hunting, baby," he'd say, as if that explained everything. "We'll eat as soon as we can."

We did the dishes with stream water that had so much silt

in it that they looked muddier every time we washed them. The cabin was only eight by ten and we took turns standing in the center of the floor over the washbasin to brush our teeth, and then one at a time we got ready for bed. Two half-cots/half-hammocks folded out of the wall into something like bunk beds. The hunter slept in the top bunk and I got the bottom. Boone spread his ground pad and sleeping bag on what was left of the floor.

Every night we'd wait until the hunter started to snore and then Boone would climb into my bunk and we'd make slow and utterly silent love. There was barely enough room for my shoulder blades across the cot, barely enough room for both of our bodies under the hunter's sag, but we managed somehow to complete the act and I discovered, for the first time in my life, that restraint can be very sexy.

Boone would usually fall right asleep and I'd be so tired from the day's hunting that I'd sleep too, even crushed like that under the weight of him. Sometime before 3:30 we'd wake up, stiff and numb, and he would slip out of my bunk and onto his knees on the floor. He'd stay there, kneeling for a while, rubbing my temples or massaging my fingers until I fell asleep again. When the alarm went off he was always buried in his sleeping bag, everything covered but one arm reaching toward my cot, sometimes still up and on the edge of it.

I don't think any of the hunters knew what was going on except for Russell, who got so crazy for Boone in his own way that he was afraid to leave Boone and me alone, afraid he'd miss a moment of intimacy, afraid even to fall asleep at night. One night, close to climax, we bumped Russell hard, hard enough so that I felt it right through Boone. Boone lay still for a long time until we all fell asleep, and we never even finished making love. The next night we waited forever for Russell to start snoring, and even when he did I thought it sounded forced and fake but Boone seemed convinced by it and he crawled into my bed and made himself so flat like a snake against me that I couldn't tell my movements apart from his.

* * *

We hunted in grizzly bear country, and on cloudy nights when the transistor could pick up the Fairbanks station we'd always hear of another mauling, or another hunter's body that Fish and Game couldn't find. We didn't go anywhere without rifles, and when our bush pilot found out I didn't have a gun he pulled the smallest .22 pistol I'd ever seen out of his pocket.

"It won't stop a bear unless you put it inside his mouth," he said. "But it's better than nothing at all."

And then he told a story just like all the other stories. In this one a bear took a man's scalp off with one swipe of the paw, and then the bear crushed his skull against a tree trunk, and then he broke his back against a rock.

But it wasn't the fear for my life that I thought would get to me, it wasn't the fighting or the hard work or the bad food. The only thing I really worried about in Alaska was how I'd feel when the hunt was successful, how I'd feel watching the animal go down: the period of time, however short, between the shooting and the dying.

Boone told me it wouldn't be as bad as I expected. He told me our hunters were expert marksmen, that they would all make perfect heart-lung shots, that the rams would die instantly and without pain. He told me that the good thing about hunting Dalls was that you always harvested the oldest rams because they were the ones with the biggest horns, they were the ones whose horns made a full curl. Boone said that most of the rams we would shoot that season would have died slow painful deaths of starvation that winter. He said when they got weak they would have had their guts ripped out by a pack of wolves, sometimes while they were still alive.

Boone talked a lot about the ethics of hunting, about the relationship between meat eaters and game. He said that even though he catered to trophy hunters he had never let his hunters shoot an animal without killing it, and had never let them kill one without taking all the meat. The scraps that had to be left on the carcass became food for the wolves and the eagles. It was the most basic of spiritual relationships, he said, and I wanted so much to believe him that I clung to his doctrine like hope.

But I still always rooted for the sheep. Whenever we got close I tried to send them telepathic messages to make them turn their heads and look at us, to make them run away after they'd seen us, but so often they would just stand there stupidly and wait to be shot. Sometimes they wouldn't move even after the hunter had fired, sometimes even after the dead ram had fallen at their feet.

It was at those times, in the middle of all the hand clasping, the stiff hugs and manly pats on the back, that I wondered how I could possibly be in love with Boone. I would wonder how I could possibly be in love with a man who seemed happy that the stunning white animal in front of us had just fallen dead.

*   *   *

The first sheep that died that season was for a hunter named James. James owned a company that manufactured all the essential components of sewage-treatment plants. He was jolly and a little stupid and evidently very rich.

On the first day we were all together, James told us a story about going hunting with six other men who all had elk permits. Apparently they all split up and James came upon the herd first and shot six animals in a matter of seconds. I tried to imagine coming into a clearing and seeing six bull elk and shooting all of them, not leaving even one.

"I knew if I just shot one they was gonna scatter and we'd lose them," he said. "They was standing real close together and I knew if I just let the lead fly, I'd dust more than one."

* * *

For the first ten days of James's hunt we had so much rain and such low clouds that the sheep could have been on top of us and we wouldn't have seen them. Our clothes had been wet for so long that our skin had started to rot underneath them. Each morning we put our feet into new plastic bags.

On the eleventh morning the sun came out bold and warm. During the cloudy days the short Alaskan summer had slipped into fall, and the tundra had already started to turn from green and yellow to orange and red.

Boone said our luck would change with the weather, and it wasn't two hours and six or seven miles of hiking before we'd spotted five of the biggest rams Boone had ever seen in the valley.

They were a long way from us, maybe three miles horizontal and three thousand feet up, the wind was squirrelly, and there was no real cover between us and them. Our only choice was to go right up the creek bed on our bellies and hope we blended with the moving water and the slate-colored rocks. The bed was steep for a couple of hundred yards, and there were two or three waterfalls to negotiate, and I thought we were going to lose James to the river once or twice, but we all made it through the steep part only half soaked.

Then we were in the tundra with almost no protection, and we had to crawl with our elbows and our boot tips, knees and stomachs in the mud, two or three inches per advance, wet, cold, dirty.

I thought how very much like soldiers we looked, how very much like war this all was, how very strange that the warlike element seemed to be so much the attraction.

The crawling took most of the day, and it put us in a good position for the afternoon feeding. We got behind a long low rock outcrop where we would get a good look at the rams, and sure enough, they had started coming down off the crags they bedded on during the day. Four of the five were full curls, all with a lot of mass and depth. We couldn't get any closer without being seen, so all we could do was lie on the rocks in our wet clothes and wait for them to graze in our direction.

Every half hour Boone would raise his body just enough to see over the ridge that protected us. He'd smile or give us the thumbs-up. Three more hours passed and the numbness which had started in my feet had worked its way up above my knees. Finally, Boone motioned for James to join him on the ridge. For the first time in hours I moved, getting up on my elbows to see the rams grazing, no more than a hundred yards away. I watched James try to position himself, try to breathe deeply, try to get the best hold on the gun. Boone was talking softly into his ear and I could only hear fragments of what he was saying— "very makeable shot," or "second from the right," "one chance," "get comfortable"—and I tried to imagine some rhythmic chant, some incantation, that would sanctify the scene somehow, that would make what seemed murderous holy. Then the shot exploded in my ears and one of the rams ran back up the mountain toward the crags.

"Watch him for blood!" Boone said to me. And I set my binoculars on him but he was climbing strong and steady. I was pretty sure it was a clean miss but I didn't say so because I didn't want James to get another shot, and the other four rams were still standing, staring, trying to get our scent, trying to understand what we were and what we were doing on their side of the mountain.

James was in position to shoot again.

"What do you see?" Boone asked me.

"I haven't got a look at him from the front," I said, which was true, even if beside the point.

James relaxed his hold on the gun. A gust of wind came suddenly from behind us and the rams got our scent. Just that fast they were climbing toward the fifth ram, and in seconds they were out of shooting range.

"He's clean," I said. "You must have shot over his back."

"Okay," Boone said to James. "We're gonna let them get a little ahead and then we're gonna follow them up to the top. Baby, I want you to stay here and watch the bottom. Watch the rams, watch our progress. Once we get to the top we're going to start to move south along the ridge. I want you to stay a few hundred yards ahead of us. I want you to keep the rams from coming down."

It was another three thousand feet to the top of the ridge. The rams topped out in twenty-five minutes. Boone and James hadn't gone a quarter of the way. I knew that if the rams would just keep going, if they would drop down into the debris on the other side, Boone and James would never get to them before dark.

I watched two rams butt horns against the darkening sky and I thought that maybe the reason why the ewes and the lambs lived separately was that the rams were not so different from the hunters after all, and in some strange way I was consoled.

"Go on," I thought at them again and again, but they stayed there, posed on the skyline while the men got closer.

Finally Boone and James were at the top, about six hundred yards from the rams. But the rams saw them first and started back down on my side. If I wanted to do as Boone told me, it was time to start walking. I sat in the tundra and slowly pulled on my gloves. I knew Boone could see me from up there. I knew he would know if I didn't do my job. I took a step toward where the rams were coming down, and then another. I had their attention, and they stalled nervously on the mountainside between the hunters and me. I sat down to change my socks, which were soaked and suddenly annoying. When I stood back up I watched the five rams, one at a time, slip down into the valley floor in front of me.

* * *

It was after dark when Boone and James got down off the mountain. We decided to camp there and look for the rams again early in the morning. I made some freeze-dried chicken stew and instant chocolate pudding.

Right after dinner we met Brian. He approached our camp at dusk, hollering for all he was worth so we wouldn't think he was a bear and fire. He walked and talked and looked like a Canadian lumberjack, but sometime during the evening he confessed to being from Philadelphia.

Brian was a survival specialist. He taught survival courses in Anchorage and nationwide. When he finished his two-week solo hunt he was off to the Sonoran desert to teach people how to jump out of helicopters with scuba gear on. He was the only man I met in Alaska who said nice things about his wife.

Brian carried Jack Daniel's in a plastic bottle that said "emergency provisions" in six different languages. He told us about his students; how they were required to solo for three days at the end of his course; how he gave them each a live rabbit to take with them so they could have one good meal. He hoped they would dry some jerky. He hoped they would stitch a hand warmer together with string made from the sinews in the rabbit's legs.

"But it never works," he said, "because companionship is a very special thing."

We all thought he was going to say something dirty, and we waited while he took a long hit off the bottle.

"I check on them sometime during the second day," he said. "They've all built little stone houses for their rabbits, some of them with mailboxes. They've given their rabbits names, and carved their initials into pieces of bark and hung them above the little doors."

We all sat there for a minute without saying anything, and then the conversation turned back to the usual. A brown bear that continued to charge after six rounds with a .300 Winchester. A bull moose that wouldn't go down after seven shots, and then after eight. A bullet that entered a caribou through the anus and exited through the mouth.

I looked across the fire in time to see Boone, out of chewing tobacco, stick a wad of instant coffee between his cheek and gum. Brian passed the bottle again, his rifle across his knees, a bullet in the chamber. He said he had followed grizzly prints the last mile and a half to camp, big ones, indicating at least a seven-foot bear.

I wanted to go to bed, but the tent was almost one hundred yards from the fire, and I knew I'd never get Boone away. I was tired of hunting stories, tired of chewing tobacco and cigars and the voices of men. I was tired of bear paranoia: of being afraid to spill one drop of food on my clothing, afraid to go to the bathroom, afraid to really fall asleep. I was tired of being cold and wet and hungry and thirsty and dirty and sweaty and clammy and tired of the sand that was in our eyes and our mouths and our food and our tent and even the water we drank and of the wind which blew it around and was incessant.

* * *

We never saw those five big rams again, but on the second-to-last day of James's hunt we got close enough to some new rams for another stalk. We had the wind in our favor but only a few hours till dark. We crawled like soldiers for what seemed like a long time, the only sound besides the river James's rhythmic grunting every time he lifted his belly out of the mud.

We got into shooting position with just enough light, Boone talking softly into James's ear, James positioning his body, then his rifle, then his body again. There were eleven rams in front of us, eight high and five low. At least four or five of them were full curls. I was trying to decide which one was the biggest when the gun fired sharp and loud, and then fired again.

"Don't shoot again!" Boone said, his voice angry. "Watch that ram."

And we all watched as one of the five lower rams ran down the gravel bed, his front legs splayed and awkward.

"Let me shoot again," James said. "Let me shoot at another one."

"We need to see if the one you shot at is hit," Boone said, calm again.

"He ain't hit," James said.

"He *is* hit," I said.

"At this point I can't tell," Boone said.

James cocked his gun.

The ram hobbled farther down and out of our view. James and Boone kept talking, talking themselves into the fact that the ram wasn't injured, but I knew it was. I knew it the way a mother knows when her child's been hurt.

"That ram's been hit," I said again. "I just don't know where."

First one and then three other rams ran down to join the first.

"I didn't see any blood," Boone said. "I think he's okay."

"He's not okay," I said, loudly now. "Do you hear me?"

Both men turned suddenly, as if remembering my presence for the first time, and then just as suddenly turned away.

"Let's see if we can get closer," Boone said. And then, after all that crawling, Boone stood up and strode across the moraine toward where the five lower rams had disappeared. James and I followed. The eight rams above us watched for a minute and then started climbing, slowly but steadily, up to the top of the ridge. The sun had set behind that ridge hours ago, but the Alaskan twilight lingered and lit the backdrop as the rams, one by one, topped out and filled the skyline, each one a perfect black silhouette against a bloody sky.

One of the five lower rams ran up to join the herd on the skyline. We came over a ledge and saw three more, not fifty feet below us.

"This is my kind of shot," James said.

"Not yet," Boone said. The three rams walked out in full view. None of them was bleeding.

"The first two are full curls," Boone said. "Fire when you're ready."

"We're still missing one ram," I said. "The injured ram is still down there."

Boone didn't even turn around. His hand silenced me. The gun fired again and the first ram went down.

"Dead ram!" Boone said.

I remember thinking I shouldn't watch, and I suspect everything would have been easier from then on if I hadn't. But it wasn't the way Boone had said it was going to be.

The ram was hit in the hindquarter, leaving him very much alive but unable to stand. For ten or twelve seconds he tried to drag himself across the glacier on his front feet, and then, exhausted, he gave up and started rolling down the glacier, rolling, in fact, right for a crevasse.

"Stop, you son of a bitch!" James yelled. "Stop, you motherfucker!"

The ram was still alive, twitching and kicking its front legs, when it fell several hundred feet to the bottom of the crevasse, irretrievable, even for the wolves, even for the eagles. We all watched the place where it had fallen.

"Jesus fuckin' Christ," James said.

That's when the injured ram, the first injured ram, limped out from the place we couldn't see below us and started to run, or tried to run, across the glacier. It was faltering now, dying, and we could see the blood running down between its front legs. Without a word to either of us, Boone grabbed James's gun and took off at a dead run across the glacier. Even fatally injured, the ram made better time on the ice than Boone, but just before the ram topped out above him he aimed and made a perfect heart-lung shot and the ram fell, instantly dead.

Of course we'd left our backpacks miles behind. Boone sent me back for them alone, and I clutched the little gun in my pocket as if it would help me. I walked right to the backpacks, in the near total darkness, something that even Boone himself couldn't have done. I had learned, by then, to make mental markers each time we left the packs, to find a mark on every surrounding horizon so that even after dark the spot could be relocated.

The temperature had dropped thirty degrees in thirty minutes, and I dug for my down coat and put it on over my wet clothing, and headed back toward James and Boone.

I found them just by following the smell of the dead ram. We were all without flashlights, and Boone decided it was too dark to butcher.

"We'll gut it and come back for it tomorrow," Boone said. "If the bears don't get it, the meat won't spoil."

"Fuck the meat," James said. "Let's cut the horns off the son of a bitch and get the hell out of here."

It was true dark now and James was getting nervous about bears. He had the safety off his gun and he kept spinning around every time a chunk of ice rolled down off the glacier.

"That's against the law," Boone said. "Come help me gut this ram." He turned to me. "You stay close."

*   *   *

I found out later about Alaska's wanton waste law, designed to protect the wilderness from trophy hunters like James. I also found out later the reason the ram smelled so awful. He died so slowly his adrenaline had lots of time to get pumping; James's first shot hit him in the gut and by the time he finally died his insides were rotten with stomach acid.

That night, though, the smell just seemed like a natural part of the nightmare. Even when they were finished gutting and we all started gingerly down the glacier, the smell of the ram came off Boone like he was the one who'd been shot in the gut. For the first time ever, I wouldn't hug him. He saved me from slipping once by grabbing my hand and left the smell all over my glove. It was worse than sour milk, that smell, worse than cat piss, worse than anything.

We walked for over an hour and I could tell by my marks on the skyline that we hadn't even gone a half a mile.

"This is crazy," I said. It was so dark that we couldn't see the dirty ice we walked on. "One of us is going to wind up in a crevasse with that ram."

"Maybe we should sit for a couple hours," Boone said. "If we sit for three or four hours it will start getting light."

"I think we should keep walking," James said.

Neither option was good. We were wet and cold already, we smelled like dinner for a bear, we had one real gun and a hunter who couldn't make an accurate shot at thirty yards. But we were alive and whole and together, and each careful step I took into the blackness made my heart race.

"We'll sit until we get so cold we have to move again," Boone said.

We piled up, nearly on top of each other. I opened three cans of sardines.

"That's perfect," Boone said. "The bear will think he's getting surf and turf."

We did okay for the first half hour. There had been a light cloud cover at sunset but not a million stars dotted the moonless sky. Boone was the thinnest, and he started to shiver first. We moved even closer together.

My fantasies were simple. A long hot shower. A plate of vegetables. A bed with sheets. TV. I thought of my mother, our last conversation by satellite telephone from North Pole, Alaska, where I assured her there was no real danger, and she told me about an actor, Jimmy Stewart or Paul Newman. "He used to be an avid hunter," she said, "and now he's a conservationist. He's done a hundred-and-eighty-degree switch." And I stood there for five dollars a minute listening to myself tell her that conservation and hunting are not antithetical, listening to myself use words like "game management," words like "harvest" and "herd control."

"This," I said out loud, "is wanting to love somebody too much."

"Here come the lights," Boone said, and even as he said the words a translucent green curtain began to rise on the horizon. Then the curtain divided itself and became a wave and the wave divided itself and became a dragon, then a goddess, then a wave. Soon the whole night sky was full of spirits flying and rolling, weaving and braiding themselves across the sky. The colors were familiar, mostly shades of green, but the motion, the movement, was unearthly and somehow female; it was unlike anything I'd ever seen. I was suddenly warm with amazement. I pressed my body harder into Boone's.

Early the next morning we went back for the ram. I shot a roll of film while James and Boone hugged and shook hands over it, while they picked up the horns and twisted the now stiff head from side to side, and then shook hands again. They were happy as schoolboys and I understood that what we had accomplished was more for this moment than anything, this moment where two men were allowed to be happy together and touch.

*   *   *

James flew back to Fairbanks the next morning, giving Boone and me our first day together in more than two weeks. We needed to take another hundred pounds of food up to the cabin for the hunter who was already on his way, and bring the garbage back down to the strip. With the six miles of packing each way from the airstrip we had a full day, but I was hoping we'd have time for a nice lunch once we got up there, hoping we'd have time for some loud, rowdy sex before we had to load up our packs and come back down.

The sun came out for our walk to the cabin, and when we got there I made Boone lunch and a couple of drinks. I mixed the Tang and water separately from the rum so the drinks would taste real. I added extra butter to the freeze-dried food, some dehydrated Parmesan, some parsley flakes.

I can't remember how the fight started, or why we disagreed. I only remember the moment when we stepped, as we always did, out of ourselves, and into the roles from which we fight.

"I spent the whole day trying to make everything nice for you," I said, hearing the script in my head, already knowing the outcome of the scene.

"What did you do?" he said. "Boil water?"

And he was right, what I had done was boil water, and there still might have been a way of saving the day if it hadn't been for the fact of those parsley flakes, if it hadn't been for the fact of that Parmesan cheese.

"Go to hell," I said.

"What was that?"

"Fuck you."

And then he was there, in my face, temples bulging. He grabbed my neck and twisted it into an unnatural position. I felt one of the lenses fall out of my glasses, felt something pinch between my shoulder blades, and I screamed, trying to channel all the pain into my voice so he'd let go, and it worked. But then he came back at me, grabbed my shirt around my neck and twisted it.

"If you hurt me again," I said, "I'll shoot you." It was sort of a ridiculous thing to say, on many levels, not the least of which being that the gun in my pocket, the one that Bill had given me simply out of pity, wasn't big enough to kill a ptarmigan unless you hit it in exactly the right place. I remembered another argument of months before, where I'd said I wouldn't shoot a rapist and infuriated Boone, and I tried to decide if what was happening was somehow worse than rape, and I knew even then that Boone would never really hurt me and I would never really shoot him, loving him like I did. And I decided it was just something I said because it seemed like the next logical line in the drama, but it made Boone wilder.

He ripped my coat off and took the little gun out of my pocket. He knocked me onto the floor of the cabin and then picked me up and threw me out the front door. My knee hit the rock that was the doorstop. He threw my backpack out after me, and then my bag of dirty clothes. The wind coming off the glacier picked up one of my T-shirts, a couple of pairs of underwear, and scattered them across the tundra, which was finally, I noticed, all red and gold.

"Give me my gun," I said, as if that were the issue.

"You won't have it," he said. "And don't ask again."

Stupid in his anger, he walked to the river, leaving his rifle a few feet away from me. I stared at it for a minute and thought about my previously nonviolent life. Only rednecks and crazy people had fights with guns, people in the inner city, people on late-night news shows.

But I was fascinated by us with our dramatics, and somehow bound to the logical sequence of the scene. I picked up the rifle, carried it into the cabin, hid it under a foam pad on the bunk bed, and sat on it.

"Where is it?" he said, minutes later. "Did you touch it?" I knew in his anger he thought he might have misplaced his gun. He crashed around the cabin and then outside.

"Where is it?" he said again.

"Give me my gun," I said.

This undid him. He ripped his gun out from under me.

"If you messed up the scope . . . " he said. I eased into the corner as he examined the scope. If it had moved a fraction, even if only in his mind, I was in big trouble. We had gone too far this time, and at that instant I didn't know if and how we'd ever get back. He put his rifle down and took a step toward me.

"Don't come near me," I said.

"Now don't get upset," he said, suddenly all control and condescension. "Just get yourself together." He patted my knee.

"Take it easy now," he said. "Take a deep breath."

That was when my hiking boot moved, it seemed, all by itself and my Vibram sole connected with his thigh and I pushed with all the strength I had and sent him hurtling backwards across the cabin into the woodpile and the stove. A shelf crashed down on his head when he hit the wall. My foot hung in the air and I stared at it, amazed at its power, amazed at my life's first violent act.

Then Boone was up and coming across the cabin at me and I just balled up and let him throw me out the door again, let my knee make contact with the rock. I gathered my clothes around me, pulled my backpack over my legs to block the wind.

Boone stayed inside, shouting things I only half heard. "You're out," he said at one point. "In more ways than you know."

I thought I ought to be horrified at myself, but I felt okay, light-headed, almost elated. He was stronger but I was strong. I looked again at my boot and flexed the muscle in my leg.

His tirade ended in some kind of a question I couldn't hear but guessed was rhetorical. I said something I couldn't resist about the shoe being on the other foot, and then laughed out loud so suddenly that he came to the cabin door and stared at me.

It was going to be dark in a few hours and I didn't think Boone would let me in the cabin, so I gathered up my underwear and started down toward the airstrip, where we had a tent set up. I knew it was a bad time of night to be walking alone in bear country, but after two long weeks without even seeing one bear, the grizzly had started to seem a bit like a creature of everybody's mind.

My knee was swelling to almost twice its normal size, but as long as I watched where I was walking, and didn't let it bend too far, it didn't really hurt. It was because I was looking down, I guess, because I was walking carefully, that I got so close to the bears before we saw each other.

It was a sow, six or seven feet tall, and two nearly full-grown cubs. They were knee-deep in blueberries, rolling and eating and playing. When I saw them they weren't fifty yards away.

I froze, and reached for my little gun before I remembered that Boone hadn't given it back. I took one step backwards and that's when mama saw me. The sun was just setting, and the late-afternoon light shone off their coats, which were brown and long and frosted at the tips. Mama stood on her hind legs, all seven feet of her, and then the cubs stood too and looked my way. They couldn't smell me, I knew, and they were trying to. Mama's ears went back and I thought, "Here she comes," but then she raised one giant paw in the air and swung it at me like a forehand, and then all three bears ran up into the mountain.

*   *   *

Boone and I took three more hunters out that season and we got them each a ram. All three hunters made perfect heart-lung shots. All three rams died instantly, just like Boone said.

One of our hunters, a man named Chuck, was kind and sincere. He got his ram with a bow and arrow from thirty yards away after a ten-hour stalk that was truly artistic. Chuck seemed to have an unspoken understanding with the wildlands and I was really almost happy for him when the ram went down, and I would have shaken his hand when he and Boone got finished jumping up and down in each other's arms if he had wanted to shake mine.

Boone told me I would get used to watching the rams die, and I have to admit—not without a certain horror—that the third killing was easier than the second, and the fourth was easier yet again.

I got thinner and harder and stronger and faster, turning my body into the kind of machine I couldn't help but be proud of, even though that had never been my goal.

Boone and I stopped fighting after the day we hiked to the cabin, but we also stopped talking; what we had left between us was hunting, and making love. I knew as soon as we got back to the lower forty-eight it would be over between us, and so I spent each day hiking behind him, measuring the time by quantity and not quality. It was like sitting by the bedside of a dying friend.

The nights got longer and longer, and we spent a lot more of them stuck out and away from the cabin. But the clouds were always thick and low, and even on the nights I tried hard to stay awake the northern lights never came again.

*   *   *

It was late September when we finished. The snow line was below four thousand feet and it was getting well below zero every night, and we'd been camped on the airstrip for three days waiting for the bush plane. The last hunters had flown out days before, and Boone and I had closed up the cabin in silence, like animals preparing for winter.

It had been hours, maybe days, since we'd spoken, so the sound of Boone's voice out of the darkness, out of somewhere deep in his sleeping bag, startled me.

"You know, none of those rams had an ounce of fat on them," he said. "There's not one of them that would have lasted through the winter."

"Well," I said. "That's something."

"I've been doing this for years," he said, and at first I thought he was going to say, "And it still isn't easy to watch them die," but he didn't.

"You really hung in there," he said.

"Yeah," I said. "I did."

"But it made you stop loving me," he said. "Even so."

Somewhere up the mountain the wolves started moaning and shrieking. I hadn't told Boone about the night I saw the bears, but the scene had stayed right with me; I couldn't get it out of my mind. It was the power of the mother bear's gesture, I guess, the power and the ambivalence. Because the wave of her paw was both forbidding and inviting. Because even though I knew that she was showing me her anger, I also knew that somewhere in her gesture, she was asking me to come along.

Jane Hirshfield

THE WEIGHING

The heart's reasons
seen clearly,
even the hardest
will carry
its whip-marks and sadness
and must be forgiven.

As the drought-starved
eland forgives

the drought-starved lion
who finally takes her,
enters willingly then
the life she cannot refuse,
and is lion, is fed,
and does not remember the other.

So few grains of happiness
measured against all the dark
and still the scales balance.

The world asks of us
only the strength we have and we give it.
Then it asks more, and we give it.

Jane Smiley
FULL CRY

▼ **B**ack when I was on the very lowest reaches of the educational slopes, before any of my present opinions were formed, I used to ponder Oscar Wilde's characterization of fox hunting as "the unspeakable pursuit of the uneatable." Like almost every other expression that had to do with fox hunting, Wilde's *mot* seemed to me like a magic charm, or what I would later know as a mantra—an almost unintelligible set of words that others seemed to understand and use with ease, but that I found mysterious and fascinating. Just because I was an Anglophile (I had read all of *Mary Poppins,* Sherlock Holmes, and Prince Valiant by that time) didn't mean I knew what "view halloo," or "gone to earth," or "whipper-in" meant. "Hounds" were not dogs. They had "sterns," not tails, and they were counted in "couples," not one by one. Red woolen hunting coats (worn only by men) were actually "pink." Before the hunt everyone partook of the "stirrup cup," which came in a chased silver vessel with a pointed bottom that couldn't be set down, but had to be brought around and taken away by servants. Foxes had no tails, faces, or feet, but "brushes," "masks," and "pads," and, to foreshadow later events in this essay, these were ritually cut from the corpse after the "death" and awarded to especially avid members of the "field" who had been "in at the death."

I came to fox hunting through horseback riding, which was my overwhelming obsession. The hunt in my town, St. Louis, was called the Bridlespur Hunt, and most of the horsey types there, from the Busches on down, were members, whether they actually "rode to hounds" or not. If you were a member of the hunt and had "earned your colors," you could wear robin's egg blue on the collar of your melton jacket. The western environs of St. Louis and St. Charles Counties, just north of the Missouri River as it approaches the Mississippi, were, and may still be, good hunt country, with broad, rolling fields and open woodland, plenty of foxes, and good scenting conditions for the hounds, which I understood then to be light winds and sufficient humidity. Nonetheless, Bridlespur country was not England, and the master, the huntsman, and the members of the field spoke regular American when they weren't hunting and sometimes when they were. They were probably less afraid of breaking the linguistic rules than I was.

Anything about hunting that other sorts of hunters might cite to justify their sport is not citable about fox hunting. The fox is truly uneatable, even for the hounds, who mill about excitably after the death until the whippers-in whip them back into a pack and the huntsman and the master decide whether and where to find another. Besides, no one in the field has probably ever gone without a meal anyway. Fox hunters do not commune with nature. The whippers-in control the hounds, the huntsman looks for the fox (it is he who gives the "view halloo" when he sees one), and the members of the field spend their nongalloping time gossiping among themselves or attending to their horses. The history of fox hunting (or stag hunting) over the centuries is, in every particular, the history of a privileged class riding roughshod (the horses' iron shoes undoubtedly caulked to provide more-secure footing in the mud) over everything in its path. When I saw the movie *Tom Jones* right in the midst of my foxhunting career, I could, at least, understand the moment where the farmer emerges from his hovel after the passing of the field and lifts up his prize goose, trampled and broken by the galloping horses. These days, much better read (not only *Tom Jones*, the book, but Dickens, Eliot, George Moore, Lawrence, Marx, you name it), I understand the "unspeakable" part of Wilde's remark, and I surely wouldn't go fox hunting again, but all the same, like most of the educated, I do harbor a fondness for the sins of my ignorant past.

As a parent, I cannot image the abdication of good sense that allowed my parents to allow me to ride to hounds, but they did. Probably I wore them down drop by drop, as I did about every equestrian venture, overcoming their perfectly reasonable objections on the grounds of safety and expense with the sheer tenacity of my desire. I had gotten them to pay for the riding lessons, then to allow me to jump, then to let me enter the Pony Club rally, which entailed a lot of jumping. I had shown devotion to the horse. After breaking my arm high jumping (I never suffered a single equestrian injury, but track and field was my undoing), I'd gone to the horse every chance I could anyway, and cleaned her stall one-handed. That persuaded them to buy me the horse. She was a dark bay thoroughbred mare, with a kindly nature and a beautiful head. Under saddle, she was a little hot for me, but I had her in control most of the time. It didn't really matter, though, how good or bad she was objectively—she was my destined mate and I was ready to take the good with the bad.

I rode her and jumped her all summer and into the fall. After the fields were harvested, everyone else in the barn loaded their horses into trailers on Sundays and sometimes on Wednesdays (remember, this is the leisure class) and went out to the various areas where the master had secured permission to hunt, and they galloped and jumped for hours on end. The other girls went. Surely that must have been an element of my argument, and there was probably some phoning among parents. Thanksgiving loomed, and I set my sights on that Thursday hunt. What better way to celebrate the coming of the English to Virginia—the true origin of our country, forget those non-foxhunting Puritans—than rising at 5 A.M., riding all day, and coming home too exhausted toward the late afternoon to partake of the family feast?

It seems to be the case that experienced horses do like fox hunting. Horses will respond to the sound of the horn and hounds and the sight of the field galloping away by whinnying and fighting to join the hunt. Some horses, if they lose their rider, will keep galloping and jumping with the group until caught and led away. Writers and artists of fox hunting also maintain that the fox enjoys the hunt. There are many paintings of a fox standing alertly on a stone wall in the foreground, watching the hounds and the horses gallop into the empty distance. Certainly, the fox has plenty of warning that he or she is being hunted—fox hunting makes a virtue of noise—the liquid call of the horn, the seismic boom of forty horses galloping over the earth, and the cry of the hounds, which is neither barking nor howling, but a high, desperate, glad yodeling called "giving voice." When the hounds are fast on the trail of the fox, they are said to be "in full cry," which means that the noise and speed and adrenaline are peaking in horse, hound, human, and possibly, too, in the fox.

There are other, more efficient mechanisms for disposing of a chicken-killing fox than fox hunting, though characterizing the fox as a verminous nuisance has always been the fox hunter's single limp rationalization for the whole colorful enterprise.

And the hounds undoubtedly like it, because, as with all hunting dogs, this is what they are bred to do, and because for the rest of their time they live in the kennel, and because, unlike Labs and pointers and German shorthairs, they work in a group.

And so I set the clock for 5 A.M., and I rose and dressed carefully in my high black boots, my thick wool "canary" (yellow) breeches (in those days before stretch fabrics, wide-pegged at the thigh for ease in mounting), my black melton-wool jacket, my white cotton "stock" (a four-inch-wide tie wrapped two or three times around my neck, intended for use as a bandage or tourniquet in case of emergency), my hair net, and my velvet hard hat, in which my mother vested a great deal of faith concerning head injuries (though unlike riding helmets today, it had no chin strap and was untested for actual impact effectiveness). I was chauffeured by my mother in her robe to the stable, where I accompanied my horse and the other members of the elect to the wildlife area in St. Charles County where the hunt was to commence. We were mounted by eight.

Maybe the best thing about a fox hunt is the sight of all the horses and riders gathered together early in the morning, waiting to set off. The horses are impeccably clean and fitted out—in any equine endeavor, there is a high premium placed on making a pristine appearance that I see now is a sort of conspicuous consumption rooted in the days of many grooms and servants—and they are fresh and eager, too, striding about in an informal ballet, long necked and long limbed and long tailed, giving off their horsey scent to the accompaniment of the happy chatter of many riders who know one another and are secure in sharing social rituals of long standing.

When the huntsman and the whips bring in the hounds, the hounds introduce an entirely different energy, noisy and single-minded, that focuses the field on the task at hand and reminds them that this isn't just a ride in the park. They are giving themselves up to the fox, who, once found, will lead them across all sorts of country, and they and their horses will have to be ready for anything—any sort of ground, any sort of fence, any sort of incline, any sort of woodlot. This is the "chase," not the "stalk." Not much care will be taken once the apotheosis is achieved: the hounds in full cry.

I was nervous about the jumping. I had heard, though I hadn't told my mother, that the fences could be as high as four feet, and I wasn't used to jumping much higher than three feet. I fixed my hard hat more firmly on my head. Four feet and solid. Unlike jumps in a ring, these were not made of poles on standards that would fall if hit. They were telephone poles and chicken coops and railroad ties. I kept my fears to myself, but I did happen to hear someone else say, "Usually there's a lower part to one side that you can go for." I decided to stay close to that woman, and discreetly fell in not far from her.

I was proud of my mare. She looked sleek and fit, rangy and eager, which is often the special charm of a thoroughbred. She was somewhat calmer than usual, probably taking pleasure and reassurance from the presence of the other horses. She had never hunted before, but she had raced. Perhaps the situation she found herself in suggested to her that there would be the opportunity to GO. Most thoroughbreds, even failed racehorses, like very much to GO.

The huntsman set off with the hounds and the whips. When they were just out of sight, the hounds began to give voice. That was the master's signal to follow, and we followed him—more experienced members of the field in front, less experienced or less eager ones behind. It was a dank, late-autumn day. The sky promised to be a clear, platinum blue, but mist rose from the muddy brown fields and leafless dark woodland, softening the chilly air. The riders and the horses gave off a mist, too, of breath and evaporating perspiration. Like duck and deer hunting, fox hunting is a sport that gives late autumn and early winter a point, that lures the hunter out of the warm house into the strange, coldly lit charms of the dying year. Soon we were cantering after the hounds, which we could hear but not see. I wasn't looking for anything except the tails of the horses in front of me. I thought I would manage my horse for now and learn about the niceties of actually chasing the killing a fox at some later date.

I should mention here that in England fox hunting is often carried out without the fox, revealing that galloping and jumping and listening to the hounds is the real point of the sport. "Drag hunts" are common in England—the day before the hunt, someone drags a sack impregnated with fox scent over the countryside, more or less diabolically mimicking foxy strategies, taking care to challenge the field (or not, if the drag hunt is intended for children). And drag hunting isn't the only death-free alternative. In her memoirs, Jessica Mitford (another left-winger who once adored fox hunting) recalls that her father, Lord Redesdale, was especially fond of hunting his children, a memory corroborated by Nancy Mitford in her novels.

Here is where education interferes with narrative. I know what we would have done next, but the nugget of memory has accreted too many images from later riding experiences, later experiences of horse manuals, English literature, social class, England itself, and even conversations with others. Images that arose as a response of the imagination offer themselves as memories. All I know about what happened next is that we did some galloping and jumping, following the hounds for an hour or more, and that I grew more self-confident and relaxed.

The next thing I remember is the sight of a large fence built of three telephone poles and myself pausing to wait for other riders to clear it. We gathered at the edge of the field, under the overhang of the woodland, trying to avoid the mud. My turn came up. I followed four or five strides behind the woman in front of me, knowing her horse's willingness would influence my horse. But I didn't have anything to worry about. My mare was happy to jump. The fence loomed, brown and upright, in front of us, got larger, and was gone. I felt her forelegs land and saw that we were in a wide, muddy lane that veered to the right toward a dirt road. I saw the other horses galloping away.

Of course, accompanying these visual memories are sensory ones, particularly the feeling of the presence of the horse as I gripped her sides with my legs, moved my own body with the rhythm of her gait, leaned close to her neck, felt the tug of her mouth through the reins in my hands. Two strides after the fence, our momentum was still carrying us forward. I twitched the right rein to remind her to follow the others, and I felt her right hind leg slip in the mud and go out from underneath us.

The fall was a slow one; not a toppling or a pitching forward off the horse, but a sideways fall with the horse. The mud was soft and I was on my feet almost before I hit the ground, reassuring those who followed that I was all right. Perhaps I remember the sensation of pulling my leg from under my mare, but perhaps I don't. She was on her feet nearly as fast as I was. I do remember the strangeness of the feeling that now we were no longer going, now we were stopped, and I was standing on my feet rather than mounted on my horse. One step forward revealed that my mare was limping badly, so it was clear that going was over for the day, and waiting was to be the new activity.

The next thing I remember is the diagnosis, a break at the stifle joint of the left hind leg. The stifle joint is the joint at the top of the hind leg close to the body, comparable to a human knee. I knew from all the horse stories I had read by then (*Black Gold, The Black Stallion, King of the Wind,* and every other horse story then in print) that a broken leg was fatal to a horse. I knew that all discussion of healing her and maybe breeding her was done for my benefit, to put off the final blow. But a broken stifle joint was too much of a challenge to veteri-

nary science of the period. After pretending to consider other
alternatives, my stepfather and the vet told me that the mare
would be trailered out to the kennel where the Bridlespur
hounds were kept and put down. An electrical device of some
sort would be put to her head, the current would run to her iron
shoes, and she would die, be butchered, and be fed to the
hounds, a common and entirely appropriate use for old
hunters.

Early in the fall, when it was still almost summer, I had
been riding my mare alone one Sunday afternoon when I saw
my summer riding friend, Dorothy, being driven past in her
mother's car. Dorothy's family raised Connemara ponies, and
Dorothy rode a gray mare named Larkspur. She had been riding
for years, and had shown me all the trails and fields round about
the club where I kept my mare. Dorothy, teary and disheveled,
didn't respond when I called out to her, but her mother stopped
the car and leaned across her daughter toward the open passenger window. She said, "Dorothy's pony's just been killed hunting. She fell at the fence and broke her neck." They drove off.
I'm sure I looked stricken and sympathetic, although I don't
know whether, at fourteen, I knew the right thing to say. Later I
heard that Dorothy had given up riding entirely, even though
her family had ten or fifteen other possible mounts for her. I certainly considered forsaking all equestrian activity a reasonable
reaction to the death of one's destined equine mate, rather like
taking the veil upon the death of one's spouse.

But I found myself cool and remote from my own mare.
She stood still in her stall, her eyes half shut, her head down,
her coat staring. She had lost her very horseness, a larger than
human vitality that makes equine alertness and beauty compel-
ling to people like me. I sat with her and groomed her and gave
her carrots, but I wasn't drawn to her. A day and a half after her
accident she was gone from her stall, and I was back to square
one, horse-wise. I did not think it likely that my parents would
replace her.

None of this meant that I had learned anything about the dangers and difficulties of my chosen sport. My obsession flourished as green as ever; unlike Dorothy, I was uneducable. Experience did nothing to me.

Now for the peripeteia. The damp, muddy fall progressed into a crisp, frosty winter. The once-distant gray blue sky became a brilliant glare that surrounded us with light. I was again in the field, this time on a rented horse, also a bay mare. We all, riders and horses, seemed to shine in the sunlight, from our glossy black velvet caps down to the caulked shoes of our mounts that glinted and winked with each stride and rang on the frozen gravel roads. This was the New Year's hunt, and its venue a part of the wildlife area that had no fences. For some reason, I resolved to stay near the master and watch the actual chase after the fox. I don't remember what the chase looked like. I know there was a fox out there, but I don't remember what it looked like. I know the sterns of the bunched, coursing, vocalizing hounds pointed up like miniature pikes as the pack ran and scrabbled over the countryside in glorious full cry. I do remember the sight of the master's horse in front of me as well as the sunlight on the white stock and gold stock pin of the rider beside me. I remember the long, tireless gallop and the relief I felt at there being no jumping. Then I remember the way we came upon the hounds and the huntsman and the whips just where a clearing gave way to light oak woodlands. The liver and white hounds were yodeling and whining, and the huntsman vaulted off his mount and waded into the pack while the whippers-in unfurled the long lashes of their whips and began driving the hounds away from the focus of their attention. The huntsman was leaning down, and then he held the quarry aloft, a dead gray fox.

Yes, I felt exhilarated at the sight, pumped up by the vigor of the galloping and the sensation of having ridden in front of the field, of having been in at the death. I wasn't at all repelled or moved by the sight of the dead fox, and my reaction was en-

tirely visceral, not at all intellectual. We had wanted to kill him
and now he was dead, a stillness at the center of human, canine,
and equine tumult. Good for us, good for me, good for my
rented mount, who had been both willing and controllable. The
huntsman drew forth his hunting knife.

Maybe this is the ugliest face of fox hunting, the group
blood lust. How is the field different from any other mob, except that its members are mounted? A significant portion of my
subsequent education would invite, and even force, me to con-
clude that the pink coats and the high boots, the elaborate costume and ritual and language of fox hunting, the very expense
of it, are really the merest film of respectability designed to
camouflage the mob and allow it to reassure itself that it is more
civilized than other mobs, when it is actually far worse—caught
up in irresponsible and destructive blood lust the object of
which is not social justice or even retribution for felt wrongs,
but the trivial pursuit of unworthy prey. I could talk myself into
class hatred here.

On the other hand, fox hunting is a form of aggression, and
it seems clear by now that human aggression is so inherent that
it must and will take a form. Inclination, cultural history, and
education, too, predispose me to prefer elaborate forms that
break down inherent drives into parts, ritualizing them and pre-
senting them for both appreciation and interpretation. Beauty,
always morally neutral, resides in rituals of aggression as much
as it does in rituals of religious faith or love or art. Fox hunting
need not be unmediated or mindless aggression, partly because
the hunt must receive permission to ride over land owned by
others. The responsibility of the master, the huntsman, the
whips, and the field is to understand the potential for destruction that fox hunting presents and to mitigate the destruction—
riding fit and experienced horses, taking responsibility for
younger members of the field, never galloping across agricultural ground, but always keeping to its margins, hunting in winter when much of the agricultural and natural world is dormant,

never blocking the fox's escape strategies, promoting courtesy among the members of the field through severe social strictures. In traditional fox hunting, as in the Catholic Church, there is a name for every occasion of sin as well as every occasion of transcendence. The aggressive impulse is developed and restrained by form, which may look like obscure and arbitrary formality.

My fifteen-year-old self wasn't engaging in any of these arguments. She was panting and excited, warmed in the chilly sunlight by the exertion of the chase. When the huntsman came around to "blood" me, that is to dab my cheek with the fox's blood to signify that I had witnessed by first death, the warmth and thickness of it on my check and neck was an unalloyed thrill. Of course, now I read many meanings into that gory signifier—the end of virginity, blood on my conscience, feeling death as well as seeing it, making the fox's self part of my own.

I also clearly remember seeing the master look around and smile as the huntsman was taking the trophies from the fox—he smiled at me, and told the huntsman to give me one of the pads, rewarding my eagerness and interest in the progress of the chase. Perhaps in addition to keeping close to the master, I had peppered him with (respectful) questions? I was known for asking a tiresome number of questions in those days. If I did, I don't remember it now.

I took the pad in my hand. It was the small, dark foreleg of the fox, maybe three inches long, with toes and nails like those of a little dog. It hadn't stiffened yet. It seemed marvelous to me, as exciting as any silver cup or blue ribbon. But the hunt was moving on, looking for another fox, and so I put it in my pocket. Later, I wrapped it in plastic and put it in the family freezer. Over the next two and a half years, while it stayed, untaxidermied, in the freezer, my mother would unwrap it from time to time, wondering what sort of meat was in the small package. I would unwrap it from time to time, too, and stare at its wonderfulness. I considered it very important that the freezer was close to the back door, because, should the house catch fire, the last thing I would do after saving our dogs would be to snatch my fox pad from the inferno.

Education interfered with later fox hunting in the most literal way—when I got to college, I found I had neither the time nor the money to keep riding, and I hated the dangers of hitchhiking to the stable (I had no other mode of transportation). My mother had pressed me to go to Vassar instead of one of those horse colleges in Virginia that had been my original inclination. She beat the lure of the horses and set my walking feet on the path of learning and art. Pretty soon I was too well-educated for either blood sports or Anglophilia, and so I remain. The equestrian activity that interests me now is dressage, which is to fox hunting rather what ice dancing is to hockey. Horses rarely if ever break their necks or their legs at dressage, and dressage, like all the arts (trout fishing, ballet, novel writing) is full of theorists and intellectuals, as well as practitioners, both human and equine, who are advanced in years.

My present horse is also a thoroughbred though, and I sometimes sense beneath his self-restraint that inbred urge to GO, to join the galloping herd, to be caught up in headlong forward motion. And I sometimes sense that inborn urge in myself, too.

Kim Barnes
CALLING THE COYOTES IN

Dark green ravines run like lava
through the canyon's fissured humps,
and it is here they come, late
in winter's good cold to find
the seventy-dollar pelts.
Crouched in a shadowing hedge
of sumac and sap-leeched syringa,
she waits. Five nights
they have worked the ridges, calling

the coyotes in. From the camouflaged recorder
cries of a dying rabbit play
again and again, a chant
she rocks to, feet numbed to stone.
Beside her, the man squats trigger-ready,
the white orbit of his eyes blueing
in half-moon light.
He's been in Nam, and though she won't say it,
there's an enemy somewhere. Even his breath
seems cloistered, the way his jaw slacks
to quiet the rush of air.
This time, two split
from the tangle of brambled cottonwood,
trot forward, high-stepping the snow.
He signals for her to take the right one.
Raising the rifle, liquid from knees to cheek,
she shoots easy, good at limiting damage:
behind the ear, a finger-sized hole.
The man stands, the blue flame
he holds to her blinding
as she draws the smoke deep.
Kneeling at the first belly, he begins
the skinning, cigarette clenched
between his teeth.
She'll take her time with hers,
slip the knife between muscle
and hide, follow the leg's curve
to cobbled spine.
There's a moment when he'll call her, in his hands
a bundle rolled tail to nose, and she'll see
how his lips have tightened to hold
the last biting fire, how he hasn't moved
to stop the calling, and neither has she,
knee-deep in dark dappled snow,
feeling all around them the closing eyes.

Mary Morris
THE GLASS WALL

Rosa rested on the steps of the Cookie Dream Factory, her mother's bakery, wondering why Uncle Tio's pet pig ran away two nights ago. The moon had been full when Uncle Tio opened the door of their house, peering in with red eyes to inquire if they'd seen the old pink-and-black sow he'd never had the guts to slaughter, whom he called Petunia. She was a destructive pig, eating clothes and ripping out fences. Every year she ruined the vegetable patch, but what else did Uncle Tio have but that rambled-down shack, his sledgehammer, and the dried-up sow? Rosa shuffled the lottery tickets she held in her hand, staring at the numbers; no one had bought from her all day. She told Uncle Tio that if she won the lottery, she'd buy him a new pig but he just shook his head, disappearing back into the shadows of the alleyway as he fumbled along toward his shack. He wanted the old pig.

Trapper's jeep pulled up and Rosa saw he had two men with him, tourists from across the border, probably from the East, who came to hunt. Trapper led them into the high country. Rosa's mother, Dolores Two-Step, slumped on a ratty armchair in the back of the bakery, watching a soap opera she'd been following for seven years, thinking some day it would end. When the jeep drove up, Dolores moved to the front of the store while Rosa shouted back that it was just Trapper with some more men. Trapper squeezed her shoulder the way he did once or twice a week when he made these rounds. He'd bring the tourists into town for supplies and always he'd see Rosa, not like he used to, but he'd always pass by the store.

The three men walked into Dolores Two-Step's Cookie Dream Factory. They called her Two-Step because her word was like poison from a two-step snake, but in the Cookie Dream Factory, she hardly spoke. Trapper kissed her on the cheek calling her Tia, even though he knew she was angry with him. He always brought his hunters here to buy bread because he knew they needed the money and because it was a big tourist attraction—the only real tourist attraction in town, outside of a visit to the nuclear reactor and the abandoned silver mine, each an hour away in opposite directions. Dolores extracted sugar from fruits and made cookies out of ground flour and these she shaped into objects. People came in, thinking they'd get chocolate chip or peanut butter cookies but they grew entranced with the funny objects, sculpted from dough, which were supposed to predict the future. Dolores watched as the eyes of the men scanned the strange pouncing animals, the wild sprawling trees, the shanties, the little villages and their cookie denizens. To the tall man, she gave a fireman cookie, saying he was a man of great passion and would always be loved. To the stocky man, she gave a deer cookie and said he was going on a long journey that would prove profitable. And to Trapper she gave a tree cookie, as she had consistently for the past three months, saying he'd be buried under one soon.

The stocky man slapped his friend on the back; he'd just gotten a transfer last week to his bank's Tokyo branch. The tall man smirked a little, casually admitting that he was very passionate, letting his gaze fall on Rosa as she sat on the front steps. Then they both glanced morbidly at Trapper, asking if her predictions ever came true. "All the time." He munched on his tree cookie and Dolores gave him another, glancing over her shoulder to see what was happening with her soap opera. It was six months and still no one knew where the doctor's daughter had gone or with whom.

Trapper was eating a prairie dog and a policeman when Rosa wandered in. "Uncle Tio's on the hill."

Trapper went to the entranceway, looking up in the direction of Uncle Tio. "What's he doing?" he mumbled.

"Petunia ran away two nights ago," Rosa replied. In the distance Uncle Tio groped his way further and further up the hill.

The tourists wanted more dream cookies but Trapper told them they only got one shot. Trapper kissed Dolores on the cold cheek which she turned quickly away from him. He walked to the porch with Rosa behind him and put his arm on her shoulder but she moved away. Lately everyone he touched moved away. He was starting to get used to it. But Rosa knew Trapper, knew him like the back of her hand, with the instinct that animals know and fear one another. He was Trapper because that's what he did, caught poor helpless things. He was also El Negro because he was black inside and out, and no one knew it like Rosa because she'd known him since they were three. She knew him in the woods, in the dark; many nights his skins had kept her warm and she still slept draped in the fox, the beaver, the raccoon, left over from a time when she'd done anything to stay warm. He yearned for her and she knew that. She knew that depriving him was the worst thing she could do and deprive him she did. And she knew that as long as she deprived him, he'd keep passing by the store. It was the only way to keep him.

The stocky man took a Coke from the Coke machine and the tall man took an orange drink. Sweat poured down their necks, moistening their collars. The tall man wiped his neck with a handkerchief as he drank the orange drink.

"Tell Uncle Tio I'll look for Petunia on the road up to the mountains," Trapper said, swinging back into the jeep. He was huge and brawny, with enormous feet. Rosa smiled, trying to imagine the pig taking a road somewhere.

"Maybe we should let her come along to cook for us," the tall man joked, gloating over the fact that Dolores Two-Step had called him a passionate man.

"Shut up," Trapper mumbled under his breath but loud enough so Rosa could hear, "I loved that girl once."

Dolores Two-Step always left the bakery early because that's what she'd done when her husband was alive and because she was accustomed to getting dinner. It was eight-thirty when Rosa closed the Cookie Dream Factory. She closed at the same time every night. Then she took a few pesos from the till and bought two lottery tickets, one for herself and one for El Negrito. Sometimes, if they had a good day, she bought more. Sometimes she even bought one which she mentally gave to Trapper but she never told anyone.

It was dark in the night and the skies were very black because the full moon had passed when Rosa set out on her way home. In Esperanza they say that if you fall to the ground, you go to hell, and that if a dog barks all night at the moon, he talks to the devil. Even though Rosa wasn't superstitious, ever since Petunia ran away, some yellow dog had been barking all night, and the night before on her way home, Rosa had tripped over something in the road and fallen. She didn't quite hit the ground but her hands did and she wondered if only her hands could go to hell. And just last night, she'd seen a cat with the face of a child sitting on a wall.

There were two ways to go home. Her barrio was San Rafael and she could take the long way, up toward the highway near where her brother had been killed, then cut over to the Calle Zapata, down the cobble streets, and up the very steep hill to the Calle Hidalgo which had the wall around it. This way was almost three miles and she didn't get home until well after nine. Then there was the other way, the way she came every day when she went to work for the Señora and the way she walked home when she came back late every night. It was the easy way, it was the way she liked, not because it was easy and the path was smooth but because it took her past people's houses and not only along the dark streets and she felt safer. This way, which she walked along now, took her home as the crow flies. She would cut through the Colonia Riodoro, following a straight path until she came to the wall. In the wall there was a hole, and when they built Riodoro two years ago, they had left the hole in the wall, and this was the way people who lived in San Rafael went home.

As she walked along the dirt path through Riodoro, she looked at the houses. She liked to look at these white and pink houses which at night looked even bigger than they did in the day. In San Rafael, the houses were all very small, just piles of wooden slats and sometimes cement, and chickens and donkeys walked all around the houses, but here there weren't any animals making noise and walking around and the paths were very clean. In San Rafael, you could see the lights from fires but the houses were dark and cold and when she looked at the houses in San Rafael, she didn't feel warm the way she did when she walked through Riodoro. But she never could see the whole house. Each house was hidden behind a stucco wall or row of hedges followed by a stucco wall, and if she didn't work for the

Señora, she wouldn't know what it was like inside. Rosa always liked to see the lights on in other people's houses. She pictured big dogs, a man by the fire, a couple snuggled in bed. She liked to walk in the dark night and look into the windows, to see silhouettes moving inside, and sometimes as she walked by, she would see them looking down at her from behind their picture windows and she knew that in the daytime from those windows they could see across the whole valley, to the border even. She had to climb the steep hill in order to see that far. And now as she walked, she saw people looking down at her from the picture windows, noses pressed to the glass.

A dog kept howling somewhere and that made her nervous. She looked down at the ground, careful not to fall. It was late and she was going to be late getting home, which meant she might not see El Negrito until the following evening, because when she left in the morning he was usually still asleep. She'd reached the wall. The short way took her fifteen minutes to walk from the bakery to the wall and another fifteen from the wall to her house. If she were lucky and hurried, she could put him to bed herself.

She reached the wall and stared. For a long time she stared and stared. She touched it. The stone in front of her was a paler shade and the cement between the stones wasn't quite dry. It took several minutes for her to understand that there was no more hole, no way to pass through. Someone had closed the hole so that the people who lived in San Rafael could no longer take the shortcut through Riodoro. Rosa looked at the houses behind her, the lights coming from the windows, the few faces staring down. She wondered if they could see her from where they stood. She assumed some could see her but most couldn't. The wall wasn't that high, only five feet or so, and there were stones lying on the ground in front of where the hole had been. If she turned and went back she'd be another hour getting home. She climbed up on a rock, hoisted herself onto the wall and flew over, landing hard on the cobblestone like a heavy bird, careful not to let anything but her feet touch the ground. Rosa gasped, catching her breath as she landed. It was day on one side and night on the other. The San Rafael barrio was almost pitch black with no street lights on the cobble walk, except for the light that came from a few houses set back off the road. The Colonia Riodoro was always lighter than the barrio San Rafael but she'd never quite noticed it as she did at that moment.

She walked up the Calle Hidalgo. Whenever it looks as if things could be getting easier, something makes them harder, she thought. It was just two months ago when she got the job with the Señora and could stop selling Kleenex out by the intersection where her brother had gotten run over by the dump truck. And that was after that very bad time when her mother told her about Trapper and the woman up north and when El Negrito was born. She climbed the hill slowly, feet clicking against the cobblestone. I'm not afraid, she told herself. This is the only part of my walk home when I could be afraid because it's so dark here and there are walls on both sides and no place to go if someone jumps out at me like that crazy Naranjo boy did that night, but I was with Trapper who was taking a leak in the bushes a few yards back. Never saw anyone jump so high as the Naranjo boy when Trapper came up behind him and thrust his pocket knife up against his spine. This is the only part of the walk that's bad, the last stretch or so up the hill on the road that's walled in on both sides. Otherwise there's no problem at all. Rosa walked straight on, not looking over her shoulder, not wanting to see if anyone was behind her or to the side of her or standing on the wall peering down at her.

Uncle Tio brought his sledgehammer down hard on a new pole for his fence as Rosa walked by. Everyone knew that "uncle" meant "tio" and "tio" meant "uncle" and that his name didn't mean anything, but Uncle Tio was all mixed up because their house had straddled the border in Nogales when he was born. He was no one's uncle that anyone knew about but he belonged to everyone in San Rafael and that's what they'd called him since before Rosa was born. He paused, stared blankly at Rosa, then raised the sledgehammer and brought it down again. It was how Uncle Tio spent most of his nights, hammering new fences to keep his chickens in. All the chickens had names that Rosa could never keep straight. If you went to Uncle Tio's for dinner, he'd often say, "We're eating Cyclone tonight." Or Redhead or Henpecked. There was something strange about eating an animal whose name you knew but Uncle Tio talked about Cyclone or Redhead as he ate them, discussing the kind of life they'd lived right up until the end. He brought the sledgehammer down again, then turned to Rosa.

"Uncle Tio, they filled up the hole in the wall. Why do you suppose they did that?"

Uncle Tio shrugged his shoulders. "Have you seen my pig?" he asked.

The next morning before dawn Rosa walked around the wall to go to the Colonia Riodoro because she was afraid she'd get caught. When she got to work the Señora told her she had to go to the dentist in El Paso for the day and might not be back the next day either. The Señora had married a Mexican who gave her two children before he married her, and half the town, too, the half that had running water, by the time he died. The Señora paid her almost three dollars for the morning's work, and the only thing Rosa didn't like was that she wouldn't let Rosa in the house unless she was there to watch her, so when the Señora went to El Paso Rosa didn't get paid. The next morning Rosa jumped the wall but the Señora was still in El Paso and the next day too so Rosa only worked at the bakery those days and sold lottery tickets when she was done baking. And at the end of the day she sat alone in the bakery, listening to the night sounds—boys dribbling basketballs up and down the street, Uncle Tio hollering about his lost pig, cars whizzing by on their way to Texas.

The third morning, the morning when the Señora came home and Rosa went back to work, she saw men working on the wall so she had to walk around. It was only six in the morning when she passed where the hole had been and she saw them, preparing to do some work. It didn't look like they were going to make the hole back again because they had plaster with them. That morning Dolores took El Negrito to the bakery because Juana, Rosa's older sister who had twins and had been nursing El Negrito while Rosa worked, had something wrong with her throat and didn't know if she could nurse her own until she got back from the clinic. Rosa carried the baby in her arms and her mother hobbled along beside her. Dolores Two-Step, as sharp as was her tongue, had bad ankles and often fell on the cobblestones so Rosa never let her carry El Negrito when they took him somewhere. Everyone knew that Dolores wouldn't go to hell for falling because she had special connections and powers no one else could understand but which they all believed in. Dolores looked at the place where the hole had once been in the wall and spat on the ground in front of the men who were arranging their plaster and tools on the ground. The workers were sons of friends, all from the barrio San Rafael, and she looked at them as she spat and they didn't say anything to her because they knew Dolores could put a curse on anyone she wanted.

When Rosa reached the house, the Señora was waiting for her. She complained that Rosa was late and she had been waiting for almost half an hour. "I didn't know if you'd be here," Rosa said. "I came the other days and you weren't here so I didn't know."

The Señora was angry. "If you don't want to work, there are other girls who do," the Señora said, but Rosa didn't say anything back because she needed the three dollars a day.

"It's because of the wall," Rosa said. "They filled in the hole in the wall and I have to walk around."

"What are you talking about?" the Señora asked. "What hole?"

Rosa was sitting in the back of the bakery, cutting animal cookies for the Dream Factory with El Negrito sleeping on the couch, when she heard the jeep drive up. She heard the sound of footsteps coming up the steps of the bakery. She knew as the jeep pulled around the corner, she knew from the way it shrieked on its tires, from the way it pulled to a halt, from the way the door slammed and the feet climbed the steps, that it was Trapper and he was drunk. She heard him pacing the front of the bakery but she kept cutting her animal cookies. Then she heard him tapping his fingers, calling, moving behind the counter. He opened the curtain and stepped into the back room. She was watching *Kung Fu* and did not take her eyes from the set.

Trapper walked in and slumped onto the couch beside El Negrito. He patted the baby on the head like a dog, he caressed its cheek. Rosa watched carefully, not saying a word. She watched to make sure he didn't touch the boy too hard. Slowly Trapper looked her way. He was a somber man with curly black hair and very black eyes. His body was firm and Rosa's, he always told her, was soft and plump. Trapper spent the years of his youth trying to prove his prowess by arm wrestling as often as possible in Rosa's presence. His skin always looked dirty even if he'd just bathed and no matter how long he slept he always seemed tired. When he was a boy, she remembered, he had few friends and mostly kept to himself, unless he was playing games with her. When they played doctor, he always had some invisible ailment she could never cure.

He looked up at her and sighed. "I'll marry you," he muttered. "That's what I came to say."

She shook her head. He looked at her hard and she knew what he was thinking. She can be stubborn if she wants. Sometimes he hated her. Sometimes he went up into the hills when the fish were biting or it was time for the rut and never wanted to see her again. He rose and rook from the oven some donuts that had just finished baking. He took milk from the refrigerator. He knew where everything was. He sat across from her. "We can get married. All right? Is that what you want?"

"Leave me alone," she said softly but emphatically.

He ate a donut whole, popping it into his mouth. "You don't understand, do you? I can't live without you. I don't want to live without you. There's no woman up north and if there was, there isn't now and won't be again. I want to be with you. I want to live with you. I can't stand it any more."

She was beginning to enjoy depriving him and that worried her. It had become a sacred mission in her life, to deny him. It had become some wonderful, fantastically contrived test of will and now it was no longer a test but the most natural thing in the world. As long as she could earn ten dollars a day, she didn't need him. She loved him and always would but she'd never need him again, not the way she had. Juana said she was a fool. "Marry him," she yelled at her in the evenings. "What else are you going to do with your life?"

"I want you to go away," she spoke firmly. "I don't want you any more."

He fumbled with a piece of dough on the long wooden table, twisting it into a million shapes, grabbing cookie cutters and cutting it into houses and dogs and flowers and rivers and trees and cars, into all the things he liked and couldn't stand, the things he wanted or could have been. He made a Coke bottle and smashed it. He made tourists and the Grand Canyon. He made a woman and smashed her. He made a baby and smashed it. Rosa sat and watched him move as if his life were going by in a swift succession. Then he took the dough, rolled it up in his hand and hurled it onto the table as if it were dice, and smashed it into a pancake so flat and thin that Rosa could almost read the newspaper headlines that lay underneath. Then he leaned forward, perched on his knuckles like a great ape, and stared her square in the eye. "What do I have to do?" Rosa didn't know what he had to do. She didn't know if she wanted him to do anything. "What do I have to do?" He slammed his fist onto the pancake dough, then held his palm out to her like a beggar pleading for alms, his face twisted like the dough in rage and humiliation.

Rosa paused and thought for a moment. "Blow up the wall," she mumbled.

"What wall?" Trapper looked around him, thinking it might be nearby. "What are you talking about!"

"The wall that's in my way," she said. "The one that blocks the shortcut; the one that makes me late for work."

He reached across and tried to grab her. He put his hand against her shirt and tried to pull her to him. She pushed him away. "And don't touch me," she shouted, pointing at him. "Don't touch me until you blow up that wall."

"Is that all?"

She nodded. "And drive me home."

Trapper took the road through town, swung around and circled past Riodoro, then drove up Insurgentes until he came to Calle Hidalgo. It was much faster in a car, Rosa thought. Maybe she should marry him so he could bring her home in the car. A month ago she would have married him; a week ago maybe; but suddenly now she wouldn't marry him for all the money in the world, unless he put a hole back in the wall for her. A hole she'd never use because she'd marry him and he'd drive her home every night in the jeep and drive her to work every morning in it too. She looked at Trapper from the side without really looking at him. There were two kinds of people to her. The kind who were dark and you couldn't see into them at all; then there was the other kind, the ones who were transparent and you could see everything. Even when they tried they couldn't hide what they felt. Trapper was the see-through kind. Her mother was the opaque kind. There was a part of her that was proud she now could get Trapper to do exactly what she wanted, after so many years of waiting for him to come around. Now that she didn't care.

They were driving past the wall and suddenly she saw the bright, shimmering fragments in the moonlight—lime green, a soft, coffee brown, a bright yellow gold, and white, and an almost blood red. They were shiny and pointed and they stuck up

in the moonlight like cactus on the prairie. She grabbed
Trapper's hand on the shift and motioned for him to stop. "That
wall?" he said, watching as Rosa stared, then jumped down from
the jeep. "Is that the wall?" She walked over to the wall, El
Negrito in her arms. She let her hands slide over the sharp,
pointed shards of glass which stuck out of the still-moist plaster
on the top of the wall and along the sloping sides, glass from
Coke bottles and Seven-Up bottles, bright blue mineral water
and dull brown beer bottles, broken on barroom floors, Fanta
and Pepsi Cola, glass from the bottles she drank all day, bottles
from companies her people didn't own. In the moonlight the
wall shimmered and the light that passed over the fragments
turned into stars. It shone like those wonderful rocks Trapper
used to bring down from the mountains and chop in half so that
inside you saw crystals of all colors and shapes that had been
hidden inside there for so many centuries, growing inside the
rock. And it stood up like shark's fins, bright and wet out of the
water. The men had put pieces of sharp glass along the top of
the wall so that the people who lived in San Rafael couldn't
jump the wall on their way to and from town where most of
them worked and so that the streets of Riodoro would be very
clean. Rosa let her fingers run over the glass, feeling the sharp
edges biting her hand. Then she climbed back into the jeep.
Trapper drove along. "So, as soon as the hunters leave, I'll get
some dynamite and knock a hole big enough for an elephant to
pass through."

The next morning Rosa walked around the wall and lost
her job. She'd gotten up at five-thirty but El Negrito was sick
and she didn't want to leave him until Uncle Tío, who once
worked on an ambulance, came to take a look. She left her
house at seven but didn't reach the Señora until after eight.
"You're erratic," the Señora said. "I don't like undependable
people." She said there were other things too that she didn't
like about the way Rosa did things and she closed the door. For
a few moments Rosa stood staring at the door, then she spat at

it the way her mother had taught her to do, putting a curse she knew wouldn't work because she didn't have the power her mother had.

Late that night when she was making dough, Trapper walked into the store. He startled her because she hadn't heard his jeep drive up and she hadn't heard his footsteps as he walked into the store; he'd come in silently like an Indian. She jumped up. She pushed her hand over her chest and felt her heart pounding inside. Usually when he came in he made a big noise. Usually she could hear him a mile away.

He didn't say anything but moved silently through the back of the bakery, moving around and around in circles. He pounded his fist into cupboards, on counters and tabletops; Rosa moved back. "You're drunk." She saw, as he moved toward her, that he was worse than he'd been the night before.

"I'm going to take El Negrito away," he said, still moving toward her while she kept backing up against the wall. On the counter there was a knife and slowly she worked her way toward it. The baby started crying, his face turning blue. Trapper slammed his fist into the wall, into the cupboard. He moved beside where she stood at the counter and Rosa reached behind her back for the knife. She pulled the knife in front of her and stared at him. Then suddenly Trapper leaned his head against the counter and started to cry. He sobbed big heavy sobs so that his whole body shook and when Rosa thought he was done, he started again with heavier sobs. She picked up El Negrito and went to Trapper who now cried silently, his mouth open in a grotesque laugh which brought tears down his cheeks and from which no sound came. Rosa went to him, wrapping his head up with her hands and pulling him close to her. "I wouldn't take him away," he mumbled through his sobs. "But you're making me crazy." She wanted to say that he never wanted her when she wanted him, she wanted to say that he never was there when she needed him, but there was something about seeing him, sobbing against her chest, that made her stop thinking those things. Suddenly she wanted him again, not as she'd wanted him before, not the kind of wanting that made it so she couldn't sleep but the kind that made her want to sit by a big fire with him at her side. "As soon as the hunters leave," he said, "I'll blow up the wall." Trapper was very good with dynamite.

Just before dawn the tall passionate man was startled from his restless sleep and, without thinking, shot Trapper through the shoulder as he made his way back to their campsite. The stocky man, who didn't want any trouble with the authorities, stuffed some money in Trapper's shirt pocket, took his jeep, and headed for the border. It took Trapper a full day to make it down the mountain on foot to Dolores Two-Step's cabin. When he staggered in, Dolores screamed as she had when her oldest boy was killed, and nothing could convince her that Trapper wasn't going to die.

When Rosa walked in after nine, she saw the doctor who tended the San Rafael people cleaning Trapper's wound and she saw her mother, tears streaming down her cheeks, heating herbs on the stove. El Negrito slept peacefully in his crib. Her first thought was that she hadn't seen the jeep out front and she knew it was gone. Now she'd have to walk around the wall forever. Her second thought was disbelief. That one of her mother's predictions almost came true. And then she thought that she didn't know what she wanted and she was mad. She didn't know if she wanted him or not. Last night she wanted him; suddenly she didn't know. But she didn't want him to die, she knew that. She walked over to where he lay, breathing heavily. She touched him and seeing he'd live, she stormed out of the cabin. She screamed back at him, "Why didn't you blow it up when you said you would?" Trapper started to cry again. She walked down the road until she came to Uncle Tio's shack. Uncle Tio was out cold, head on the table, drunk, and she took his sledgehammer from under the table and moved fast down the road, her feet flying over the cobblestone, dragging the sledgehammer behind her.

She walked until she came to where the hole had been. She looked for a moment at where the pale, new cement and stone met with the old and the new stone took shape next to the old. First it was a lady, dressed up for church or a parade. Then it was a jockey, riding his horse fast over the finish. She ran her fingers over the glass as if it were piano keys she was about to play. Then she brought the sledgehammer over her head with both hands and smashed it into the wall. Glass splintered all around her like tiny fish darting through dark water. She closed her eyes tight and brought it down again. She smashed at the sharp edges, grinding them find as sand. She smashed the way Trapper had smashed dough and she smashed just as easily. The people in Riodoro came to their windows when they heard the sound but no one dared come down and see what was happening. All they saw was the hammerhead coming up and glass flying in tiny, brilliant splinters. She kept at it. When the glass was gone, she worked on the stone. She saw the people staring down at her with darkened faces she could not recognize. She knocked out one stone, then another. She knocked out a hole large enough for a child to pass through. Then she stopped. Trapper could finish the job. She knew she had him where she wanted him now and that he would do this for her. She had broken him as she'd broken the wall.

She started slowly back up the hill, tired this time, dragging the sledgehammer so that it bounced on the cobbles. She stopped when she heard a sound she knew she did not make. At first she thought it was men who'd come to harm her, the ones she'd always feared would hide and jump out at her when she didn't expect it. She thought it was they who'd just pushed their way through the hole she opened in the wall, but she saw nothing. She started walking again, but then she heard the sound again and knew she was being followed. She turned, gripping the hammer, ready to smash whoever it was, when she saw, walking behind her on the last dark stretch of road, Petunia methodically working her way home. From behind their windows of glass, the Riodoro people now watched the pig. Pigs, they say, are smart, and this one, who seemed to recognize either Rosa or the sledgehammer, caught up with her and together they walked the rest of the way up the hill.

Kelly Cherry
THE FAMILY

The father has been killed in an accident during a hunting expedition.

The Mother Speaks
The day they came home without you,
I was teaching Mara to thread the bone needle:
chew leather, I said, the way a giraffe chews grass.

Mara's teeth are strong,

her smile is strong;
she has long lashes.

I teach my daughter the art of survival,
the home-keeping art: sweep spider webs away,
pick the twigs up from the hearth, pray.

Keep a sharp lookout: light is a snake
the color of cream, coiled
in the crotch of a tree; it spits

poison in your eye and you die.

The Brother, a Cripple, Speaks

I was doing my tricks
for the children, beating sticks
with sticks, singing a song
on one note like a bird
with one word: "Me, me, me."

My legs are air but I can't fly.
I sit in the shade of a tree,
plucking my weedy knee.
The children turn somersaults;
sun sticks to their hair like bits of straw.

I used to hunt boar,
my spear tipped with blood,
mud on my back and arms,
a necklace of sworn charms
painted across my breast

with a brush dipped in dung.
I used to hunt elephant. . . .

Elephants shed real tears for their dead,
and during the long drought I once saw a bull cry
silently, as his calves choked on yellow dust like lye.

Children: water the earth with your eye.

The Son Speaks

I remember the air was dry
as earth in summer,
or a cake of wheat baked in ashes—
but my bones were cold;
they froze in my flesh like icicles.

Mother was teaching Mara to sew.
My uncle dozed under the sycamore.

* * *

I have a dog;
his vest is white,
his feet are white;
at night, he curls by the fire,
and his hind legs jerk
in his sleep; does he dream
of chasing rabbits, squirrels?
And you—do you dream?

Uncle says dreamless sleep
is the darkest. I keep
my eyes open,
I prop my lids with my fingers
and prick my skin with the quill
of a porcupine, I swallow sand
so I won't sleep.

All night I walk
to and fro in our cave.
I leave my handprint
on the walls of our cave.
I draw the great deer
on the walls of our cave.
Firelight burns color
into the walls—
red and yellow,
the shape of shadow.
The walls of our cave
secrete beads of moisture;
I will wear a necklace of cold water.

*   *   *

An extravagance:
my sister will wear earrings
of raindrops

*   *   *

Her eyes are as blue as the pool
at the lip of a waterfall
at twilight;
I swim in them
like a fish,
I dive down to dark.
I nap in a bed
of mud and silt
on the floor of my sister's eyes;
I rise on a sun-warmed current
to air, where forsythia
hangs over the bank in bright clumps,
like clumps of light,

dripping petals like water.

I am a willow
growing beside the pool
of my sister's gaze.
My roots sip her sweet springs
and drain her dry.
I weep with my sister's eye.

All That Mara Knows

These are the lessons I have learned by heart; give
mandrake
for deep sleep, willow bark for headache;
to chase away nightmares, take
the peony's seeds by mouth.

If your man leaves you, go south.

If food is scarce, feed
on your own tongue;
what words bleed?

The celebrated stone showing my mother's form shows
        mine:
my stomach is lava,
my breasts are limestone,
my skin is like mica.

My hair is as red as an August poppy—

These lessons I have learned,
but I don't know why I'm loved.
Why am I loved?

My brother sleeps with his head on my shoulder;
my uncle has no legs, but he walks beside me like the
    wind,
embracing me as a strong wind embraces a tree.

They teach me to dig under the boulder for grubworms
    and mice;
they teach me where to find wild rice.

I am the best student,
the student of surpassing brilliance;
I am the first genius.
I live among the cold rocks,
tending our small fire,
cooking bear and deer.
I am learning history
by watching others die.
I know where our souls fly after death:
to the dark shelf that oozes wet salt
at the rear of the cave,
where my father's blind spirit hangs upside down
and harks to the echo
of its own thin cry.

Mara Speaks

I was sewing a shirt of animal skins,
when the hunters returned.
This is the lesson I learned:
the dead are buried sitting up;
the living lie down with one another,
uncle, mother, brother.

Kelly Cherry
HUNTING: A STORY

I

We headed north,
summer at our backs,
living on roots and water,
following the unmistakable tracks
of the elk, as they advanced our party
day after day, all of us weary,
the Giant-winged Moth
gleaming on the oak's

breeze-blown leaves, the river
green and sparkling, liquid jewels,
the sun in it like a fish with a million flashing fins.

I forget why we had come.
It had something to do with food,
something to do with a child who died.

I could smell your shoulder at my side,
could lick salt from your arm.
At night, in the wood,
I slept wrapped in your arms
like a cob in its husk,
like a plant
breathing only the air you breathed out in your dreams,
a man's musk,
thinking, *Want*—
until you heard what I couldn't say
and answered me, kissing.

II

Our bodies' fire: the quick
spark of desire in the dark,

leaping like deer or silver trout
to the hole at the top, and out—

I warm my hands in the hollow space
between your neck and the ground's hard face,

or in the hair on your back
like a mane, and the black

night erupts into flame in our brilliant tent:
your flesh igniting mine like a flint.

III

Morning.
I fed you berries and bark.
Oh, I remember your hand on my arm
like the sun on a branch,
your eyes like hunting knives!

There was weather:
a smell of rain on the wind,
clouds racing like a herd of antelope,
thunder . . .
leaves clattering like horses' hooves on limestone.
The ground was as hard as bone,
and the sky black as a crow feather.

Don't go,
don't go.

I was hitting you
because the only words were in my fists,
I spoke them on your chest,
but you held my wrists
with one hand, and with the other drew
a ring around my breast,
thinking—what were you thinking?

I watched you go.

IV

The V of the geese
is like the dent at the base of your throat.
Their rain-color is the color of your eyes.
I am in love with geese.
I go looking for geese,

spend my long days in marshes and swamps,
scanning the sky for geese.
I dream that I am sleeping
in your wide black-fringed white wings,
and your hot, enthusiastic heart beats under my ear
but it is only the river
running,
far off, the sound rolling underground.
He-Who-Drums-Has Drowned.

V

Winter.
The light hard as ice,
frozen between the wind-pumiced branches
like blue water between chestnut shoots,
still and solid,
the sky like a lake . . .

Winter.
I am thinking a question.
It lies curled in my brain,
waiting to be born:
sons and daughters will spring
from my mouth, I will be called
Mother-of-Many Words. . . .

The question ends in a loop like a lasso.
Or: it is a question like a fever,
hot to the touch,
cold inside.

I shiver.

I feel the wind that is like a warrior
marking a path in the sides of trees

cutting into my legs,
and I think: I will bleed ice crystals,
there will be nothing between my legs,
only coldness and cutting.

—*But why?*

VI

Years go by—

The north wind whispers
under the mud hut walls,
it tongues my ear.
What I can't say,
only wind can hear.

There was a word once
danced in my body
sang through my throat
lived in my brain
saying itself
over and over: *you.*

The word went away,
leaving only the sound of the wind,
lonesome, mocking, sneak-sound,
old Eavesdropper, old Tattletale,
old Snake in the Grass,
wind.

VII

Now I live
like an animal,
where it is March

and April forever,
where the white sun's arch
and fall
are both so thin that noon never
quits, and dawn and dusk arrive
unannounced, mere
light dustings of shadow
on the day's long year.

VIII

Snow geese, blue geese, the greylag . . .

One by one,
shadows are peeled from the sycamore,
from the counsel-holding evergreen.

Now the pond's surface ripples
with a swift paddling of wings like oars.
Light-sweetened air, cool
as melting snow on the tongue,
drops over the still-hard ground.
Touch-me-not springs.

And when wet snow stipples
dark bark, poetry pours
from the sky, forming a pool
I wade out in, sung
to by the wind, water-kissed, hugged, and drowned.
Wind in the water's locks sings.

Sings: *The day's long year, blue snow,*
the gray geese, pale lights, the evergreen
secretive as snow, the blue lag
between then and now, rippling. . . .

Sings these same things,
for nothing ever really happened
but comings and goings,

comings and goings,

and goings again, until
not even that happened
and love was still

as a stone. O love (if anyone reads),
here is my heart,
trapped among snow-tipped reeds.

Susan Griffin

HIS POWER:
HE TAMES WHAT IS WILD

Is it by its indefiniteness it shadows forth the heartless voids and immensities of the universe, and thus stabs us from behind with the thought of annihilation when beholding the milky way?
—*Herman Melville*, Moby-Dick

And at last she could bear the burden of herself no more. She was to be had for the taking. To be had for the taking.
—*D. H. Lawrence*, Lady Chatterley's Lover

The Hunt

She has captured his heart. She has overcome him. He cannot tear his eyes away. He is burning with passion. He cannot live without her. He pursues her. She makes him pursue her. The faster she runs, the stronger his desire. He will overtake her. He will make her his own. He will have her. (The boy chases the doe and her yearling for nearly two hours. She keeps running despite her wounds. He pursues her through pastures, over fences, groves of trees, crossing the road, up hills, volleys of rifle shots sounding, until perhaps twenty bullets are embedded in her body.) She has no mercy. She has dressed to excite his desire. She has no scruples. She has painted herself for him. She makes supple movements to entice him. She is without a soul. Beneath her painted face is flesh, are bones. She reveals only part of herself to him. She is wild. She flees whenever he approaches. She is teasing him. (Finally, she is defeated and falls and he sees that half of her head has been blown off, that one leg is gone, her abdomen split from her tail to her head, and her organs hang outside her body. Then four men encircle the fawn and harvest her too.) He is an easy target, he says. He says he is pierced. Love has shot him through, he says. He is a familiar mark. Riddled. Stripped to the bone. He is conquered, he says. (The boys, fond of hunting hare, search in particular for pregnant females.) He is fighting for his life. He faces annihilation in her, he says. He is losing himself to her, he says. Now, he must conquer her wildness, he says, he must tame her before she drives him wild, he says. (Once catching their prey, they step on her back, breaking it, and they call this "dancing on the hare.") Thus he goes on his knees to her. Thus he wins her over, he tells her he wants her. He makes her his own. He encloses her. He encircles her. He puts her under lock and key. He protects her. (Approaching the great mammals, the hunters make little sounds which they know will make the elephants form a defensive circle.) And once she is his, he prizes his delight. He feasts his eyes on her. He adorns her luxuriantly. He gives her ivory. He gives her perfume. (The older matriarchs stand to the outside of the circle to protect the calves and younger mothers.) He covers her with the skins of mink, beaver, muskrat, seal, raccoon, otter, ermine, fox, the feathers of ostriches, osprey, egret, ibis. (The hunters then encircle that circle and fire first into the bodies of the matriarchs. When these older elephants fall, the younger panic, yet unwilling to leave the bodies of their dead mothers, they make easy targets.) And thus he makes her soft. He makes her calm. He makes her grateful to him. He has tamed her, he says. She is content to be his, he says. (In the win-

ter, if a single wolf has leaped over the walls of the city and ter-
rorized the streets, the hunters go out in a band to rid the forest of the whole pack.) Her voice is now soothing to him. Her
eyes no longer blaze, but look on him serenely. When he calls
to her, she gives herself to him. Her ferocity lies under him.
(The body of the great whale is strapped with explosives.) Now
nothing of the old beast remains in her. (Eastern Bison, extinct
1825; Spectacled Cormorant, extinct 1852; Cape Lion, extinct
1865; Bonin Night Heron, extinct 1889; Barbary Lion, extinct
1922; Great Auk, extinct 1944.) And he can trust her wholly
with himself. So he is blazing when he enters her, and she is
consumed. (Florida Key Deer, vanishing; Wild Indian Buffalo,
vanishing; Great Sable Antelope, vanishing.) Because she is his,
she offers no resistance. She is a place of rest for him. A place
of his making. And when his flesh begins to yield and his skin
melts into her, he becomes soft, and he is without fear; he does
not lose himself; though something in him gives way, he is not
lost in her, because she is his now: he has captured her.

Mary Pinard

GATHERINGS

I

A pebble dropped down a well
or a small arm pulled from its socket.
It's a hollow sound, my father
plucking feathers. Flesh pores open

each like a nostril flared with breath
or fury. Floodlight splits
over carcasses, off the beveled edge
of his glasses. He doesn't see me perched,

this railing. With every snap, I flinch:
it's my skin, the shame, and I wonder
how I might free this pheasant's soul
from its bone cage.

II

I shuffle photos of dead birds, mourning
doves, mallards, ring-necked pheasants,
like a card player. Here are the hunters,
my French uncles, layered in gear and leaning

on a jeep. Sometimes they kneel
at broken necks, bloody breasts, torsos
posed. Brothers, this their annual
gathering. Tradition. This is Spink County,

Redfield, South Dakota. These sons kiss
land with rifle butts, move across stubble,
a column of soldiers in early fog, in smoke.
They forget me in the car. I wait, lean

out the window. White air bursts at his mouth,
Uncle Monty's heard the rustle, kicks the brush.
They're up. Metallic whir of wingflaps,
the blast, and a horizon, a hundred rainbows.

III

Sounds of gunshot—pinged off saltwater
and the breast of a pintail or mallard—
are also hollow. My father coaches me,
flunky hunter. I am better, he sighs,

at collecting decoys or retrieving
the dead ones, better than a dog.
My chance: from the blind I fire,
I miss. The bird flees with a grace

that humiliates. Banished then to shore
where lichen spills over logs, I squat
to look, hide from the death that falls,
has always fallen, too heavy around me.

Alice Hoffman

FROM *SECOND NATURE*

By April most people had already forgotten about him, except for some of the nurses on the floor, who crossed themselves when they walked past his room. The guard stationed outside his door, who had little to do but read magazines and drink coffee for more than three months, bragged to his friends that on nights when there was a full moon he needed a whip and a chair just to set a dinner tray on the other side of the door. But in fact, the guard had never even dared to look around the room, where the metal bed was made up with clean white sheets every week, though it had never once been slept in.

The man who occupied the room had no name. He refused to look anyone in the eye or, even after months of work with the speech therapists, to make any sound whatsoever, at least not in the presence of others. Officially he was listed as patient 3119, but among themselves the staff called him the Wolf Man, although they were expressly forbidden to do so. He was underweight and had a long scar along the inside of one thigh that had healed years before but still turned purple on cold or rainy days. For two months he'd needed to wear a cast on his reconstructed foot; but otherwise he was in surprisingly good health. Since he had no birthday, the staff at Kelvin Medical Center had assigned him one. They'd chipped in to buy him a sweater, blue wool, on sale at Bloomingdale's, and one of the cooks had baked and frosted an angel food cake. But that was back in January, after he learned to use a fork and dress himself, and they'd still had hope for him. Now, they left him alone, and when he sat motionless, and sunlight came through the bars on his window, some of the nurses swore that his eyes turned yellow.

The evening before his transfer upstate, the barber was sent to his room. There would be no need to sweep the floor after his shave and haircut; the raven that had been perching on the window ledge was waiting to dart through the bars and gather up the hair to wind into its nest. One lab technician, who had been brave enough to look through the glass window in the door, had once seen the raven eating right out of his plate while the Wolf Man calmly continued with his dinner. Now, the raven watched as the attendants strapped the Wolf Man into a metal chair and held his head back. The barber wanted no chances taken; a human bite was the most dangerous of all. In the interest of speed, he used a razor rather than scissors, and while he worked he quickly recited a blessing.

The following morning, two attendants helped the Wolf Man into a black overcoat, which would be taken away once he settled into the state hospital, since he'd never need it again and another patient could make use of it. The cook who had baked the angel food cake for his birthday wept. She insisted he had smiled when she lit the candles on the cake, but no one believed her, except the guard stationed at his door, who had been made so anxious by this bit of news that he took to biting his fingernails, close enough to the skin to draw blood.

The cook had discovered that the Wolf Man would not eat meat unless it was raw. He liked his potatoes unbaked as well, and would not touch a salad or a pudding. For his last meal, an early breakfast, she had simply passed a hamburger patty over a flame for a moment. So what if uncooked meat was bad for you, and most of the patients liked cereal and toast, she wanted him to have what he liked. She had an impulse to hide a knife or a screwdriver inside the folded napkin, because she knew that as soon as he'd eaten his breakfast, he would be handcuffed, then released into the custody of a social worker from the state hospital for the ride along the Hudson. By afternoon he would be signed into a ward from which no one was ever released. But she didn't follow her impulse, and after the Wolf Man had his meal, the attendants dressed him and helped him into the black overcoat, then clasped the handcuffs on him, quickly, from behind, before he could fight back.

Outside the door, the guard turned his Walkman up to the highest volume, and he slipped his sunglasses on, though the April sky threatened to storm. His friends liked to hear stories about the Wolf Man—how he crouched and circled three times before he curled up to sleep with his back against the wall, that five strong men were needed to hold him down each time they drew blood or inoculated him against measles and tetanus—and the guard was always happy to oblige. But what he never mentioned, as he drank cold beer with his friends, was that on nights when there was thunder he often heard a whimpering behind the door, a sound so pitiful it turned his bones cold and his heart inside out.

That was the sound the trappers had heard on the last day of December, when the snow was ten feet deep and deer stuck in the drifts and froze solid. There, at the edge of northern Michigan, much of the land had never been charted and trees were so dense they blocked out the sun. Beneath the ice, streams were filled with green water. Bears in these mountains grew to seven feet, and their hides were so thick a whole hive of bees couldn't sting them. It was dark as night on winter afternoons; trappers had to carry flashlights and leave lanterns hung on their snowmobiles in order to find their way back. Most of these men never poached enough to get caught by the rangers, and anyone looking for them would have had a difficult time. In the spring, moss appeared overnight and covered any footprints completely by morning. In winter, no one but a maniac or an experienced hunter would venture into the forest. For those men who didn't fear the woods, there was little chance of legal action against them. Trapping was, after all, a criminal act without a witness. There was no one to hear a shotgun fired, or the peculiar cry made by a fox when a piece of cyanide-laced lamb takes effect.

The men who found him were an uncle and nephew who had worked the forest for more than ten years and who were not nearly as greedy or cruel as some of their neighbors. They worked in silence, not with poisoned meat but with steel traps, and they were always particularly careful to stay together, even when it made sense to split up, since they had seen, several times, huge paw prints, three times as big as a dog's. In these mountains all sorts of things were said on winter nights, some to be believed, some not. A man they knew, over in Cromley, had a wolf-skin rug on his living room floor, head and all. He told everyone he'd shot the wolf, a male of more than a hundred and ten pounds, head-on, but his wife had let it slip that he'd simply found it the spring before, dead of natural causes, preserved all winter long by the cold. Wolves were rare, even this far north; you could probably count on your fingers the ones that had come down from Canada and stayed.

Still, their tenuous presence made for good talk and real

fear. An old trapper who hadn't been caught once in sixty years of making a living liked to scare some of the boys who were just starting out by swearing that it was possible for some wolves to become human. He'd seen it himself on a night when there was an orange hunter's moon. A wolf was crouching down with the pack one minute and standing on two feet like a man the next. That happened with old trappers sometimes—they had killed more animals than they could number and, now that they were senior citizens who couldn't eat anything but oatmeal, they suddenly started to have some kind of funny regret that mixed them up so badly they didn't even notice people were laughing at them.

The uncle and his nephew didn't listen to stories and they didn't take foolish chances. As far as they were concerned, they weren't breaking the law so much as taking care of their families. They were interested in deer for the meat, foxes and raccoons for their skins, but they got much more than that on the last day of December. This was the season when the sky turned black at four-thirty and the cold made breathing painful and sharp. They were inspecting the traps they had left out the day before when they heard the howling. Normally they would have backtracked, but they had worked all day with nothing to show and still had one trap left to check. As they walked forward, it wasn't the cold that made them shiver, and their brand-new parkas from Sears couldn't help them one bit. The nephew's teeth were hitting against each other so hard he thought he'd chip the enamel right off them.

It was hard to tell from the howling exactly how many wolves there were until they saw them. What sounded like a dozen turned out to be three, up above, on the ridgetop. All three were silver, brothers by the look of them. They seemed to be waiting for the uncle and his nephew, because as soon as they saw the men, the wolves stopped their racket. Yet they stayed where they were, unprotected up there on the ridge. When the uncle saw a pool of blood, he thought the wolves

were after a deer or a fisher caught in the last trap, and he fig-
ured it might be best just to let them have it. The temperature
had begun to drop and the sun would soon be going down. The
uncle would have turned back then if his nephew hadn't
grabbed his arm.

The last steel trap was a good one; kept oiled and cleaned,
it would last another fifty years. When they heard the whimpering sound, they assumed they were simply suffering from the
cold. Hallucinations occurred in severe weather; they sprang up
from the ground fully formed. Jack Flannagan insisted he'd
been visited by his dead mother one day in the woods, when the
temperature was ten below zero. A friend of the nephew's
would not hunt after dark, convinced that a deer he had shot
one snowy day had cried real tears, just like a baby. So the wail-
ing they heard might have been caused by twilight and ice. The
notion of going home began to feel about right, even necessary.
Then they saw the thing in the trap, struggling and bleeding, its
foot partially crushed, and they might have shot it then, to put
it out of its misery, if they hadn't realized, all at once, that the
struggling thing had the shape of a man.

The wolves took up their howling again, while the uncle
labored to open the trap. The nephew fired his gun in the air,
even though he knew it was bad luck to shoot at wolves, and
they took off, across the ridge and through the pine trees. It
took almost two hours to get the poor creature out of the trap
and carry him back to the snowmobiles. A trail of red blood
burned through the snow. The drifts were now much higher, so
that a mile seemed to go on endlessly. The nephew wondered
aloud whether they'd be charged with murder if their unin-
tended victim should die. He was already unconscious and his
skin had turned blue. How had it been possible, the nephew
asked his uncle, for him to have survived through the winter,
wearing only skins on his body and wrapped around his feet?
Why had they never seen him before, when they knew every
man for a hundred miles around?

The uncle didn't bother to answer, he was too busy tying the limp body into the snowmobile with thick brown rope. Clouds were moving in fast, threatening more snow. They had to get to the rangers' station, where a helicopter ran an airlift to St. Joseph's Hospital in Cromley. The uncle's breathing was ragged. He knew for a fact that the trap had shattered the left foot; bone jutted through the skin. As the uncle was positioning the head onto a blanket he realized how young their victim was, younger than his nephew. Once he looked at the pale face, with its high cheekbones and knots of dark hair, he couldn't look away, even though he had removed his gloves to lash the rope to the snowmobile and his fingers were freezing. If he'd seen anything like this face before, it was in the chapel at St. Joseph's, where he'd waited while his wife was being operated on for something wrong inside her stomach a few years back. To the right of the pews, in a dark alcove, there had been a statue made of white wood with a countenance so calm it had made him weep.

He pulled his gloves back on and started his snowmobile. In less than three hours, work would begin in the only operating room in St. Joseph's as an orthopedic surgeon repaired the bones the steel trap had shattered. Two weeks later, the patient would be flown to the Kelvin Medical Center on East Eighty-sixth Street in New York, a hospital that dealt exclusively with victims of traumatic stress. There he would stay, in a locked room, for the next few months, while some of the best doctors in the city tried to ascertain what they were dealing with. But the uncle knew what they had right then and there. It didn't matter what people said on winter nights this year or the year after or the one after that. It didn't matter what people believed. The uncle knew exactly what it was they were dealing with, on this night and forever after. They had caught themselves a wolf.

Carol Frost
RED DEER

The red deer in summer sunlight
browses slowly in the landscape
we make of the forest. It is beautiful
and slays me with its delicacy,
its ankles. Bugs dance above the briars,
and fleshy raspberries are tinged black;
sun is falling. The Indians saw this contour
of land and the red deer,
stalking it through pines,

bits of brown like piles of little eggs
its trail to the river
where the last lights come.
Its bones and sinews sewed the shoes
for silence where I keep vigil now,
on the same ground, listening for a rustle
that is louder than the weight of birds
in the underbrush, wanting to see
the alarmed head turn, the large eyes.
I walk, and stop, and walk,
my body thinking, what does
the deer matter except it is flesh
and I have smelled it?
If I cut open the red coat,
I could live in it.
Green going gray going black,
I stand in violence, in death,
and I am happy—with the chill of fear.
The light withdraws; chills me; alters
nothing. At the root of humanness
a cup of blood
nature spills. And this is part
of everything I see or make or am.
I can hide it in a closet like a gun
to be shown in all its hiddenness
or paste it over with yellow, for sanctity,
and cool greens. But this once
let me tell the truth
that can't be told
outright. I had no pity.
The deer's last breath
crawled out like a clear beautiful ray
of sun on stones. I kissed
its head. I couldn't help myself.

Carol Frost
WILD PARTRIDGE

The same bird over and over again,
quiet so long I had passed by,
drums from the last crisped leaves

up through the branches that had been fire.
Treading moss and stopping my breath,
I've gotten as close as to the russet brink

of an autumn sky and lost it

to the disheveled light . . .
a few wood berries, barley seed

under some pines, a liquid chuckling
somewhere ahead, then on the northern air—
beauty, autumn, vision burning

their overlapping images into dusk.
Can I stalk the wild partridge
and forget, seeing the fallen ash,

the leaves scattered and rotting,
how each moment soars, in truth,
in mortal surprise, away from us always?

Joy Williams
THE KILLING GAME

Death and suffering are a big part of hunting. A big part. Not that you'd ever know it by hearing hunters talk. They tend to downplay the killing part. To kill is to put to death, extinguish, nullify, cancel, destroy. But from the hunter's point of view, it's just a tiny part of the experience. *The kill is the least important part of the hunt,* they often say, or, *Killing involves only a split second of the innumerable hours we spend surrounded by and observing nature. . . .* For the animal, of course, the killing part is of considerably more importance.

José Ortega y Gasset, in *Meditations on Hunting*, wrote, *Death is a sign of reality in hunting. One does not hunt in order to kill; on the contrary, one kills in order to have hunted.* This is the sort of intellectual blather that the "thinking" hunter holds dear. The conservation editor of *Field & Stream*, George Reiger, recently paraphrased this sentiment by saying, *We kill to hunt, and not the other way around,* thereby making it truly fatuous. A hunter in West Virginia, one Mr. Bill Neal, blazed through this philosophical fog by explaining why he blows the toes of tree raccoons so that they will fall down and be torn apart by his dogs. *That's the best part of it. It's not any fun just shooting them.*

Instead of monitoring animals—many animals in managed areas are tagged, tattooed, and wear radio transmitters—wildlife managers should start hanging telemetry gear around hunter's necks to study their attitudes and listen to their conversations. It would be grisly listening, but it would tune out for good the *suffering as sacrament* and *spiritual experience* blather that some hunting apologists employ. *The unease with which the good hunter inflicts death is an unease not merely with his conscience but with affirming his animality in the midst of his struggles toward humanity and clarity,* Holmes Rolston III drones on in his book *Environmental Ethics.*

There is a formula to this in literature—someone the protagonist loves has just died, so he goes out and kills an animal. This makes him feel better. But it's kind of a sad feeling-better. He gets to relate to Death and Nature in this way. Somewhat. But not really. Death is still a mystery. Well, it's hard to explain. It's sort of a semireligious thing . . . Killing and affirming, affirming and killing, it's just the cross the "good" hunter must bear. The bad hunter just has to deal with postkill letdown.

Many are the hunter's specious arguments. Less semireligious but a long-standing favorite with them is the vegetarian approach: you eat meat, don't you? If you say no, they feel they've got you—you're just a vegetarian attempting to impose your weird views on others. If you say yes, they accuse you of being hypocritical, of allowing your genial A&P butcher to stand between you and reality. The fact is, the chief attraction of hunting is the pursuit and murder of animals—the meat-eating aspect of it is trivial. If the hunter chooses to be *ethical* about it, he might cook his kill, but the meat of most animals is discarded. Dead bear can even be dangerous! A bear's heavy hide must be skinned at once to prevent meat spoilage. With effort, a hunter can make okay chili, *something to keep in mind,* a sports rag says, *if you take two skinny spring bears.*

As for subsistence hunting, please . . . Granted that there might be one "good" hunter out there who conducts the kill as spiritual exercise and two others who are atavistic enough to want to supplement their Chicken McNuggets with venison, most hunters hunt for the hell of it.

For hunters, hunting is fun. Recreation is play. Hunting is recreation. Hunters kill for play, for entertainment. They kill for the thrill of it, to make an animal "theirs." (The Gandhian doctrine of nonpossession has never been a big hit with hunters.) The animal becomes the property of the hunter by its death. Alive, the beast belongs only to itself. This is unacceptable to the hunter. *He's yours . . . He's mine . . . I decided to . . . I decided not to . . . I debated shooting it, then I decided to let it live . . .* Hunters like beautiful creatures. A "beautiful" deer, elk, bear, cougar, bighorn sheep. A "beautiful" goose or mallard. Of course, they don't stay "beautiful" for long, particularly the birds. Many birds become rags in the air, shredded, blown to bits. *Keep shooting till they drop!* Hunters get a thrill out of seeing a plummeting bird, out of seeing it crumple and fall. *The big pheasant folded in classic fashion.* They get a kick out of "collecting" new species. *Why not add a unique harlequin duck to your collection?* Swan hunting is satisfying. *I let loose a three-inch Magnum. The large bird only flinched with my first shot and began to gain altitude. I frantically ejected the round, chambered another, and dropped the swan with my second shot. After retrieving the bird I was amazed by its size. The swan's six-foot wingspan, huge body, and long neck made it an impressive trophy*. Hunters like big animals, trophy animals. A "trophy" usually means that the hunter doesn't deign to eat it. Maybe he skins it or mounts it. Maybe he takes a picture. *We took pictures, we took pictures*. Maybe he just looks at it for a while. The disposition of the "experience" is up to the hunter. He's entitled to do whatever he wishes with the damn thing. It's dead.

Hunters like categories they can tailor to their needs. There are the "good" animals—deer, elk, bear, moose—which are allowed to exist for the hunter's pleasure. Then there are the "bad" animals, the vermin, varmints, and "nuisance" animals, the rabbits and raccoons and coyotes and beavers and badgers, which are disencouraged to exist. The hunter can have fun killing them, but the pleasure is diminished because the animals aren't "magnificent."

Then there are the predators. These can be killed any time, because, hunters argue, they're predators, for godssakes.

Many people in South Dakota want to exterminate the red fox because it preys upon some of the ducks and pheasant they want to hunt and kill each year. They found that after they killed the wolves and coyotes, they had more foxes than they wanted. The ring-necked pheasant is South Dakota's state bird. No matter that it was imported from Asia specifically to be "harvested" for sport, it's South Dakota's state bird and they're proud of it. A group called Pheasants Unlimited gave some tips on how to hunt foxes. *Place a small amount of larvicide* [a grain fumigant] *on a rag and chuck it down the hole . . . The first pup generally comes out in fifteen minutes . . . Use a .22 to dispatch him . . . Remove each pup shot from the hole. Following gassing, set traps for the old fox who will return later in the evening . . .* Poisoning, shooting, trapping—they make up a sort of sportsman's triathlon.

* * *

In the hunting magazines, hunters freely admit the pleasure of killing to one another. *Undeniable pleasure radiated
from her smile. The excitement of shooting the bear had Barb
talking a mile a minute.* But in public, most hunters are becoming a little wary about raving on as to how much fun it is to
kill things. Hunters have a tendency to call large animals by
cute names—"bruins" and "muleys," "berry-fed blackies" and
"handsome cusses" and "big guys," thereby implying a balanced jolly game of mutual satisfaction between the hunter and
the hunted—*Bam, bam, bam, I get to shoot you and you get to
be dead.* More often, though, when dealing with the nonhunting public, a drier, businesslike tone is employed. Animals become a "resource" that must be "utilized." Hunting becomes "a
legitimate use of the resource." Animals become a product like
wool or lumber or a crop like fruit or corn that must be "collected" or "taken" or "harvested." Hunters love to use the
world *legitimate.* (Oddly, Tolstoy referred to hunting as "evil le-
gitimized.") *A legitimate use, a legitimate form of recreation, a
legitimate escape, a legitimate pursuit.* It's a word they trust will
slam the door on discourse. Hunters are increasingly relying
upon their spokesmen and supporters, state and federal game
managers and wildlife officials, to employ the drone of a solemn
bureaucratic language and toss around a lot of questionable sta-
tistics to assure the nonhunting public (93 percent!) that there's
nothing to worry about. The pogrom is under control. The mass
murder and manipulation of wild animals is just another business. Hunters are a tiny minority, and it's crucial to them that
the millions of people who don't hunt not be awakened from
their long sleep and become antihunting. Nonhunters are okay.
Dweeby, probably, but okay. A hunter *can respect the rights* of
a nonhunter. It's the "antis" he despises, those *misguided, emotional, not-in-possession-of-the-facts, uninformed zealots who
don't understand nature . . . those dime-store ecologists cloaked
in ignorance and spurred by emotion . . . those doggy-woggy
types, who under the guise of being environmentalists and con-*

servationists are working to deprive him of his precious right to kill. (Sometimes it's just a *right;* sometimes it's a *God-given* right.) Antis can be scorned, but nonhunters must be pacified, and this is where the number crunching of wildlife biologists and the scripts of *professional resource managers* come in. Leave it to the professionals. They know what numbers are the good numbers. Utah determined that there were six hundred sandhill cranes in the state, so permits were issued to shoot one hundred of them. Don't want to have too many sandhill cranes. California wildlife officials reported "sufficient numbers" of mountain lions to "justify" renewed hunting, even though it doesn't take a rocket scientist to know the animal is extremely rare. (It's always a dark day for hunters when an animal is adjudged *rare.* How can its numbers be "controlled" through hunting if it scarcely exists?) A recent citizens' referendum prohibits the hunting of the mountain lion in perpetuity—not that the lions aren't killed anyway, in California and all over the West, hundreds of them annually by the government as part of the scandalous Animal Damage Control Program. Oh, to be the lucky hunter who gets to be an official government hunter and can legitimately kill animals his buddies aren't supposed to! Montana officials, led by K. L. Cool, that state's wildlife director, have definite ideas on the number of buffalo they feel can be tolerated. Zero is the number. Yellowstone National Park is the only place in America where bison exist, having been annihilated everywhere else. In the winter of 1988, nearly six hundred buffalo wandered out of the north boundary of the park and into Montana, where they were immediately shot at point-blank range by lottery-winning hunters. It was easy. And it was obvious from a video taken on one of the blow-away-the-bison days that the hunters had a heck of a good time. The buffalo, cool says, threaten ranchers' livelihoods by doing damage to property—by which he means, I guess, that they eat the grass. Montana wants zero buffalo; it also wants zero wolves.

Large predators—including grizzlies, cougars, and wolves—

are often the most "beautiful," the smartest and wildest animals
of all. The gray wolf is both a supreme predator and an endangered species, and since the Supreme Court recently affirmed
that ranchers have no constitutional right to kill endangered
predators—apparently some God-given rights are not constitutional ones—this makes the wolf a more or less lucky dog. But
not for long. A small population of gray wolves has recently established itself in northwestern Montana, primarily in Glacier
National Park, and there is a plan, long a dream of conservationists, to "reintroduce" the wolf to Yellowstone. But to please
ranchers and hunters, part of the plan would involve immediately removing the wolf from the endangered species list. Beyond the park's boundaries, he could be hunted as a "game animal" or exterminated as a "pest." (Hunters kill to hunt,
remember, except when they're hunting to kill.) The area of
Yellowstone where the wolf would be restored is the same
mountain and high-plateau country that is abandoned in winter by most animals, including the aforementioned luckless bison. Part of the plan, too, is compensation to ranchers if any of
their far-ranging livestock is killed by a wolf. It's a real industry
out there, apparently, killing and controlling and getting com-
pensated for losing something under the Big Sky.

Wolves gotta eat—a fact that disturbs hunters. Jack
Atcheson, an outfitter in Butte, said *Some wolves are fine if there
is control. But there never will be control. The wolf-control plan
provided by the Fish and Wildlife Service speaks only of protecting domestic livestock. There is no plan to protect wildlife
. . . There are no surplus deer or elk in Montana . . . Their numbers are carefully managed. With uncontrolled wolf populations,
a lot of people will have to give up hunting just to feed wolves.
Will you give up your elk permit for a wolf?*

It won't be long before hunters start demanding compensation for animals they aren't able to shoot.

* * *

Hunters believe that wild animals exist only to satisfy their wish to kill them. And it's so easy to kill them! The weaponry available is staggering, and the equipment and gear limitless. *The demand for big boomers has never been greater than right now, Outdoor Life crows, and the makers of rifles and cartridges are responding to the craze with a variety of light artillery that is virtually unprecedented in the history of sporting arms* . . . Hunters use grossly overpowered shotguns and rifles and compound bows. They rely on four-wheel-drive vehicles and three-wheel ATVs and airplanes . . . *He was interesting, the only moving, living creature on that limitless white expanse. I slipped a cartridge into the barrel of my rifle and threw the safety off* . . . They use snowmobiles to run down elk, and dogs to run down and tree cougars. It's easy to shoot an animal out of a tree. It's virtually impossible to miss a moose, a conspicuous and placid animal of steady habits . . . *I took a deep breath and pulled the trigger. The bull dropped. I looked at my watch: 8:22. The big guy was early. Mike started whooping and hollering and I joined him. I never realized how big a moose was until this one was on the ground. We took pictures* . . . Hunters shoot animals when they're resting . . . *Mike selected a deer, settled down to a steady rest, and fired. The buck was his when he squeezed the trigger. John decided to take the other buck, which had jumped up to its feet. The deer hadn't seen us and was confused by the shot echoing about in the valley. John took careful aim, fired, and took the buck. The hunt was over* . . . And they shoot them when they're eating . . . *The bruin ambled up the stream, checking gravel bars and backwaters for fish. Finally he plopped down on the bank to eat. Quickly, I tiptoed into range* . . . They use decoys and calls . . . *The six–point gave me a cold-eyed glare from ninety steps away. I hit him with a 130-grain Sierra boat-tail handload. The bull went down hard. Our hunt was over* . . . They use sex lures . . . *The big buck raised its nose to the air, curled back its lips, and tested the scent of the doe's urine. I held my breath, fought back the shivers, and jerked off a shot. The 180-grain spire-point bullet caught the buck high on the back behind the shoulder and put it down. It didn't get up* ... They use walkie-talkies, binoculars, scopes ... *With my 308 Browning BLR, I steadied the 9X cross hairs on the front of the bear's massive shoulders and squeezed. The bear cartwheeled backward for fifty yards* ... *The second Federal Premium 165-grain bullet found its mark. Another shot anchored the bear for good* ... They bait deer with corn. They spread popcorn on golf courses for Canada geese and they douse meat baits with fry grease and honey for bears ... *Make the baiting site redolent of inner-city doughnut shops.* They use blinds and tree stands and mobile stands. They go out in groups, in gangs, and employ "pushes" and "drives." So many methods are effective. So few rules apply. It's fun! ... *We kept on repelling the swarms of birds as they came in looking for shelter from that big ocean wind, emptying our shell belts* ... A species can, in the vernacular, be *pressured by hunting* (which means that killing them has decimated them), but that just increases the fun, the *challenge.* There is practically no criticism of conduct within the ranks ... *It's mostly a matter of opinion and how hunters have been brought up to hunt* ... Although a recent editorial in *Ducks Unlimited* magazine did venture to primly suggest that one should *not fall victim to greed-induced stress through piggish competition with others.*

But hunters are piggy. They just can't seem to help it. They're overequipped ... insatiable, malevolent, and vain. They maim and mutilate and despoil. And for the most part, they're inept. Grossly inept.

Camouflaged toilet paper is a must for the modern hunter, along with his Bronco and his beer. Too many hunters taking a dump in the woods with their roll of Charmin beside them were mistaken for white-tailed deer and shot. Hunters get excited. They'll shoot anything—the pallid ass of another sportsman or even themselves. A Long Island man died last year when his shotgun went off as he clubbed a wounded deer with the butt.

Hunters get mad. They get restless and want to fire! They want to use those assault rifles and see foamy blood on the ferns. Wounded animals can travel for miles in fear and pain before they collapse. Countless gut-shot deer—*if you hear a sudden, squashy thump, the animal has probably been hit in the abdomen*—are "lost" each year. "Poorly placed shots" are frequent, and injured animals are seldom tracked, because most hunters never learned how to track. The majority of hunters will shoot at anything with four legs during deer season and anything with wings during duck season. Hunters try to nail running animals and distant birds. They become so overeager, so *aroused*, that they misidentify and misjudge, spraying their "game" with shots but failing to bring it down.

The fact is, hunters' lack of skill is a big, big problem. And nowhere is the problem worse than in the new glamour recreation, bow hunting. These guys are elitists. They doll themselves up in camouflage, paint their faces black, and climb up into tree stands from which they attempt the penetration of deer, elk, and turkeys with modern, multiblade, broadhead arrows shot from sophisticated, easy-to-draw compound bows. This "primitive" way of hunting appeals to many, and even the nonhunter may feel that it's a "fairer" method, requiring more strength and skill, but bow hunting is the cruelest, most wanton form of wildlife disposal of all. Studies conducted by state fish and wildlife departments repeatedly show that bow hunters wound and fail to retrieve as many animals as they kill. An animal that flees, wounded by an arrow, will most assuredly die of the wound, but it will be days before he does. Even with a "good" hit, the time elapsed between the strike and death is exceedingly long. *The rule of thumb has long been that we should wait thirty to forty-five minutes on heart and lung hits, an hour or more on a suspected liver hit, eight to twelve hours on paunch hits, and that we should follow immediately on hindquarter and other muscle-only hits, to keep the wound open and bleeding,* is the advice in the magazine *Fins and Feathers*. What the hunter does as he hangs around waiting for his animal to finish with its terrified running and dying hasn't been studied—maybe he puts on more makeup, maybe he has a highball.

Wildlife agencies promote and encourage bow hunting by permitting earlier and longer seasons, even though they are well aware that, in their words, *crippling is a by-product of the sport*, making archers pretty sloppy for elitists. The broadhead arrow is a very inefficient killing tool. Bow hunters are trying to deal with this problem with the suggestion that they use poison pods. These poisoned arrows are illegal in all states except Mississippi *(Ah'm gonna get ma deer even if ah just nick the little bastard)*, but they're widely used anyway. You wouldn't want that deer to suffer, would you?

*   *   *

The mystique of the efficacy and decency of the bow hunter is as much an illusion as the perception that a waterfowler is a refined and thoughtful fellow, a *romantic aesthete*, as Vance Bourjaily put it, equipped with his faithful Labs and a love for solitude and wild places. More sentimental drivel has been written about bird shooting than any other type of hunting. It's a soul-wrenching pursuit, apparently, the execution of birds in flight. Ducks Unlimited—an organization that has managed to put a spin on the word *conservation* for years—works hard to project the idea that duck hunters are blue bloods and that duck stamps with their pretty pictures are responsible for saving all the saved puddles in North America. *Sportsman's conservation* is a contradiction in terms (We protect things now so that we can kill them later) and is broadly interpreted (Don't kill them all, just kill most of them). A hunter is a conservationist in the same way a farmer or a rancher is: he's not. Like the rancher who kills everything that's not stock on his (and the public's) land, and the farmer who scorns wildlife because "they don't pay their freight," the hunter uses nature by destroying its parts, mastering it by simplifying it through death.

George ("We kill to hunt and not the other way around") Reiger, the conservationist-hunter's spokesman (he's the best they've got, apparently), said that the "dedicated" waterfowler will shoot other game "of course," but *we do so much in the same spirit of the lyrics, that when we're not near the girl we love, we love the girl we're near.* (Duck hunters practice tough love.) The fact is, far from being a "romantic aesthete," the waterfowler is the most avaricious of all hunters . . . *That's when Scott suggested the friendly wager on who would take the most birds* . . . and the most resistant to minimum ecological decency. Millions of birds that managed to elude shotgun blasts were dying each year from ingesting the lead shot that rained down in the wetlands. Year after year, birds perished from feeding on spent lead, but hunters were "reluctant" to switch to steel. They worried that it would impair their shooting, and ammunition manufacturers said a changeover would be "expensive." State and federal officials had to weigh the poisoning against these considerations. It took forever, this weighing, but now steel-shot loads are required almost everywhere, having been judged "more than adequate" to bring down the birds. This is not to say, of course, that most duck hunters use steel shot almost everywhere. They're traditionalists and don't care for all the new, pesky rules. Oh, for the golden age of waterfowling, when a man could measure a good day's shooting by the pickup load. But those days are gone. Fall is a melancholy time, all right.

Spectacular abuses occur wherever geese congregate, Shooting Sportsman notes quietly, something that the more cultivated Ducks Unlimited would hesitate to admit. Waterfowl populations are plummeting and waterfowl hunters are out of control. "Supervised" hunt are hardly distinguished from unsupervised ones. A biologist with the Department of the Interior who observed a hunt at Sand Lake in South Dakota said, *Hunters repeatedly shot over the line at incoming flights where there was no possible chance of retrieving. Time and time again I was shocked at the behavior of hunters. I heard them laugh at the plight of dazed cripples that stumbled about. I saw them striking the heads of retrieved cripples against fence posts.* In the South, wood ducks return to their roosts after sunset when shooting hours are closed. Hunters find this an excellent time to shoot them. Dennis Anderson, an outdoors writer, said, *Roost shooters just fire at the birds as fast as they can, trying to drop as many as they can. Then they grab what birds they can find. The birds they can't find in the dark, they leave behind.*

Carnage and waste are the rules in bird hunting, even during legal seasons and open hours. Thousands of wounded ducks and geese are not retrieved, left to rot in the marshes and fields . . . *When I asked Wanda where hers had fallen, she wasn't sure.* Cripples, and there are many cripples made in this pastime, are still able to run and hide, eluding the hunter even if he's willing to spend time searching for them, which he usually isn't . . . *It's one thing to run down a cripple in a picked bean field or a pasture, and quite another to watch a wing-tipped bird drop into a huge block of switch grass. Oh nasty, nasty switch grass.* A downed bird becomes invisible on the ground and is practically unfindable without a good dog, and few "waterfowlers" have them these days. They're hard to train—usually a professional has to do it—and most hunters can't be bothered. Birds are easy to tumble . . . *Canada geese—blues and snows—can all take a good amount of shot. Brant are easily called and decoyed and come down easily. Ruffed grouse are hard to hit but easy to kill. Sharptails are harder to kill but easier to hit* . . . It's just a nuisance to recover them. But it's fun, fun, fun swatting them down . . . *There's distinct pleasure in watching a flock work to a good friend's gun.*

Teal, the smallest of common ducks, are really easy to kill. Hunters in the South used to *practice* on teal in September, prior to the "serious" waterfowl season. But the birds were so diminutive and the limit so low (four a day) that many hunters felt it hardly worth going out and getting bit by mosquitoes to kill them. Enough did, however, brave the bugs and manage to "harvest" 165,000 of the little migrating birds in Louisiana in

1987 alone. *Shooting is usually best on opening day. By the second day you can sometimes detect a decline in local teal numbers. Areas may deteriorate to virtually no action by the third day* . . . The area *deteriorates.* When a flock is wiped out, the skies are empty. *No action.*

Teal declined more sharply than any duck species except mallard last year; this baffles hunters. Hunters and their procurers—wildlife agencies—will *never* admit that hunting is responsible for the decimation of a species. John Turner, head of the federal Fish and Wildlife Service, delivers the familiar and litanic line. Hunting is not the problem. *Pollution* is the problem. *Pesticides, urbanization, deforestation, hazardous waste,* and *wetlands destruction* are the problem. And drought! There's been a big drought! Antis should devote their energies to solving these problems if they care about wildlife, and leave the hunters alone. While the Fish and Wildlife Service is busily conducting experiments in cause and effect, like releasing mallard ducklings on a wetland sprayed with the insecticide ethyl parathion (they died—it was known they would, but you can never have enough studies that show guns aren't a duck's only problem), hunters are killing some 200 million birds and animals each year. But these deaths are incidental to the problem, according to Turner. A factor, perhaps, but a *minor* one. Ducks Unlimited says the problem isn't hunting, it's *low recruitment* on the part of the birds. To the hunter, *birth* in the animal kingdom is *recruitment.* They wouldn't want to use an emotional, sentimental word like *birth.* The black duck, a very "popular" duck in the Northeast, so "popular," in fact, that game agencies felt that hunters couldn't be asked to refrain from shooting it, is scarce and getting scarcer. Nevertheless, it's still being hunted. *A number of studies are currently under way in an attempt to discover why black ducks are disappearing, Sports Afield* reports. Black ducks are disappearing because they've been shot out, their elimination being a dreadful example of game management, and managers who are loath to "displease" hunters.

The skies—*flyways*—of America have been divided into four ad-
ministrative regions, and the states, advised by a federal government coordinator, have to agree on policies.

There's always a lot of squabbling that goes on in flyway
meetings—lots of complaints about short-stopping, for example.
Short-stopping is the deliberate holding of birds in a state, often by feeding them in wildlife refuges, so that their southern
migration is slowed or stopped. Hunters in the North get to kill
more than hunters in the South. This isn't fair. Hunters demand
equality in opportunities to kill.

Wildlife managers hate closing the season on anything.
Closing the season on a species would indicate a certain amount
of *mis*management and misjudgment at the very least—a certain
reliance on overly optimistic winter counts, a certain overap-
peasement of hunters who would be "upset" if they couldn't kill
their favorite thing. And worse, closing a season would be considered victory for the antis. Bird-hunting "rules" are very com-
plicated, but they all encourage killing. There are shortened
seasons and split seasons and special seasons for "underuti-
lized" birds. (Teal were very recently considered "underuti-
lized.") The limit on coots is fifteen a day—shooting them, it's
easy! They don't fly high—giving the hunter something to do
while he waits in the blind. Some species are "protected," but
bear in mind that hunters begin blasting away one half hour before sunrise and that most hunters can't identify a bird in the
air even in broad daylight. Some of them can't identify birds in
hand either, and even if they can *(#%*! I got me a canvasback,
that duck's frigging protected . . .)*, they are likely to bury un-
popular or "trash" ducks so that they can continue to hunt the
ones they "love."

Game "professionals," in thrall to hunters' "needs," will
not stop managing bird populations until they've doled out the
final duck *(I didn't get my limit but I bagged the last one, by
golly . . .)*. The Fish and Wildlife Service services legal hunters
as busily as any madam, but it is powerless in tempering the

lusts of the illegal ones. Illegal kill is a monumental problem in the not-so-wonderful world of waterfowl. Excesses have always pervaded the "sport," and bird shooters have historically been the slobs and profligates of hunting. *Doing away with hunting would do away with a vital cultural and historical aspect of American life,* John Turner claims. So, do away with it. Do away with those who have already done away with so much. Do away with them before the birds they have pursued so relentlessly and for so long drop into extinction, sink, in the poet Wallace Stevens's words, "downward to darkness on extended wings."

"Quality" hunting is as rare as the Florida panther. What you've got is a bunch of guys driving over the plains, up the mountains, and through the woods with their stupid tag that cost them a couple of bucks and immense coolers full of beer and body parts. There's a price tag on the right to destroy living creatures for play, but it's not much. *A big-game hunting license is the greatest deal going since the Homestead Act,* Ted Kerasote writes in *Sports Afield. In many states residents can hunt big game for more than a month for about $20.* It's cheaper than taking the little woman out to lunch. It's cheap all right, and it's because killing animals is considered *recreation* and is underwritten by state and federal funds. In Florida, state moneys are routinely spent on "youth hunts," in which kids are guided to shoot deer from stands in wildlife-management areas. The organizers of these events say that these staged hunts *help youth to understand man's role in the ecosystem.* (Drop a doe and take your place in the ecological community, son ...)

Hunters claim (they don't actually believe it but they've learned to say it) that they're doing nonhunters a favor, for if they didn't *use* wild animals, wild animals would be useless. They believe that they're just *helping Mother Nature control populations. (You wouldn't want those deer to die of starvation, would you?)* They claim that their tiny fees provide *all* Americans with wild lands and animals. (People who don't hunt get to enjoy animals all year round while hunters get to enjoy them only during hunting season . . .) Ducks Unlimited feels that it, in particular, is a selfless provider and environmental champion. Although members spend most of their money lobbying for hunters and raising ducks in pens to release later over shooting fields, they do save some wetlands, mostly by persuading farmers not to fill them in. *See that little pothole there the ducks like? Well, I'm gonna plant more soybeans there if you don't pay me not to* . . . Hunters claim many nonsensical things, but the most nonsensical of all is that they *pay their own way*. They do not pay their own way. They *do* pay into a perverse wildlife-management system that manipulates "stocks" and "herds" and "flocks" for hunters' killing pleasure, but these fees in no way cover the cost of highly questionable ecological practices. For some spare change . . . *the greatest deal going* . . . hunters can hunt on public lands—national parks, state forests—preserves for hunters!—which the nonhunting and antihunting public pay for. (Access to private lands is becoming increasingly difficult for them, as experience has taught people that hunters are obnoxious.) Hunters kill on millions of acres of land all over America that are maintained with general taxpayer revenue, but the most shocking, really twisted subsidization takes place on national wildlife refuges. Nowhere is the arrogance and the insidiousness of this small, aggressive minority more clearly demonstrated. Nowhere is the murder of animals, the manipulation of language, and the distortion of public intent more flagrant. The public perceives national wildlife refuges as safe havens, as sanctuaries for animals. And why wouldn't they? The word *refuge* of course *means* shelter from danger and distress. But the dweeby nonhunting public—they tend to be so literal. The word has been reinterpreted by management over time and now hunters are invited into more than half of the country's more than 440 wildlife "sanctuaries" each year to bang them up and kill more than half a million animals. This is called *wildlife-oriented recreation*. Hunters think of this as being no less than their due, claiming that refuge lands were purchased with duck stamps (... *our duck stamps paid for it ... our duck stamps paid for it ...*). Hunters equate those stupid stamps with the mystic, multiplying power of the Lord's loaves and fishes, but of 90 million acres in the Wildlife Refuge System, only 3 million were bought with hunting-stamp revenue. Most wildlife "restoration" programs in the states are translated into clearing land to increase deer habitats (so that too many deer will require hunting ... you wouldn't want them to die of starvation, would you?) and trapping animals for restocking and study (so hunters can shoot more of them). Fish and game agencies hustle hunting—instead of conserving wildlife, they're killing it. It's time for them to get in the business of protecting and preserving wildlife and creating balanced ecological systems instead of pimping for hunters who want their deer/duck/pheasant/turkey—animals stocked to be shot.

Hunters' self-serving arguments and lies are becoming more preposterous as nonhunters awake from their long, albeit troubled, sleep. Sport hunting is immoral; it should be made illegal. Hunters are persecutors of nature who should be prosecuted. They wield a disruptive power out of all proportion to their numbers, and pandering to their interests—the special interests of a group that just wants to kill things—is mad. It's preposterous that every year less than 7 percent of the population turns the skies into shooting galleries and the woods and fields into abattoirs. It's time to stop actively supporting and passively allowing hunting, and time to stigmatize it. It's time to stop being conned and cowed by hunters, time to stop pampering and coddling them, time to get them off the government's duck-and-deer dole, time to stop thinking of wild animals as "resources" and "game," and start thinking of them as sentient beings that deserve our wonder and respect, time to stop allowing hunting to be creditable by calling it "sport" and "recreation." Hunters make wildlife *dead, dead, dead.* It's time to wake up to this indisputable fact. As for the hunters, it's long past check-out time.

Allison Prescott
WINTER IN THE DESERT

'87

My father and grandfather hunt quail this Christmas,
taking the ailing International jeep into the mountains
of the Piñon Ranch just west of El Paso.
The coveys rise from the brush like a cloud of
kicked-up dust, then finally settle. My grandmother
prepares them the way we like: marinated, stuffed
with jalapeño, and we eat in this place where the silence
presses up from the hoofed ground, opening into

the frozen sky. We sleep to the cracking
and dying of the small fires in our rooms; I imagine
I escape like smoke through the chimney, sailing
in my white gown and woolen socks over frozen stalks of
cholla near the cave where a mountain lion winters,
head not yet trophied like the one raging from the wall.
Christmas morning, we take gifts
to the two Mexicans in the cabin nearby; they mend
    fences
and ride the land; they keep. Their radio plays a fuzzy
    ballad;
one has been whittling. My father and grandfather know
a little Spanish; mostly it is an exchange of smiles. Feliz
Navidad.   This Christmas, as every other, my brother
    wants
a pocketknife, a bow, a shotgun. He runs ahead of us
in the new snow, leading us to dinner.

'88

Traveling like a pack of strange animals, we press
into the Arizona desert, saguaro country, unsure of
the weather and the endurance of the children; we
    search
for a suitable place to offer up our awe of a birth in
    winter.
When it is found, we bury the turkey in a pit of
    smoldering coals;
several hours later we pronounce it a fine bird. We
    celebrate
that eve around the fire. The next day we are blown
    home by the wind
that stings eyes and grinds teeth with sand. This is the
    last time
I will see my uncle alive, bush-bearded and long-armed,

packing
our Christmas back to Tucson.

'90

Winter in the desert is for those who know the way; a
    night
of cold could kill a person. My father leads us through
    the sliced
fins of ancient redrock, to Devil's Garden. The ones who
    get lost here,
he says, are the ones who forget the turns they made,
    who let the sun
fall before they realize it, who look for the headlights of
    the distant,
impossible highway instead of for their path. We follow
    silently,
aware of whose ghost we are chasing among the stones
    this
gray afternoon. Taking us over a precarious pass, my
    father apologizes
for not remembering the steep cleft to our right, from
    which a spiraling
wind rises. I concentrate on the placement of my fingers,
    toes,
thinking of the deepness the hardness in the parting of
    the rock.   Christmas
is wild, with tortilla soup to humble us; we push back the
furniture in the crowded cabin and the twenty of us,
    family, dance
to the Texas Tornados alone in pairs in threes, my father
    master of ceremonies.
Outside, deer graze from the alfalfa bales my brother has
    set up for
archery practice; the cabin is lit to the loft with heat and

laughter. I imagine
that to them, on this winter night, it looks like a fire in
the desert,
sending up sparks to snap in the brittle air.

Evelina Zuni Lucero
DEER DANCE

Trini had been told not to come because nothing good ever happened at the bar. Grandma, Old Auntie Lena, all the aunts, and her mother stretched thin lips when the bar's name, the Watering Hole, was mentioned.

Now here she was in reckless disregard dancing with Reynard at the Watering Hole with his cool, distant air, and the half-moon curve of his smile. Drop-dead handsome, she thought. With that thought she almost stopped in her tracks as she remembered the Deer Man. Trini smiled when she caught herself looking at Reynard's feet. His gleaming leather boots were as fancy as the rest of him. Cross-stitched thunderbirds stretched their wings across the front yokes of his shirt, a crisp, black-and-white checkered print, neatly tucked into his blue jeans. A large silver buckle sat atop his firm belly, threading a leather tooled belt that blazed REYNARD on the back. Like a buck, he was sleek and full, well muscled, surefooted; his neck was smooth and graceful, his skin an even bronze tone. He possessed an easy smile that flashed like a lightning bolt, illuminating his face and sparking movement behind his photograys.

Yes, he was good-looking enough to fit the story that Auntie Rosalee like to spook them with as children:

The tall, handsome stranger strode into a wedding dance, commanding attention with his silent entrance, looking neither to the left or right. No one knew who he was though he looked vaguely familiar, like someone's cousin's cousin. The bride's family thought he must be the guest of the groom's family, and the groom's family assumed he was known by the bride's side. He carried himself with grace and sureness, head erect, meeting all questioning eyes and answering them with careful indifference. Large turquoise stones, conspicuously old and heavy, dangled from his earlobes. His long hair was pulled back in an old-time style. He leaned against the wall, smoking a cigarette, a glint of amusement in his dark, slanted eyes.

All the young, single women and even the restless married ones watched, ready to catch his eye, hoping to be the one he'd ask to dance. After a long time, when the dance was almost over, he asked the prettiest girl to dance. The other women sighed, tossed their heads, and pretended they didn't care, but they watched enviously seeing how he tenderly gazed into the depths of her eyes, and how he smoothly spun her across the room. He was light on his feet and she moved easily with him. Other women crossed their arms and shook their heads in disapproval at her reckless laughter.

The girl forgot who she came with, forgot that her sweetheart might have meant something to her, that he stood in the corner sulking. A woman letting her hair down, she danced on with the stranger. The songs became soft sighs, each dance a yearning. The stranger held her tighter and tighter till her boyfriend rushed forward, his eyes narrow slits. Before he could reach her, as the song was ending, screams and shouts filled the air. The band stopped. The crowd parted. The young girl lay lifeless on the floor.

In the confusion of the moment, the stranger almost slipped away, but he was stopped at the door by belligerent, red-eyed young men. Something about his movement as he stepped back from them caused one young man to look down at his feet. The young man paled, his eyes widened, causing others to follow his gaze. Once again, terrified screams paralyzed the crowd. In the sudden hush that came upon the room, someone cried out, "Look! Look at his feet! He has the feet of a deer!" The stranger smiled, brazen and fearless. He pushed his way to the door unchallenged and walked out.

Later, his deer tracks were found beneath all the windows of the hall.

Auntie Rosalee heard the story while she was at the Indian School from the matrons, who insisted that it was true, that two-legged deer tracks were still to be found in the snow on winter mornings. During the deer-hunting season, Rosalee and other women would joke, saying, "Now that the men are gone, let's go on a hunt of our own for a two-legged *dear*." It took years before Trini caught the pun. She used to wonder why they'd want to look for the Deer Man and risk being danced to death.

Only in a place like this could that happen.

Reynard smiled at her.

She looked away.

Heather McHugh
SOME KIND OF PINE

Mid-leap in her escape, the nymph has lost
momentum.
She is bushed, one hand fanned out in

branches, tropes turned
helio. The hapless god got his

comeuppance, too: he's stuck for good
in his own stalking. All the while the maker's

a remarker, casting animal as vegetable and then
as mineral. A moment's monument.

*   *   *

So now the downcast god puts forth forever
in the villa's living room

preposterous, unsinkable, his best
foremember. There it is, a figurative branching toward

her laurel literality. She can't, in time,
escape; he can't, in time, arrive.

They're caught forever in this fleeting and
ambiguous ambition:

one extending, one intending,
never to be free.

*   *   *

Right now, as I write "now,"
one happenstance of courtyard tree appears
attractively more literal than theirs (as yours,
if you have one, must seem to you

more literal than mine—by mine, I mean this actual and
    un-
possessible mid-summer something . . . what's its name,
    this

evergreen—beyond the hotel balcony whose French
    doors—do they
call them that, in Italy?—I flung wide
    open to escape

*   *   *

my rectitude of narrow-bedded room). The conifers
    outside confer
a ringing down on everything; and water whooshes

white around a bend; the branches
glimmer at the tips. (Are they

some kind of pine?) I'm moved
by them, now that I've come

to rest, from so many thousands of
words (numbed space, named time). I stand

*   *   *

at planet-speed, struck dumb
before such patiences as these, that surge for years to
    crown

in great calm altitudes, in starful prongs. How did they
    get
so far? They leave us low and babbling, they ignore

our running reasons and our human stream; they pour
into the sky. That's what they're standing for:

for standing fast. They are a sign
we shall not overcome at all,

except in undergoing more . . .

Mary Clearman Blew

A Lesson in Hunter Safety

aura stood in the doorway of the VFW Club and peered into the dark sanctuary of middle-aged men. From along the bar and from tables farther back in the gloom the drowsy regulars roused themselves to stare at her, the intruder. The overheated old cavern was thick with smoke and the smell of draught beer. Even the football game on the overhead television screen had been turned down so low that the flickering figures in uniform seemed like ghosts from a faraway world of combat come to haunt these sleepy and well-fed veterans.

The bartender hauled himself off his elbows and made his way down the bar toward Laura, squinting against the late afternoon sunshine that flooded through the door behind her.

"You bringing a kid to the hunter safety class? They're holding the meeting in the basement. Take the left-hand turn," he advised, and turned back to the game.

Apparently several parents and sons had been searching out the hunter safety course ahead of her and Robin. Self-conscious and pretending she did not see the row of sleepy eyes that opened wide enough to follow her, Laura sidled past the bar and went down the basement stairs. Robin, aloof but keeping so close that he was almost trampling her heels, clutched the paper and pencil he had been instructed to bring.

She never had been in the VFW Club before. The odor of men going about their male doings made her edgy as a hunted thing even though she had seen them replete and satiated with beer. The lighted basement, with its sheetrocked walls and echoing cement floor, recalled less taboo suppers-and-bingo, but Laura still felt alien, and an old dread of opening a door upon a roomful of strangers kept her lingering at the foot of the stairs, examining a thirty-year-old tinted aerial photograph of VFW headquarters in Pennsylvania that perhaps had been hung when the club was wide awake and active.

"Mother!" muttered Robin in her ear, and Laura opened the door.

Nothing had prepared her for the din. It still was only five minutes to seven, but the room was crowded with perhaps fifty squirming boys and a few girls. The racket made her think wildly of a giant chicken house at feeding time. She could not take her hand off the doorknob. Never had she encountered so much undirected energy. It boiled through the room, erupting in spurts of arguments or scuffles over the one or two remaining chairs. All the folding seats set out along the tables for the meeting had been taken by first comers who glared angrily at prowling invaders.

"I see now why they never advertise this class," said Laura over her shoulder to Robin.

Robin ignored her. Completing the hunter safety course was the only way he could get a license to hunt before he was sixteen, and he had made up his mind he was going to get a license.

"Over there," he said. Laura, following the jerk of his head, saw a row of filing cabinets across the back of the room. They offered a place to perch. Robin swung himself up and, after an involuntary glance over her shoulder to see if she were making herself conspicuous, Laura scrambled up beside him. Her legs dangled, exactly the same length as her son's, as like his as a twin in washed-out blue Levis and cowboy boots.

But once she was high and dry in the corner, Laura felt at ease enough to watch the crowd. In the next ten minutes another twenty or thirty boys and a few fathers came down the basement stairs, looked with bewilderment through the door, and were sucked into the maelstrom. Boys were jostling two and three deep along the walls or hunkering down in corners.

The policeman who taught the hunter safety class, Fred Flisch, was dressed in an ordinary sports shirt and pants this evening, but he gripped a short rod like a swagger stick in front of him, and everyone knew who he was. His eyes, sunken above his chops, roamed over the racketing ten- and twelve- and four-teen-year-olds, counting them; and the boys sneered back at him, bright-eyed.

The three or four other adults in the room, men, were leaning back against the walls, resigned to the few minutes they had to spend in bedlam before they could leave and have a few beers until time to pick up their kids again. Meanwhile they shrugged and exchanged glances, glad it was Flisch and not themselves who had to face this pack of cubs. Mean little devils! Oh, everybody's kid was all right by himself, of course. Really decent. Maybe prone to a little trouble, like all kids. But a pack like this, all together? Flisch might be an ornery son of a bitch himself, but hell! Who else would tackle a job like this? And Flisch continued to pace the room, his back as broad and thick as a prime steer's, his eyes on the children.

Laura glanced at her son, wondering what he was thinking. Robin's face was unreadable under his heavy thatch of black hair. That was Robin, watching the world through skeptical dark eyes that never missed a thing and never gave a thing away. When he was a toddler strangers had stopped to look at the striking little boy with the beautiful dark eyes. Now at thirteen he was slim and dark and shaggy and had the beginnings of a moustache on his upper lip. He was growing almost visibly. In a few months Laura wouldn't be able to borrow a pair of clean Levis from him the way she had this evening. But the surge of good feeling came back to remind her: *at least she had done a good job with Robin.*

She felt someone watching her from across the room and looked up to see Flisch's assistant, a beefy young man with a crew cut and jowls like Flisch's who wore a fluorescent orange hunting vest as buoyant as a life jacket. Laura had noticed him earlier, pretending to be counting stacks of hunter safety booklets but all the time stealing looks at the pandemonium behind him, and she had recognized his fidgeting as teachers' stage fright. Laura now dropped her eyes, blocking off the familiar inward taunts that rang louder than all the racket of the hunter safety class. *Does he know who you are? Something about you? Or is it just that not many women come to this class? It's probably supposed to be for fathers and sons.*

Boys kept pushing into the room, jostling others and raising tides of protest. Laura thought there must be a hundred of them. The air had gone stuffy.

At last Flisch stopped his pacing. His knuckles glistened on his short rod. "How many you kids under twelve?" he demanded.

About half the pack raised their hands. Everybody looked around to see if their friends were raising their hands, took their own hands down, argued with their neighbors over how old they were, changed their minds.

"All you guys under twelve, you're gonna have to leave. We're gonna run another class in a few weeks. You can take hunter safety then."

"Awww!" rose the wail. They wanted to take the class right now. Right now!

"If you're under twelve, you can't go hunting this year anyway. You have to be at least twelve before it's legal. You can come back in a few weeks. We'll have another class organized."

At last about thirty of the younger boys were chased out, complaining as they went. Even then there were not enough application forms to go around, and Flisch's assistant went to bring another stack.

Robin was passed an application card and an instruction manual. Laura got an orange NRA booklet entitled "When Your Boy or Girl Asks for a Gun." The sketch of the smiling American family on the cover reminded her of a picture from a child's primer. Robin scowled at the booklet from under his dark shag of hair.

"They ought to have a picture of the old man in his undershirt, yelling how he'll break the kid's rifle over his head if he don't leave him alone," Robin hissed.

"You'd better be quiet," said Laura. But to herself she was pleased. Robin never had bogged down in the slough of the predictable where so many of her students seemed permanently mired. He never would be sucked into a pack. At least she had taught him to question, to consider. The implied criticism of his father she probably ought not to allow; her twinge of guilty pleasure told her so. But it was Robin's own assessment. At least he thought for himself.

Flisch's assistant, sounding angry as he raised his voice to be heard, explained how the application card must be filled out, where the parent or guardian must sign, and how the kids could get their hunting licenses at half price if they asked for student tags and showed their hunter safety cards. Robin had filled out his card before the assistant could finish his explanation. He handed it to Laura to sign.

"Where'd you say to put our names?" shouted a very small boy in the back of the room. His cry loosed a torrent.

"We supposed to turn these in now?"

"What'd you say?"

"What'd you say?"

"Hold it down!" Flisch bellowed. He patrolled the room, stepping over legs and gripping his little rod, while his assistant explained everything all over again. Laura turned the application card over and looked at the blanks Robin had filled with his cramped penmanship.

"Do you really want to do this?" she asked. At first she had thought he was joking when he had announced that he was going to attend the hunter safety class and get his hunting license. She still could not be certain he was serious. Looking at him now, she was struck as she had been a thousand times at how much Robin was like her. The velvety fringed eyes and the soft dark skin, even the rounded limbs exactly the same size as hers under the denim shirt and the blue Levis washed to velvet. A part of her, exactly like her except for the silken moustache beginning to claim his upper lip like insidious, growing maleness.

"Mother!" said Robin, annoyed. "We already talked about that. And Granddad's counting on it." He reached over and repossessed the card she already had signed.

Now Flisch was explaining the requirements for passing the hunter safety course while the assistant took a turn at prowling up and down, bumping into legs and elbows, and glaring down impudent grins. His resentful gaze strayed to Laura on her file-cabinet perch, and she willed herself still.

All the children had to pass the hunter safety course before they could get a hunting license. That much Flisch could hold over them. Otherwise no legal hunting, no rifle until they were sixteen.

He read aloud a list of rules called the Ten Commandments of Hunting.

"You will know these by heart," he said, glaring around at the smirking boys who had crawled around behind him. "Word for word. We're gonna give you a test, and you have to get 88 on it to pass. The national requirement, it's only 8o, but here in Hill County we say you have to have 88."

One boy raised his hand. "What if we don't?" And his friends tittered, as delighted as if he had posed an unanswerable dilemma.

"Then you don't get no hunting license. And furthermore. It don't matter what you get on that test. Even if you get 1oo percent on that written test, it still don't matter. We got to sign it where it says you passed. And we catch one of you pulling *some stunt*—" he paused to let the words sink in, walking the length of the room with his stick gripped hard in front of his belly while the boys behind him caught each others' eyes and quivered with the held-in giggles—"we catch you pulling *some stunt*, you're never gonna get no license. We'll pull your card and that'll be the end of it, no matter what you get on that written test. No way you'll get to hunt till you're sixteen."

The boys began to snicker. Scuffles broke out all over the room, intensified by the heat and the crowd of young bodies intruding against others. They punched each other, pretending they were being funny about it, but the glitter of their eyes gave them away. Application cards were snatched, torn, spun from hand to hand. Noise rose like a tidal wave and Laura, crouching back on the file cabinet, remembered the men in the bar upstairs, entrenched over their beer and lulled by the silent combat of the televised football game. It was a wonder the ceiling didn't buckle under them.

"All right, all right! Let's keep it down!" shouted Flisch. He and his assistant stalked up and down the room, their faces pulled into masks threatening a grim fate to whelps who failed to take hunter safety seriously. The weight of their faces dragged order among the children nearest them, but chaos and laughter broke out as soon as the adults moved on. But there was a change; their inward antagonism had turned into united defiance of the adults.

"That prick Flisch is gonna get his!" hissed Robin. Laura, glancing up, saw that her son's eyes gleamed out of a face as flushed as the other children's.

"Robin!" she said, appalled.

"Well, you know what he did to Mike Worrick's brother! I suppose you think that's hot stuff! I suppose you think a kid *deserves* to have his ribs broken—"

"I didn't say anything of the kind!" began Laura in an angry whisper, but Robin already had withdrawn from the argument. He was listening intently to Flisch, who somehow had been drawn off on a patriotic tangent.

"We live in a great state. The greatest. You want to appreciate Montana, you go someplace else to live for a while and try to go hunting or fishing there. You're gonna run into garbage everywhere, and you're gonna meet people who got no respect for nobody or nothing. You gotta go see it to believe it."

Robin was expressionless, but his eyes slid around to see how Laura would respond.

"What's the matter?" she whispered, knowing it was a test.

"Nothing." He withdrew again, offended. Laura could feel from the stiff flesh of his young neck and arms that he was pained at her refusal to share his disgust. And yet she sensed still another barrier. Would Robin *let* her agree with him? From across the room Flisch's assistant, almost submerged by the turbulence of the pack in spite of his billowing orange jacket, also was watching her. Laura kept her own face carefully blank.

The current story about Fred Flisch going around the college campus had to do with a house party he had raided a few weeks ago. The kids had had no warning and couldn't get rid of whatever it was, mescaline or something—or worse yet, according to the preferred version among Laura's students, they would have had plenty of time to flush whatever it was down the toilet except that Flisch had bulled his way inside and worked over a couple of the boys. The students said that one of the boys had had a cracked rib, another a ruptured spleen. Laura hadn't believed them. Not that Flisch was incapable of it; she could believe almost anything of those slow furious eyes and the meaty hands locked on their stick. But surely no parent would remain silent?

Or would they? For the basement tonight seethed with the hostility of sixty or more boys who, after a few meetings like this one, were to be armed with rifles and loosed on the countryside for hunting season with cards stating that the possessor knew the Ten Commandments of Hunting and had passed the test with a score of 88. Laura found herself hoping they all had responsible fathers before she realized that she, Flisch, and Flisch's assistant were the only adults in the room. The others had dropped off their children and made their escapes. For some reason the father-son sketch on the cover of the hunter safety booklet must have caught her imagination.

"After all," Flisch was telling the boys, "we've been around for a while. We've seen a thing or two. We're just telling you, same as your dads would. And we ain't perfect, I wouldn't try to tell you that. Like, we don't always bring in the game. We get skunked, same as your dads do sometimes. No," Flisch conceded, "we're not perfect."

"Don't you listen to him," the assistant spoke up. His mouth smiled while his eyes roved anxiously back and forth above the ruckus, seeking rapport with the pack at any cost. "Him—" the spaniel eyes turned to Flisch—"him, he got a nice six-point elk last year. Me, I was the one got skunked." His laugh, divided between Flisch and the pack, begged them all to be guys together, one good bunch of people.

"Wonder if I should tell him what my dad got!" sneered Robin.

"Robin!" said Laura, for once more disturbed than pleased at his jab at his father. The tide below her was swelling, and it seemed to her that not even Flisch could keep a semblance of order much longer.

Oblivious, however, Flisch had begun a lecture on how they should clean up after themselves. "It makes me sick to find garbage everywhere, even way out in the hills. Probably dumped by one of them that don't have no respect for this country or themselves either. I catch any of you throwing beer cans or *whathaveyou*—" the long rhetorical pause, the glare around the room—"or *whathaveyou*, I'll skin you myself."

Flisch's assistant began to tell a story.

"Some of you may know Steve Lambert, he runs the western goods store here in town. Well, his father, old Saylor Lambert, he's got a ranch down by Cascade. South of here."

Laura's attention was distracted from Robin. She too had lived south of Cascade, and she remembered Saylor as an old man who kept a tight thumb on all he owned.

"Old Saylor Lambert, he's got a fishing pond on that ranch of his. We went down here, me and Mr. Flisch—" the spaniel eyes made the acknowledgement—"and we fished his pond. We didn't have no luck. And beings I wasn't getting no bites, I figures I may as well do something. So I gets one of them net onion sacks like I always carry in the camper. I starts gathering up beer cans, all kinds of crap, from around that pond.

"Pretty soon here comes old man Lambert in his pickup. 'I been watching you through my field glasses from the top of that hill,' he says. 'You seen the guys that threw all this crap around my pond?'

" 'No,' I says, 'I ain't seen nobody. But I've been gathering up this garbage for an hour.'

" 'I know you have,' he says to me, 'I've been watching you. And I want you to know, any time you want to hunt or fish on my land, that's fine. You're always welcome. But that son of a bitch that left those beer cans here, I'm gonna shoot that son of a bitch if I ever catch him. And I'm layin' for him on the top of that hill.' "

Boys were yelling all over the room. Laura could not hear the end of the story, or the moral if it had a moral.

"Sick!" sneered Robin, and she turned to him, but just then a scuffle broke out in the corner behind the file cabinets. A boy, shoved by a companion, lurched into Laura and recovered himself without ever being aware of the contact. He threw himself at the boy who had shoved him. Robin launched himself silently at the invader's retreating back.

"Robin!" she cried.

"Hold it down!" bellowed Flisch. "We're just about out of time tonight anyway!"

Somehow his voice just overrode the tide. He soldiered on, giving instructions about the next class meeting and what the boys should bring with them, promising pictures of hunting accidents. "We'll let you see just what it looks like to have half of your head blown off because you used the wrong gauge shell in your shotgun."

By now every boy in the basement was howling at his neighbor, but the effect was for Flisch. Their eyes were fixed on Flisch, their mouths frozen in grins as they waited for him to make his move. Robin leaned against the file cabinets, his young shoulders quivering and his eyes shining. Even on her high perch Laura was jostled again; then Robin was shoved back against her, pinning her leg at a painful angle between his shoulder blades and the cabinets. He lunged away, pummeling the other boy.

Flisch's assistant had retreated to the row of locked gun cabinets at the rear of the basement. His widened, fearful eyes found Laura's again, and Laura abruptly drew her knees up against her chest and hugged herself on her small threatened island. The other adults had been wise to depart, she realized. Afraid of their own children and yet reluctant to brutalize them into obedience. They'd rather Flisch did it for them.

"Same time tomorrow night!" shouted Flisch. "Don't forget to learn your Ten Commandments!"

At last he yielded to volume, stepped aside, and let the pack storm the stairs.

Laura waited on her high-and-dry cabinet until the basement was cleared of all but the stragglers who already had lost their application cards or who had had them snatched away. Robin surfaced from a hooting tangle of arms and legs and went up to Flisch to turn in his card.

Laura slid off the cabinet and waited for him. Maybe she should not have signed his card. But she knew she couldn't have denied him. She would have been acting like a nervous mother hovering over the boy growing up without a father. It was her fault he didn't have a father; the least she could do was see he grew up normally.

Flisch took Robin's card. His eyes, weary in his overfed face, flicked over Laura and registered nothing. He seemed deflated in the nearly empty room. The electric light fell straight down from the ceiling; he did not even cast a shadow.

After all, nothing had happened.

"Mother!" said Robin. His face was flushed. "Can I go with Mike?"

"Mike who?"

"Mike Worrick."

"I thought you and I were going out for pizza afterward."

"Yes, but—Mother! These guys are going to the Dairy Queen. And I can walk home with Mike!"

They were halfway up the basement stairs. Robin was a step ahead of her. Laura had to look up to meet his hot, urgent eyes. "I don't know," she said. She had looked forward to the evening with Robin. She remembered how she had worried whether he would make friends his own age here.

Someone was climbing the stairs behind them. Laura hastily made way for Flisch's assistant. "Excuse me!"

"That's okay," said the young man. His arms were full of hunter safety pamphlets. Lugging the pamphlets, he followed Laura and Robin out of the basement.

"Mother!" Robin urged.

"Oh. Go ahead. Watch out for the traffic on College Avenue. It's getting dark."

"Can I have a dollar for a hamburger?"

Laura dug in her handbag and found a dollar bill. The younger Worrick boy, she saw, was waiting in the doorway of the VFW Club. A few others boys lingered on the street corner, expecting a ride or perhaps killing time on their own.

"Some class, right?"

It was the young man, Flisch's assistant.

"I wouldn't want to try to teach it," Laura agreed. Robin had snatched his dollar and run off with Mike.

"Yeah—" he leaned against the wall with his armload of pamphlets, trying to make conversation. "A lot of folks think Fred, he's too rough on them kids. But you saw what it was like."

"Yes."

"And it's worse, other places. You know there's schools where they got policemen right there in the halls?"

"Yes," said Laura.

"Hell, some adult's gotta be in charge. Only thing is, when it's you and you know you got no answers, it makes you wonder. Right?"

He risked a laugh.

"Yes," said Laura for the third time. Unwillingly she recalled the panic of her first year of college teaching. The awkward young man waited, trying to think of something else to say. Laura retained an image of him armed with a nylon net sack that once had contained onions, attacking the edge of an avalanche of debris.

"You wouldn't care to stay and have a beer?" he asked.

"No," she said politely. "I have to get home."

It was almost dark. The streetlights made a cavern of light across the town, but the September wind was sharp against the corners of buildings and the parked cars. Children still roamed the street. A parting jeer floated back through the evening gloom. Somewhere ahead was Robin. Laura shivered as she left the dusty shelter of the VFW Club and made her way into the chill.

Jane Hirshfield
In Yellow Grass

In the yellow grass
each gathers with its own kind—
and the lion-beauty cuts that invisible pen,
the bright wires trampled or leapt.

So, love, it will be with us, both
lion and prey—our mouths so deep in richness
only the wild scent of earth will be left
to tremble, after.

Barbara Kafka

DIANA, GODDESS OF THE HUNT

Hunting scares me. I grew up in the world of man the hunter, woman the hunted. The harsh crack of a rifle or shotgun on a cold crisp morning makes my stomach tense, recoil like the rifle itself. I cuddle young children and dogs to me and deck them in orange and red when I must let them out. As the snow melts in the spring, I come across long arrows with triangular barbs, sharp like old-fashioned single edged razor blades, nestled in the young, fresh, pale green grass; I feel threatened. Carefully I pick up the lethal weapon and wonder where to put it.

Chickens running, streaming blood from severed necks, Bambi and rabbits dead in nooselike traps horrified me young. I eat meat and recognize my inconsistency, my willingness to benefit from the blood sports of others. My fantasy remains firmly on the side of Peter Rabbit even as I stew my hare and relish its rich sauce. I cheer the fox and admire the grouse ruffling up in a sudden spurt, evading all but the best marksmen.

As a cook, I have learned to kill trout and lobster, eviscerate fish and cut what meat I must into neat joints. Yet I take refuge in the distance from death that a mostly urban life provides. I vainly fence my country garden against raccoons and put netting around my young fruit trees to thwart the twig-nibbling deer; but have not as yet succumbed to the lust for revenge that spurs on my neighbors. Given my lack of consistency, it is good that I am not totally dependent on my own land and hunting and fishing to feed my family. I have trouble with the worm on the hook and, later, the panting, bleeding fish.

I am not of the class that rides to hounds. Romance novels in which androgynous, beautiful young women separated from their rightful name and fortune ride and shoot as well as the handsome lords they inevitably meet will always remain romances to me because impossibly remote. I can admire a portrait of a pale-skinned (how do they stay that way when riding to hounds?) English noblewoman, her long, black sidesaddle skirt caught up nonchalantly in a gloved hand that also holds a crop, as she sits a glossy chestnut, its neck arched, its reins looped; but I feel no stirring in my blood as if at the sound of a distant horn.

I am of the gatherers in the hunter-gatherer dichotomy, sexually linked to the mushroom pickers, the dandelion and ramp uprooters, the brewers of simples from collected herbs, and I am the cook. Where I wonder did I lose my lineage from Diana. Diana was a young and beautiful goddess, who protected and nurtured young animals but who was also shown with bow and arrows and saluted with dead animals from the hunt. Is hers also the aristocratic prerogative, or was a tradition as strong as that of the warrior Amazons lost as women became domesticated along with the animals?

The person who hunts to eat is certainly more of a piece than I who have no intention of becoming a vegetarian but cannot kill. A woman who can hunt as well as any man has a primitive equality I will always lack. I am no warrior and no hunter; I like my garden and my casserole; but some part of me mourns the lost Diana in my birthright.

Joanne Allred

EVERY STORY REWRITES ITSELF

Turkey vultures sail in on the early sun,
shuffle lightly into the oaks
behind the pond, changing everything.

My son, sent to silence the barking dogs,
finds them near the back gate where a quorum
of huge birds in monk's robes congregate.

They have come to absolve the clump
of fur sprawled on the dry hillside—
a casualty of trespassing hunters
I heard shooting days ago.

A spice of crushed marigolds drifting
in last night through my window sharpens

to a stench of rotting flesh.
As we move nearer

the shape shifts, becomes a mountain
lion stretched in a last sprint
nowhere.

The bullet hole in her
unscarred body knits
to snakebite, then, as we look
closer, to the bite of old age.

Those woman-being-tortured-screams
that have wakened friends a mile away
fade to fly-buzzing quiet.

With her fierce power stilled, I see how
we've moved in her mercy, the live lion's
invisibility the grace of her restraint—

the blonde paws, wide as my spread fingers,
retract their stilettos.

A dog shot for gutting sheep
last spring arises
in wronged innocence.

Beneath six shifting buzzards
a branch ready to snap in the next
windstorm cracks, a dark alert

depriving them of the spoils
they've come to gorge.

The blisters my husband's hands will wear
shoveling her grave have already healed,
star thistle grown over the earth torn
to receive her. The pond

I'd thought a refuge is death's
quenching place. In the end
every story rewrites itself.

Betty Fussell

ON MURDERING EELS AND LAUNDERING SWINE

M urder we must. If not cows and pigs and fish, then cabbages and rutabagas. We flay bananas, violate oysters, ravage pomegranates. Our lot is beastly and there's no help for it, for feed we must on creature kinds. Our hands are stained with carrot blood and not all the seas of Noah's Flood will wash them clean, not after God's pact with Noah: "Every moving thing that lives shall be food for you." That's a lot of territory in which to assert our puny manhood and decree that this is fit and this not, this food pure and that dirty. No, all that lives is food for man who, dead, is food for worms. That's the deal.

Some living things are harder to kill than others, even though some things beg to be killed. Snakes, for instance. Their very shape mirrors our throttled circumstances, the narrowness of our confines, the anguish of our passage. The same root, *ango*, generates *anguis* (snake) and anguish (pain). The same root generates *anguilla* (eel), a fish in snake's clothing. Its snaky form makes some eaters queasy and others ravenous, but to eat an eel you must kill him first and quite deliberately, with the zeal of an ax murderer, because he is well armed against us.

I have killed many snakes in the desert when it was their life or mine, but killing an eel in cold blood, on the fourth floor, in a New York City apartment—that's different. The eel and I were already intimate, for I had carried him in my lap in a large plastic bag on the subway from Chinatown, and he had rolled against my belly as if I were pregnant with eels. Watching the bag slither with speed across my kitchen floor, I was afraid to deliver him. I was, in fact, deathly afraid of snakes.

My father had kept them in cages in our basement, next to the laundry tub, the newfangled washing machine, and the old-fashioned clothes wringer. Dumping laundry from tub to washer to wringer to basket for hanging on the line, I kept my eye on the snakes. Whether harmless as garters or lethal as rattlers, they were the Serpent *anguiformes*, the One cursed by God to creep without legs or wings on its belly, condemned without mercy to the darkness of a basement with a burnt-out bulb. Their skins, if you touched them, were cold as death and, though dry, wet as an oyster. Because of them I was damned, as my grandfather had read me in the Book of Genesis, "For the imagination of man's heart is evil from his youth." I was young and therefore evil. The logic was impeccable: the snake and I were kin.

Nothing in my basement past, however, had prepared me for murdering an eel. I needed time to think and threw the bag in the freezer overnight. When I opened the bag in the sink next day, he looked stone cold dead. When I turned the water on to remove the slime, he came suddenly to life. I grabbed a Chinese cleaver and tried to grab his thrusting head, but he was all muscle and I was not. With both hands I slammed the cleaver down on what might have been his neck but may have been his shoulders. A mighty whack barely nicked him. I whacked again as, tail thrashing, he tried to worm his way down the minnow-sized drain. "I'm sorry," I apologized with every whack, and I was. But I needn't have been because I had not even scotched the snake, let alone killed him.

I looked for a blunt instrument and found a wooden mallet that I used for pounding meat. I cracked the mallet on his head and the wood split, but nothing else. He was breathing heavily, gulping air that filled a pouch below his jaws. Was he strangling? I didn't want to know. Like Raskolnikov, I wanted him dead. Like Rasputin, he refused to die. I looked to the freezer for respite and held the bag open for him to slither in. He went halfway, then with a quick U-turn wrapped his tail around my arm and began to slither out. Engulfing him with a second bag, I flopped the works onto the ice trays and slammed the freezer door.

I needed time for research and reflection, my brain against his muscle. I consulted books. "To kill eels instantly, without the horrid torture of cutting and skinning them alive, pierce the spinal marrow, close to the back part of the skull, with a sharp-pointed skewer," William Kitchiner advised in the *Cook's Oracle* in 1817. "The humane executioner," he added, "does certain criminals the favour to hang them before he breaks them on the wheel." A kind thought, but what if the criminal refused to hang? Madame Saint-Ange, in *La Cuisine*, advised French housewives to grab the eel's tail in a dishtowel and bash its head violently against a stone or wall. So much for sentimental Brits.

Surely there was some practical, efficient, clean—American—way to kill. The best way to kill an eel, A. J. McClane wrote in his *Encyclopedia of Fish Cookery*, was to put him in a container of coarse salt. I poured two large boxes of coarse kosher salt into a large stockpot, pulled the eel bag from the freezer, and slid the mound of icy coils into the pot. Before they could quiver, I blanketed them with salt and waited. Nothing stirred. Salt, McClane said, also "deslimes" the eel, but my hands and clothes were already covered with an ooze that would not wash off. When I finally inspected my victim, I found the deed was done, his mouth marred by a single drop of blood.

Skinning was yet to come. McClane suggested I attach his head by a string to a nail pounded in a board. I had neither nail nor board. What I wanted was an electric 7¼-inch circular saw with a carbide-tooth blade. What I had was a pair of poultry shears. I pierced his thick hide and cut a jagged circle below his head, then scissored the length of his belly. With one hand I held his head and with the other pulled back the skin with a pair of stout pliers. It was slow work, but the leathery hide finally slipped off the tail like a nylon stocking. Naked, he was malleable as any flesh.

With one clean stroke I severed his head and hacked him into lengths. He was a three-pound meaty boy, thick and fat. He was everything one could ask for in an eel. I put him in a pot and baptized him with white wine and vinegar, vegetables and herbs, and butter whipped to a froth. He was delicious, as fat eels always are, and crowned my murderer's feast with blessing. For the order of eels are in nature born and buried in salt. Enduring a lifetime's banishment to freshwater pastures and the long journey there and back, they return to their cradle in the salt Sargasso Sea to die in a burst of sperm and roe. "It is a covenant of salt forever": God's covenant with Levi matched the one with Noah. The salt that blesses and preserves also deslimes and kills. The eel and I were bound by the same double deal. His life for mine, salt our shared salvation.

A serpent dead, however, did nothing to scotch my deeper anguish. "Shit is a more onerous theological problem than is evil," Milan Kundera wrote in *The Unbearable Lightness of Being*. "Since God gave man freedom, we can, if need be, accept the idea that He is not responsible for man's crimes. The responsibility for shit, however, rests entirely with Him, the Creator of man." If murder is man's crime, shit is not. Shit is God's joke, yet shit we must even as we feed.

What was my relation to the ten pounds of frozen hog's guts, thawing and spreading like drowned Ophelia's hair, in my apartment bathtub? The chitterlings, ten times the length of my own inner tubing, were pastel yellow, white, and pink. They spread like dubious laundry, triggering memories of washing dirty socks and underwear in the bathtubs of innumerable French and Italian hotels that invariably forbade guests to launder. With guts as with underwear, it were better to do as a French cookbook instructs, "Take the stomach and intestines to the nearest stream or river." Women once washed guts as they washed linen, rising at dawn to carry their baskets of offal to the communal gathering place, to laugh and quarrel, a medieval poet said, as they washed "inwards" at the stream.

It is laundry that connects pig's inwards to man's outwards. The ruffles on a shirtfront were once called chitterlings, "exuberant chitterlings," as Washington Irving said, "puffed out at the neck and bosom." Our foppish frills were once the ancients' omens, when offal was deemed awe-ful and the parts most worthy of the gods. A beast's inwards then put man in touch with the stars, the outermost circle of our confinement. But we who see in serpents no more than snakes, in guts no more than garbage, in destiny no more than a gambler's shake—to our narrow and straightened palates, chitterlings are the food of slaves.

I suppose it's the smell that does it, a pervasive stink that clings to hands and hair, slightly sweet, slightly sour, like dank earth turned over, like rotting bodies in a trench, like human shit. It rubs our noses in all we would deny. Washing guts, I found clusters of fat stuck to the inner lining, along with specks of what dignified recipes call "foreign matter." Some guts are thick and rubbery, others thin and limp as wet hankies. Guts are not smooth like plastic tubing, but gathered lengthwise along invisible seams, to puff like parachute silk with gas. They are gathered the way a seamstress gathers cloth for ruffles. To reach the translucent membrane of the casing, I had to strip and strip again the clogging fat until, held to the light, the stretched skin showed leaf patterns, clouds, sea scum, palely mottled and beautiful. Only by laundering the guts of swine did I discover that shit comes wrapped in a layer of clouds trapped in a membrane resilient as nylon. Still, my lustrations were brief. Most of the cleansing had been done for me at the slaughterhouse, before the guts were frozen by the Gwaltney Company, a son of IT&T. The corporate master that sent me hog's guts puts satellites in space, making however inadvertently the cosmic connection of shit and stars.

From Lily of the Valley, Virginia, a slave's granddaughter told me that she cooks chitlins in their own yellow juice with onion and garlic and vinegar, until the guts are tender enough to chew. Chewy they are, rich on the tongue like all rejected vitals—heart, liver, lights, or haslet—all those messy inwards that remind us uneasily of our own. "Cut them chitlins in small lengths, or knot 'em, and cook 'em up with collards or rice in the pot of chitlin gravy, or fry 'em deep in bubblin' fat till they float up crisp and light," she said.

Even crisp and light, a little inwards go a long way. They go a long way as vitals, en route to shitty death. Bre'r hog knows better than I the rhythm that melds eating and shitting in every moving thing that lives, in the dung birth and death of cabbages and swine, men and snakes. "We must pitch our tents in the fields of excrement," cried Crazy Jane, who liked the way my fingers smell, my stove, my bathtub. The smell of chitterlings clings to the air the way the taste of chitterlings sticks to the tongue. It is a lingering power that gives, my Lily of the Valley friend says, satisfaction.

But I am a child of deodorized air and Lysol drains. My pasteurized senses are not ready for the excremental smell of my bathtub. I poured "Fragrant Pine" bubble bath into the water and was ashamed to read the labeled contents: sulfates, chlorides, formaldehydes, succinates, and an ingredient called "fragrance." I am too sanitized for the fragrance of pig shit. I can turn murder into blessing by symbolic salt, but excrement into sacrament is a harder trick to turn. God owes me there. My guts are serpentine as a mess of eels, but the inward darkness of Genesis shakes out as farce. Farce is my Exodus. I know that after a lifetime's wandering through a wilderness of snakes and swine, no amount of murdering, no amount of laundering, will change my promised end as meat and gravy for rutabagas, pudding for worms.

Mary Pinard

Du Pont's Black Powder Mills: Self-Guided Tour

The Brandywine River ribbons darkly
through Du Pont's estate, millhouse stones
mossed over near the powder plows, still and
innocent as push brooms. Like fists with ears, some
morels in the grass. They burst when I pick them.

On faded plaques, the words read: *Crack*
Pulverize   Saltpeter   Carbon   Graphite
right to hard gates that end my self-guided

tour, where a photo shows women pressed into bars,
knuckles tight there, hems ragged in dirt, and I

want to feel their eyes. Do they wait for word?
Whether their men lucked into that space between
fuse and explosion, stood at the tripwire
of pause, the dangle of beats, their bodies puffs
of breath, one boot set hard on stone,

the other edged above black? Or whether
friction teased open a blast that blew them
with the tin roofs into wobbling flight?
It must have seemed as if flesh could fly to safety
through the smoking holes, like birds in that great

flap of wings whistling out of water as they flee
a hunter's gun. I've felt its kick, seen my
barrel's end warp from the burn. And in the after
silence of my spent shell casings, I dreaded
the fall. So when that one mallard pulled itself

skyward out of my blast—hovering in the chill—
it *did* seem to look for its flock, expectant,
like a word waiting to be spoken,
a word like *and*. But I made it *so*
as I pulled death's impatient trigger in that

space where waiting is, as I gave motion
to rupture. And when it fell, the body seemed
to pull down with it the sky, a splash long and
hollow. I paused, one leg anchored in the blind,
the other hooking a punt, as if I could

straddle the before and after of my killing.
In a turning tide, it floated toward me,

water split behind it like a wound. Thin
and flat, the air around me leaked away,
blood staining the water crimson. I pushed

into that current, guiding myself through,
as I do now, except my end begins this time
with these women who look clear through me
as if I'm not here, and whose waiting
creates a sky.

Kimberly M. Blaeser
LIKE SOME OLD STORY

I

"We got that deer way up by Strawberry Mountain, skinned it out, butchered it, and packed it out, all the way back to Twin Lakes. I remember thinking how much warmer I felt wrapped in that deer meat. But it weren't vury long 'fore it began to feel awfully heavy. Jeezus we was sure happy to get home that night. All youse little kids woke up and wanted to eat right then."

We sit at the old man's table. I trace the knife cuts in the oilcloth as he talks. His hands remember that journey in the air. His chin, his lips, know the directions. I see the dance in his cloudy eyes and hear him laugh at the memory of that feast. "How-wah, we sure took the wrinkle out of our bellies that night!"

We hunt this way together often now. We clean and oil the guns, sharpen the knives. He brings a new box of shells out of the kitchen cabinet. (Good thing about being a bachelor he always said—you can keep your bullets handy.) We make us a lunch. He shuffles around the trailer, breathing pretty hard as he gets dressed. I pretend not to notice the way he has to lift his bad leg with his hand to get it into the boot. We sit down to a cup of coffee before going out. It's still dark and too early anyway.

"Wonder if you could show me how to make snares."

He answers in that way that he has. Gesturing with his neck and chin, his head bopping slightly, a throaty series of ahhs, and then a long-drawn-out "Well, sure I kin show you. You know what pitcher wire is?" I bring him things from here and there about the trailer. He shows me each of his tools, remembers just what he used to use and how he came to get the ones he has now. By the time I get the hang of the cutting, the tying, the sun's been up a while.

"Well lookit that. Them deer musta wondered what heppened to us. Spose they're out there looking at their clocks saying, 'Where is that ole hunter?' Jeez, what kind of hunter you gonna make, if you forget all about going out? I spose you gonna hunt just like my girls—out of my freezer. Well we mighd's well eat these sandwiches. Heppened to dad and me like this one time we was camping where that ole McDougall used to have his sugarbush. I remember it was raining jest hard. . . . "

II

The boys came in looking kind of funny. Awfully quiet, too. No teasing. Just set themselves to cleaning up. Boiling water to wash, emptying their pockets of spare shells and the matchsticks they always carried. Soon your dad went to get some tobacco and a kind of a mumbled argument was going on in the back room. Tried to keep it secret they did, but Mum and Dad would-n't have it. Sent for one of the uncles. Sent us little kids upstairs to the loft. Then they got the story out.

It was that man-deer spirit that's said to come out when them graves have been disturbed. Happens every forty years or so. Someone forgets. Gets too cocky. Pretty soon it's there on the edge of the clearing, antlers catching the early evening light. It looks straight at you when you take aim. Some reason you pause. Get a chill, a funny feeling. Talk yourself out of it. And, just as you set your finger to the trigger, the thing stands up on its man legs. And then is gone. Don't seem it was really there. But you're shaking.

III

The short, squat little man comes out from behind a tree, walks furtively across the little field to position himself on the edge of some small wetlands. He's wearing the classic camouflage clothes in browns and tans and waders that are fastened now just below his knees. Perhaps it's the duck-hunting hat or the way that he wears it with the earflaps down, but something seems a little comical in his appearance, reminiscent somehow of one of the Disney characters.

He doesn't wait long before two mallards fly over. Perhaps he hasn't gotten settled yet, because his aim is off and he misses—twice. The gunfire must be muffled somewhat by the morning dampness, because the birds seem strangely unruffled as the shots ring out and seem to fly on easily out of sight. His next shot brings down a honker, but the fourth, at a low-flying goose, hits a tree and ricochets, cartoon fashion. Soon the hunter seems to have found his rhythm, and he brings down four more of the birds which arrive miraculously in swift succession.

Suddenly the action stops. But the little man seems satisfied. He walks about picking up the birds from where they have fallen, putting the ducks in the large pockets of his hunting jacket. Like a magician he produces a small square cloth, which, with a single flourish, turns into a shoulder pack. Into this he deposits the geese. Then, his weapon pointed down like he was taught in gun safety class, he walks off in the opposite direction from which he had come. The wetland scene seems hardly disturbed by the episode.

The the tempo of the music picks up and a clone of the first man emerges again from the right edge of the screen.

IV

It was when the women were cooking together that I'd hear the other side of those stories. Like the one about the year the two deer were stolen from that tree down in the hollow. You know who always got blamed for that, don't you? I wondered at first why Aunt Maggie let those boys take the blame. But then I thought, well it was true often enough and could just as well have been true this time, too. "Good enough for them," Maggie would have said. But I never did let on or ask her about it. Later I realized how it *was* good for them—you know, to realize what a reputation they had earned. So I never told.

You remember how it happened? The men were all at

Gram's having the big dinner the women had cooked in between their card games that day. Those pies were on the cookstove, looking jest juicy and waiting to be cut into. I saw when the blue pickup went by 'cuz I was sitting on the steps outside the screen door, you know, jest far enough away so they would forget I was around but close enough to hear the stories. Anyway, pretty soon someone was walking up the path from where Ron's house used to be. It was June Bug's uncle, I forget his real name, but us kids used to jest call him Antler 'cuz he had that funny bump on the side of his head and it was covered with pale soft hairs so it looked to us like an antler jest beginning to pop out in velvet.

He never said bejou or nothing. "Somethin's after yer deer." Thems the only words I remember him saying as he stood outside on the steps looking in on those happy hunters. His nose was against the screen door when he spoke, but he jumped back pretty quick 'cuz the chairs started scraping inside and six guys came out in a real hurry. Not mad, yet, 'cuz they thought dogs or maybe a bear.

I was jest about to run after them when my aunt showed up, coming from the other side of the house, wiping her hands on a rag. "Your ole man sure can tie 'em up tight. Thought sure I was going to get caught there. Then what would we have said?"

"You manage?" It was my mom asked that.

"Ayah. Got that Brown boy to haul 'em. Said he could have a hindquarter."

Plenty of kids would have tole, you know, right that night. But I was patient, even then. I knew if you wanted to find things out you had to wait. Turns out I didn't have to wait long. Next day the women couldn't tell it enough, how they tricked their husbands into hunting for that half-blood woman Sarah Goes Lightening. She was a Sioux, you know, and had those five kids. Used to live out on the Snyder Lake road, way back. I guess the men had it in for Sarah 'cuz they thought she done wrong by one of their own, LeRoy Beaulieu. But the women thought differently. I'm still hunting that story, but it'll come along someday. I know how to wait for stories.

V

The old man is standing there just where he said we should pick him up. He has his gun and a stick about a yard long which he holds up when he sees us approach. "Looks like he got him one," Auntie says in the back.

"Wonder how long he's been waiting," my mom says. "Wish he wouldn't go out like that alone."

"You could go with." We all laugh at that. "This one ain't my hunter," Grandpa used to say about my mom. "Sure about that?" Grandma would ask. "That girl is gonna surprise you with what she brings home someday." I guess she did, too. Brought home my dad. But I don't think that's what Grandpa meant, although it might be what Grandma had in mind. Never could tell about that woman either.

He holds up his stick when we get out and lifts his head toward what's hanging on it—a deer heart pierced through. "Had to fight a great big animal to save this heart for youse girls." It takes him a long time to say this, because his words are always surrounded by gestures and because certain sounds he draws out, moving them up and down in his throat. He laughs then at what he's said, but doesn't tell us the story until later, until we've managed between the four of us to drag a small buck out of the woods where he left it, until we've heaved it into my trunk onto the gunnysacks I've laid out to catch the blood drippings, until we've driven back into the little village and sit inside drinking coffee and getting ready to butcher.

"It was a little weasel. Come out and tried to steal that heart right off the stick. You know how them little buggers are.

Tough. Sure was mad at me, and didn't want to give up his supper. So I cut him a little piece." He looks over at me. "Shoulda
said, 'Do your own hunting.' " He knows I'll take the part of the
weasel. We both pretend I have to convince him.

I dream about the weasel that night. He's a least weasel in
my dream and he's old. He sits on a log in the sun watching the
birds, thinking of the time he was quick enough to snatch a bird
before it could launch itself out of his reach. Dreams always
come that way from life and life from dreams, don't they? I saw
a least weasel snatch its dinner just that way once, a bird twice
its size, too. That time becomes this time when I sleep, but it's
only the weasel's dream. He's too old now. He needs some help,
too, just like any old hunter.

I wake up to deer meat frying and come out to find him
cleaning his gun again at the table. "Thought you were gonna
sleep all day." I look outside. It's still dark, maybe 5 A.M. I smile
when he cranes his neck toward the stove. I take the cups from
the counter where he's laid them, pour in some canned milk,
take the hot pad, letting myself sniff its stale flour smell, before
I reach for the coffeepot.

"Spose we could be out and back before them ladies even
wake up," I say pretty casual like when I put the cups and plates
on the table, like this is part of something old we've always
done.

He nods, pretending with me again. "There's some boots
you kin wear behind that wood stove there. You gut gloves?"

We both begin to eat fast and hearty, as if we hadn't just
stuffed ourselves last night. "How-wah, pretty good stuff."
We're laughing too loud and wake up my mom.

"What are you two doing," she drawls between yawns.

"Going hunting," I say, dropping my voice like it's the last
line in some old story—like someone is going to answer "Aho."

Margaret Gibson
STALKING THE LIGHT

I

Where ridge falls away to thicket
and brook borders field,
I settle into a still hunt,
heavy with rest-energy,
at one with the unshaken grace
of stone. However still, I may not
win a glimpse of the shy
habitual deer, the spotted thrush,

the owl, nor be enough within
the company of things, withdrawn
to a common depth, so that I know
the halting and singular solace
of being equivalent and simple.
Restless, my way is to rise
and go into the stand of light
between the stand of trees,
without knowing what draws me
there, within the light,
stalking it, my own light hidden.

II

But for the moment I sit, recalling
one gold-toned photograph
of Black Belly, Cheyenne—
        her face
a map of ten thousand journeys.
She worked in the sun,
hard work, long concentration—
of the kind no one praises
or would think to praise,
work too necessary, too close
to the body's survival, a discipline
that's made her skin craze.
I study her burning solitude,
her disregard for pain,
and try not to compare.
If there are wordless histories
we share, I let them come
to common focus in a split seed,
beech or oak—by root descending,
stalk ascending, riven.

III

Whether I stalk or still hunt
or simply walk, I take with me
these guides—old Black Belly,
whose steps are slow,
and the split seed that opened
for me the root of *glad*
and *glade*, a shimmering space
that spills here and there
among the trees. I also call
to mind a young Vietnamese
who walked into my life
with a sunflower on its long stalk
as his walking stick, who taught me
to count and to breathe
so that within each step a fresh
breeze rose. I'd go alone,
but my solitude spins me
in circles—I read compass
and moss and the wind all wrong.
Rivers seem to flow backwards,
known outcroppings fade. I lose
my bearings, pressing into
the illusion of getting there—
somewhere, anywhere—
on the long way up the tangled
ridge toward sun and open rock.

IV

Walking, I dream of that pure land,
Ladakh, bare rock mountains,
gravel slopes, bare sandy plains
where silence and light conjoin,
and all things are backlit

by the infinite—Kangri La,
a stupa, a sandal tree, apricots
spread on a flat roof to dry,
a stone—things justly placed
in a mandala imagined for so many
centuries, it's there. There,
a quiet shift of light moves
mountains. There, I lay
all my books into the stream
that flows down from the mountain
and watch words rinsed of their
griefs and hungers. I listen
for the still small voice
that follows windstorm and fire—
a voice before whose whisper I cover
my face in a mantle, impersonal,
unable to fear devastation—
broken houses, blackened fields,
the forest reduced to an oak
whose holy seed is its stump,
the city down to its last, a child
whose seed is a crooked helix,
a source from which no energy
spills, that bleak singularity
where light, as we know it, ends.

V

The wind makes the sound of hours
in the trees, a flash of sun
between hemlock and beech
the only blaze that marks
the lower rise. Higher up—
a flare of mica, ribs of birch,
a skin of water over rock.

I collect the names of the lowly,
my companions—self-heal,
hobblebush, fireweed, frail sedge—
flowers close to green, colors
that do not carry, mountain
surfaces that resemble the worn
weave of prayer rugs.
When the wind comes at me
blindside, I give up the search
for a home here, become
properly alone. Walking,
I push up from the earth
and feel my weight. Mass
after mass, the mountains heave,
holding firm. Somewhere,
hidden by all this light,
part of it, the planets
fall freely, traveling as straight
as they can through curved space.
At the core of what I am,
in that sacred space, light
does its work, as it will
without my consent
or blessing—and better so.
I climb, and the sun climbs,
at midday abundant, brief.

Ann Beattie

DEER SEASON

There had been very few times in their lives when they lived apart, and now, for almost three years, Margaret and Elena had shared the cottage in the Adirondacks. In all that time, things had gone smoothly. The only time in their lives things had not gone well was the time before the sisters moved to the cottage. Elena and Tom, the man Elena had been living with, had broken up, and Tom had begun to date Margaret. But Tom and Margaret had not dated long, and now it had become an episode the sisters rarely mentioned. Each understood that the other had once loved him.

Elena had lived with Tom in his brother's high rise on the East Side of Manhattan, but when Tom's brother came back from Europe they had to leave the borrowed apartment, and Tom suggested that it might be a good idea if they lived apart for a while. It had not come as a surprise to Elena, but Tom's dates with Margaret had.

Margaret had never lived with Tom; she had dated him when she was going to nursing school, telling Elena that she knew living with a man would be a great distraction from her work, and once she had decided what she wanted to do, she wanted to concentrate hard. It hurt Elena that Tom would prefer Margaret's company to her own, and it hurt her more that Margaret did not seem to really love him—she preferred her work to him. But Margaret had always been the lucky one.

Tom visited every year, around Christmas. The first year he came he talked about a woman he was dating: a college professor, a minor poet. If the news hurt either of them, the sisters didn't show it. But the next year—they were surprised that he would come again, since the first year he came his visit seemed more or less perfunctory—he talked to Elena after Margaret had gone to bed. He told her then that it had been a mistake to say that they should live apart, that he had found no one else, and would find no one else: he loved her. Then he went into her bedroom and got into bed. She thought about telling him to get out, that she didn't want to start anything again and that it would be embarrassing with Margaret in the next bedroom. But she counted back and realized that she had not slept with anyone in almost a year. She went to bed with him. After that visit, a sentence in one of his letters might have been meant as a proposal, but Elena did not allude to that in her letter to him, and Tom said nothing more. Finally his letters became less impassioned. The letters stopped entirely for almost six months, but then he wrote again, and asked if he could come for what he called his "annual visit." He also wrote Margaret, and Margaret said to Elena, "Tom wants to visit. That's all right with you, isn't it?" They were standing in the doorway to the kitchen, where Elena was putting down a saucer of milk for the cat.

"What are you thinking about so seriously?" Margaret said.

"We need a new kettle," Elena said. "One that doesn't whistle." She lifted the kettle off the burner.

"Is that what you were really thinking about? I thought you might have been thinking about the visit."

"What would I be thinking? I don't care if he comes or not."

"I don't either. Maybe next year we should just say no. It does sort of stir up memories."

Margaret poured water into a cup and added instant coffee and milk. She put the kettle down and Elena picked it up. It irritated Elena that Margaret always added the coffee after she had put the water in. It also irritated her that she had time to be bothered by such things. She thought that as she got older, she was becoming more and more petty. She had a grant, this year, to write about Rousseau's paintings, and she kept bogging down in details. After a few hours' work she would be bored and leave the house. Sometimes she would see no one but Margaret from week to week, except for the regulars at the village store and an occasional hunter walking through the woods, or along the roads. In the summer she had dated an older man named Peter Virrell, one of the summer people who had stayed on, but they had very little to say to each other. He was a painter, so they could talk about art, but she got tired of researching and writing and then talking all night about the same subject, and he drank more than she liked and embarrassed her the next day by calling and begging forgiveness. She found excuses not to see him. Once, when she did, he drank too much and insisted on holding her when she didn't want to be held, and with his lips softly against her ear whispered, "Stop pretending, stop pretending . . . " She had been afraid that when he stopped whispering, he was going to strike her. He looked angry when he let go of her and stood there staring. "Pretending what?" she said, trying to keep her voice even. "You're the one who knows," he said. He sat in front of his open fireplace, tossing in bits of paper that he had shredded and worked into little balls.

"I don't have to explain myself to you," she said.

"I'm forty years old and I drink too much," he said. "I don't blame you for not being interested in me. You don't intend to sleep with me, do you?"

She had not been asked that so bluntly since college, when a few crazy boys she knew talked that way. She didn't know whether to resent it or to try to answer him.

"That's what I thought," he said. "Next do you say that you want to go home, and do I drive you?"

"You're trying to make me a puppet," she said. "You're making a mockery of me before I even speak."

"I'm sorry," he said. He got up and put his coat on, and she heard his keys jingle as he lifted them from the table. She was humiliated to be sent home, like a child being sent from the room after it has cutely performed for all the guests. She continued to stand by the fire, but he continued to stand in the hallway.

"I didn't know you were dating me for sex," she heard herself say.

"I wasn't," he said.

That was in August, and she had not seen him since. Sometimes when she was depressed she would think of Peter and wonder whether she shouldn't have tried harder so that she and Margaret wouldn't end up together forever. They seemed to Elena to be old people already, the way they carried on about the cat: how clever it was, how much personality it had.

* * *

Tom came at eight o'clock, as Elena and Margaret were finishing dinner. Tom's hair had grown long. He wore a black coat and black boots. He had a friend with him, a fellow named Max, who stood by shyly. Max was taller than Tom, and nowhere near as good-looking. He had on a denim jacket with layers of sweaters underneath, and his face was mottled pink from the cold. Tom brought him forward and introduced him. Tom presented his usual assortment of odd gifts: a basil plant, a jar of macadamia nuts, a book of poetry called *Gathering the Bones Together*, a poster of Donald O'Connor and Debbie Reynolds and Gene Kelly from *Singin' in the Rain*. After the admiring, and the laughing, and Margaret adopting Debbie Reynolds' posture and expression, no one seemed to know what to say. Margaret offered to show Max the house. Elena told Tom how much he had changed. She didn't think that she would have recognized him on the street. When they lived together he had been thin, with a beard and short hair. Now, she saw, as he took off the coat, he had put on weight. His hair was as long as hers.

"Would you like a drink or a cup of coffee?" Elena said.

"Where have Margaret and Max gone?" Tom said.

They were silent, and could hear talking in the far room, the room where Margaret grew plants under lights in the winter.

"I might have a beer," he said. "There are some in that bag Max carried in."

They bent together to pick up the bag. Their heads bumped. She thought, again, that this was going to be an impossible visit.

"Have one?" he said.

"No thank you."

"Okay if I get a fire going? You're the only person I know who's got a fireplace."

He went to the fireplace and crumpled newspaper and stuffed it in and began building a pile of kindling and logs. Elena sat on the floor, holding the box of matches. She thought back to the night in August when she had last seen Peter.

"You said you were writing about Rousseau," Tom said. "How's it coming?"

"Not very well. I think I might have chosen the wrong topic."

"What's your topic?" he said, striking a match and putting it to the newspaper. She had told him in the letter what it was.

"Ah, beautiful," Tom said. "Look at it go." He sat beside her and smiled at the flames. "Are you going to take a walk with me later? I want to talk to you."

"What about?"

"Max has talked me into going to the West Coast. I want to talk you into going with us."

"You come to visit once a year, and this time you want me to move to the West Coast with you."

"I don't have the nerve to visit you more than once a year. I treated you like hell."

"That just occurred to you."

"It didn't just occur to me. My shrink said to tell you."

"Your shrink said to tell me."

"You sound like my shrink," Tom said. "I say something, and he repeats it."

By the time they went for a walk, several records had been played and they had all eaten cheese and crackers, and then Margaret and Max had wandered out of the room again, back to the plant room to get stoned. Elena and Tom sat drinking the last two cans of beer. She admitted defeat—she told him all the problems she had with writing, the problem she had concentrating. He confessed that he had no intention of going away with Max, but that he thought if he told her that, she might come back.

"I'm nuts. I admit I'm nuts," Tom said.

He was beginning to seem more familiar to her. Underneath the black coat had been a plaid shirt she remembered. The shoes were the same black motorcycle boots, polished.

Tom stood and pulled her up with one hand. Then, weaving, he headed for the chair to get his coat. Elena went to the closet for hers. The temperature gauge outside the door read thirty-four degrees. There was a full moon.

"Rousseau," Tom said, looking at the moon. "I think that gypsy's sleeping just to flip out the wolf."

He buried their clasped hands in the pocket of his coat. He didn't let go as he unbuttoned his coat and turned sideways to urinate on the leaves. Elena stared at him with amazement. When he finished, he buttoned his coat with one hand.

"Hang on!" Max called, running with Margaret down the field to the edge of the woods. Elena saw that Margaret had put on the white poncho their grandmother had sent her as an early Christmas present. Max and Margaret were laughing, close enough now to see their breath, running so fast that they passed Tom and Elena and stumbled toward the woods.

"I've got the tape!" Max called back, holding a cassette.

"He has a tape he borrowed from a hunter friend," Tom said.

"Recording of a dying rabbit!" Max called to Elena. "Once I get this thing going we can hide and see if a fox comes."

Max put the machine down and clicked the cassette into place, and was hurrying them into the woods and whispering for them to be quiet, although his loud whisper was the only noise. Max crouched next to Margaret, with his arm around her. Tom took Elena's hand and plunged it into his pocket again. Elena was spellbound by the noise from the cassette player: it was a rabbit in pain, shrieking louder and louder.

"You see a fox?" Max whispered.

Soon an owl landed in a small peach tree in the middle of the field. It sat there, silhouetted by the moon, making no noise. Max pointed excitedly, cupped his hands over his eyes (though there was no reason for it) to look at the owl, which sat, not moving. The screeching on the cassette player reached a crescendo and stopped abruptly. The owl stayed in the tree.

"Well," Max said. "We got an owl. Don't anybody move. Maybe there's something else out there."

They sat in silence. Elena's hand was sweaty in Tom's pocket. She got up and said, "I'm going to finish my walk." Tom rose with her and followed her out of the woods. When they had gone about a hundred feet they heard, again, the sounds of the dying rabbit.

"Is he serious?" Elena said.

"I guess so," Tom said.

They were walking toward the moon, and toward the end of the field. There was a road to the left that went to the pump house. She was thinking about going there, sitting on one of the crates inside, and telling him she would come back to him. Imagining it, Elena felt suddenly elated. Just as quickly, her mood changed. He was the one who had broken off their relationship. Then he had begun to date her sister.

"Let's go to the pump house," Tom said.

"No," Elena said. "Let's go back to the house and get warm."

Their indecision had been a joke between them when they lived together; it got so bad that they could not decide which movie to see, which restaurant to eat at, whom to invite over for an evening. Tom's solution had been to flip a coin, but even after the flip, he'd say, "Of course, we could still do the other. Would you rather do that?"

They talked for hours that night before they went to bed. They were squeezed into a chair he had hauled in front of the fireplace, both sitting on one hip to fit in.

"How could you think you're not on my mind when I write you a letter a week?" Tom said, kissing her hair.

"You only come once a year."

"When have you invited me?"

"I don't know."

"You never have. I've asked you to visit me."

"You asked Margaret, too."

"I did when I thought that you wouldn't come under any other circumstances."

"Does Max like Margaret?"

"I guess so. Max is a real charmer. Max likes women. I don't know many of his women friends. I just know he likes them, period." Tom lit a cigarette. He threw the match in the fireplace. "And anyway, you're not Margaret's keeper."

"The lease on the house goes until June," Elena said.

"They can find somebody. And if they don't, we can pay for it until then."

"You're being so matter-of-fact. It's a little strange, don't you agree? I don't know. Let me think about it."

"We'll flip a coin."

"Be serious," Elena said.

Tom stood and got a nickel out of his pocket. He tossed it, turned the coin upside down on the back of his hand. "Heads. You come back," he said.

"How do I know it was heads?"

"Okay, I'll flip again. If it's heads, you agree to believe that I was honest about the flip."

He flipped the coin again. "Heads," he said. "You believe me."

He came back to the chair.

Elena laughed. "What have you been doing the last three years?"

"I put it all in my letters."

"You never told me about the women you were seeing."

"I was seeing women. Tall women. Short women. What do you want to know?"

He took out his pocket watch and opened it. Two o'clock. Margaret and Max and been asleep for about an hour. The front of the gold watch was embossed with a hunting scene: a hunter taking aim at a deer leaping toward the woods. He pushed the watch back into his pants pocket.

"I think you want to stay here out of some crazy responsibility to Margaret," he said, "and there's no reason for it. Margaret wrote me."

"What did she write you?"

"That things weren't going well out here, and neither of you would admit it. And, as a matter of fact, I wasn't lying about the coin, either. It came up heads both times."

"Does Max like her?"

"We just discussed that."

"But does he?"

"Max charms, and screws, every woman who has a pretty face. Look: I asked her in a letter what she'd do if you went back with me, and she said she'd stay on with her job at the hospital until the lease ran out."

The fire was dying out. The side of Elena's body that was not turned toward Tom was cold.

"Come on," he said and pulled her out of the chair. Walking down the hallway to the bedroom, he stopped and turned her toward the mirror. "You know what you're looking at?" he said.

"A sheep in wolf's clothing. In the morning you just say, 'Goodbye, Margaret,' and drive away with me."

She said it, but a bit more elaborately. Max and Tom took a walk while Margaret and Elena had coffee. She told Margaret that she was going to spend the week with Tom, that after the week was up, she would be back, to decide what to do.

Margaret nodded, as if she hadn't really heard. Just as Elena was about to repeat herself, Margaret looked up and said, I always thought that Daddy like me best. Although maybe he didn't, Elena. Maybe he teased you so much because you were his favorite."

Max came into the kitchen, followed by Tom.

"We ought to get moving," Tom said. "Thank you, Margaret, for your hospitality." He held out his hand.

Margaret shook his hand.

"Snow forecast," Max said. "I heard it on the radio when I was warming up the car."

The car was running. Elena could hear it. This departure was too abrupt. Earlier Tom had carried out two boxes of books and her papers. Max was swinging her suitcase.

Max kissed Margaret's cheek. Perhaps earlier he had said he would call her. Perhaps Margaret already understood that, and it wasn't as bad as it looked. After all, Margaret had been pretty silent about other things. Hadn't Tom made that clear?

Max held open the back door. Elena hugged Margaret and told her again that she'd be back.

"Stay put if you're happy," Margaret said. It was hard to tell with what tone she said it.

They walked single file to the car. Elena sat between them. The radio was on, and Max turned up the volume. Margaret disappeared from the door, then reappeared, waving, wind blowing the white poncho away from her body. Elena could not tell who was singing on the radio because she never listened to country music. When the song ended, she changed stations. There was a weather forecast for snow before evening. She looked up through the tinted glass of the windshield and saw that the snow would start any minute; it wasn't only the gray glass that made the sky look that ominous.

"God, I'm happy," Tom said and hugged her. Max moved the dial back to the country music station and began to sing along with the song. She looked at him to see if that was deliberate, but he was looking out the window. As he sang she looked at him again, to make sure that he wasn't teasing her. Her father had loved to tease her. When she was small, her father used to toss her in the air, to the count of three. Usually he gave one toss for each count. Sometimes, though, he would throw her high and run the words together "onetwothree." That frightened her. She told him that it did, and one time she cried. Her mother yelled at her father then for going too far. "How is she going to be an acrobat if she's afraid of height?" her father said. He always tried to turn things into a joke. She could still close her eyes and see him clearly, in his silk bathrobe with his black velvet slippers monogrammed in silver, coming for her to toss her in the air.

*　*　*

They stopped at a restaurant for lunch. Max put a quarter in the jukebox and played country songs. Elena was beginning to dislike him. She already regretted leaving her sister so abruptly. But everything Tom said had been the truth. Margaret probably wanted her to go.

"Your shrink would be happy to see that smile on your face," Max said to Tom. "He'd know that he was worth the money."

"How long have you been seeing a shrink?" she asked.

"I don't know," Tom said. "Six months, maybe. Is that about right, Max?"

"His ladylove left him," Max said, "almost six months to the day."

"What the hell's the matter with you?" Tom said. "What did you say that for?"

"Was it a secret?"

"It wasn't a secret. It's just that I hadn't discussed it with her yet."

"Sorry," Max said. "I'll wash out my mouth with soap. Believe me, I intended nothing by it. If you knew how lousy my own love life was, you'd know I wasn't passing judgment."

The snow started as they ate. Elena looked toward the window because there was such a draft she thought it might be open a crack, saw that it was closed, saw the snow.

"I guess we'd better hit the road while the road's still visible," Max said, waving to the waitress. Tom took Elena's hand and kissed her knuckles. She had left almost all of her sandwich.

Outside, they all stopped. They stood staring at a van, with a deer strapped to the top. Elena looked down and fingered the buttons on her coat. When she looked up, the deer was still there, on its side on the rack on top of a blue van. Tom went over to the van. He took a piece of paper out of his pocket and wrote "Murdering Motherfucker" and swung open the door and dropped the paper on the driver's seat.

"Let's get out of here before he comes out and starts a fight," Max said.

Tom took a turn at the wheel. Max stretched out in the back seat. The driving was getting more difficult, so Tom let go

of Elena's hand to drive with both hands on the wheel. She
turned off the radio, and nobody said anything. "That bastard
was the one who should have been shot," Max said. She turned
around and saw him: eyes closed, knees raised so his feet would
fit on the seat. She no longer hated him. She hoped that Margaret had taken in wood before the snow started. The place
where it was stacked was hardly sheltered at all.

When the car started to swerve, she grabbed Tom's arm—
the worst thing she could have done—and sucked in her breath.
Max sat up and started cursing. She watched as the car drifted
farther and farther to the right, onto the shoulder of the road.
It bumped to a stop. "Goddamn tire," Max said, and opened the
back door and got out. Tom got out on his side, leaving the door
open. Snow blew into the car. No cars had been behind them
when it happened. They had been lucky. Elena heard Tom complaining that there was a jack, but no spare tire. "I'll walk back,"
Max said and kicked his foot in the gravel. "There's got to be
somebody who'll come out, snow or not. I'll call somebody." He
did not sound as if he believed what he was saying.

Tom got back in the car and slammed the door. "How stupid can we be, to take this trip without a spare?" he said. "Now
we sit here and freeze, like a couple of idiots." He looked up
into the rearview mirror, at Max walking back to where they
had come from. No cars came along the road. Elena took his
hand, but he withdrew it.

"We'll get going again," she said.

"But I can't believe how stupid we were."

"It's Max's car," she said. "He should have had the spare
with him."

"It's Max's car, but we're all in the same boat. You took
that I-am-not-my-brother's-keeper lecture too much to heart."

"You believed what you told me, didn't you?"

"Oh, leave me alone. I've had to argue and discuss all
weekend."

She turned the rearview mirror toward her to see what
progress Max was making, but the back window was entirely

covered with snow. The light was dimming. She took Tom's hand again and this time he let her, but didn't look at her.

"You'll hate me again," he said, "because I never change."

"I won't," she said.

"What about what Max said in the restaurant? You don't want to hear about all that crap, do you?"

"I guess not."

"If I bullied you into leaving Margaret, you can go back. I wouldn't hate you for it. Maybe I said too much. It just struck me that I'm not the best one to be giving advice."

"What are you trying to do?" Elena said. "Are you trying to get me to back out?"

Tom sighed. Elena moved over next to him for warmth. As they sat huddled together, a car pulled up behind them. Tom opened the door to get out. Elena looked around him, hoping to see a policeman. She saw a short man with a camouflage hat that buckled under the chin. Tom pushed the door shut behind him, but it didn't click and slowly swung open as the man talked. Elena reached across the seat to close the door, and as she did that she looked farther than she had the first time and saw that it was the blue van with the deer on top. She was terrified. Certainly the man had seen, from the restaurant, who put the note in the van. She took her hand off the handle and leaned across the seat to watch the conversation. In a while the man in the camouflage hat laughed. Tom laughed too. Then he walked to the man's van with him. Elena moved into the driver's seat and stuck her head out the door. She felt the snow soaking her hair. Max was nowhere to be seen. Tom and the man were nodding at the deer. Then Tom turned and came back to the car, and Elena moved into her seat again.

"Did he know it was us?" she said.

"How would he know?" Tom said.

"He could have looked out the restaurant window."

"No," Tom said. "He didn't know it was us."

"I thought something awful was going to happen."

"Don't be silly," Tom said, but she could tell from his voice that he had been frightened too.

"Did he make you look at it.

"No. He was nice about stopping. I thought I'd take a look at his deer and say something about it."

"What did you say?"

"Nothing," Tom said.

Elena stared ahead, into the falling snow.

* * *

When they were on the road again, Max made small talk about how smart it had been to stop to eat, because otherwise they would have starved as well as frozen. On the highway, guide lights had been turned on. Elena rubbed her window clear of fog so that she could see a little, and made a game of silently counting the lights. She got no farther than the third one before the one-two-three she had counted reminded her of her father throwing her in the air, hollering "onetwothree, onetwothree." She could remember how light, how buoyant, she had felt being tossed high in the air, and thought that perhaps being powerless was nice, in a way. She stared at the guide lights without counting, as the car moved slowly along the highway.

ACKNOWLEDGMENTS

All works not listed are printed by permission of the authors.

"The Buck" from *Heat and Other Stories* by Joyce Carol Oates. Reprinted by permission of Dutton/Signet, a division of Penguin U.S.A.

"Dream 2: Brian the Still-Hunter" from *The Journals of Suzanna Moodie* by Margaret Atwood. Copyright © 1970 Oxford University Press, Canada. Reprinted by permission of Oxford University Press, Canada.

"The Trappers" from *The Animals in That Country* by Margaret Atwood. Reprinted by permission.

"To Kill a Deer" and "Balance" from *Pure* by Carol Frost. Reprinted by permission of Northwestern University Press.

"Stalking" from *The Pilgrim at Tinker Creek* by Annie Dillard. Reprinted by permission of HarperCollins Publishers.

"Three Poems from *Cora Fry*" from *Cora Fry* by Rosellen Brown. Reprinted by permission of Farrar, Straus & Giroux.

"She Who Hunts" from *Bad Girl With Hawk* by Nance Van Winckel. Copyright © 1988 by the Board of Trustees of the University of Illinois. Reprinted by permission of the University of Illinois.

"Deerskin" from *Pieces of White Shell* by Terry Tempest Williams. Reprinted by permission of MacMillan Publishing Company, Inc.

"The Heaven of Animals" from *How I Came West and Why I Stayed* by Alison Baker. Reprinted by permission of Chronicle Books.

"Good Grease" from *The Light on the Tent Wall* by Mary TallMountain. Reprinted by permission of The Mary TallMountain Circle.

"From *Primitive People*" from *Primitive People* by Francine Prose. Reprinted by permission of Farrar, Straus & Giroux.

"The Success of the Hunt" from *Firekeeper, New and Selected Poems* by Pattiann Rogers. Reprinted by permission of Milkweed Press.

"From *The Moon by Whale Light*" from *The Moon by Whale Light* by Diane Ackerman. Reprinted by permission of Random House, Inc.

"Fair Hunt: In the Land of Men" from *In the Land of Men* by Antonya Nelson. Reprinted by permission of William Morrow & Company, Inc.

"Numberless" and "Some Kind of Pine" from *Hinge & Sign: Poems 1968-1993* by Heather McHugh. Copyright © 1994 by Heather McHugh, Wesleyan University Press. Reprinted by permission of University Press of New England.

"Dall" from *Cowboys are My Weakness* by Pam Houston. Reprinted by permission.

"The Weighing" and "In Yellow Grass" from *The October Palace* by Jane Hirshfield. Reprinted by permission of HarperCollins Publishers.

"The Glass Wall" from *Vanishing Animals* by Mary Morris. Reprinted by permission of David R. Godine Publishers.

"The Family" and "Hunting: A Story" from *Natural Theology* by Kelly Cherry. Copyright © 1988 by Kelly Cherry. Reprinted by permission of Louisiana State University Press.

"His Power: He Tames What is Wild" from *Women and Nature* by Susan Griffin. Reprinted by permission of HarperCollins Publishers.

"From *Second Nature*" from *Second Nature* by Alice Hoffman. Reprinted by permission of The Putnam Berkeley Group, Inc.

"A Lesson in Hunter Safety" from *Runaway: A Collection of Short Stories* by Mary Clearman Blew. Copyright © 1990 by Mary Clearman Blew. Reprinted by permission of Confluence Press, Inc.

"Stalking the Light" from *Out in the Open* by Margaret Gibson. Copyright © 1989 by Margaret Gibson. Published by Louisiana State University Press. Reprinted by permission.